943.0840924
FAR

DOLTON PUBLIC LIBRARY DISTRICT

ROYAL
WEB

Books by Ladislas Farago

The Last Days of Patton
Aftermath
The Game of the Foxes
The Broken Seal
Patton: Ordeal and Triumph
The Tenth Fleet

Burn after Reading
War of Wits
Behind Closed Doors
Secret Missions
Axis Grand Strategy
German Psychological Warfare

Books by Andrew Sinclair

The Breaking of Bumbo
My Friend Judas
The Raker
Gog
Magog
John Ford
The Facts in the Case of
    E. A. Poe
Prohibition: The Era of Excess

The Available Man: The Life
    behind the Masks
    of Warren Gamaliel Harding
The Emancipation of the
    American Woman
Jack: A Biography of
    Jack London
Corsair: The Life of J. Pierpont
    Morgan

❧ ROYAL ❧
WEB

Ladislas Farago
AND
Andrew Sinclair

❧❧

McGRAW-HILL BOOK COMPANY

New York   St. Louis   San Francisco   Toronto

DOLTON PUBLIC LIBRARY DISTRICT

Copyright © 1982 by Andrew Sinclair

All rights reserved.
Printed in the United States of America.
No part of this publication may
be reproduced, stored in a retrieval
system, or transmitted,
in any form or by any means,
electronic, mechanical, photocopying,
recording, or otherwise, without the prior written
permission of the publisher.

123456789 DODO 8765432

ISBN 0-07-0L994L-8

Library of Congress Cataloging in Publication Data

Farago, Ladislas.
Royal Web.
1. Frederick III, German Emperor, 1831-1888.
2. Victoria, Empress, consort of Frederick III, German
Emperor, 1840-1901.   3. Germany—Kings and rulers—
Biography. 4. Germany—History—Frederick III, 1888.
I. Sinclair, Andrew. II. Title.
DD224.F37   943.08'4'0924   [B]   81-8246
ISBN 0-07-019941-8   AACR2

BOOK DESIGN BY MARY A. BROWN

6-82 fng 12 95

To Ladislas

❧ *Preface* ❧

BY GRACIOUS PERMISSION of Her Majesty the Queen, I have been able to research in the Royal Archives at Windsor Castle and to use the letters and documents which make up the main part of this book. Her Majesty, as the owner of the copyright in Queen Victoria's letters, has also given Her gracious permission for their use in this work.

During the time which I have spent in Windsor Castle, I have been given selfless and illuminating guidance by the Queen's Librarian, Sir Robin Mackworth-Young. With his help and that of Miss Langton, I have been able to complete this work. Their wise advice has prevented me from making many errors of fact and judgment. Those which remain are my own.

I am also indebted to Wolfgang, Prince of Hesse, who is the owner of Queen Victoria's letters to the Empress Frederick, and of many other royal and imperial letters and papers at Friedrichshof, Kronberg. He has graciously granted me permission to use part of them in this book.

For their assistance in aiding me to secure and select the

illustrations, I am grateful to Sir Oliver Millar, the Keeper of the Queen's Pictures, and to Miss Frances Dimond, Curator of the Photograph Collection at the Royal Archives.

For permission to quote from the Salisbury papers, I am indebted to the Marquess of Salisbury: from the Ponsonby papers, the Malet papers, the Lascelles papers, and the Lansdowne papers, to the Public Records Office. Mr. J. M. Armstrong of the Institute of Historical Research at the University of London has helped me untiringly in the examination of these collections and at the Public Records Office.

As always, the London Library has provided the background of my work. Its staff and facilities are beyond praise.

I am also in the debt of Fulford, who is completing his edition of the private correspondence of Queen Victoria and the Crown Princess of Prussia. He has published four volumes of the correspondence, *Dearest Child, Dearest Mama, Your Dear Letter,* and *Darling Child:* these cover the years from 1858 to 1878. Although I have consulted the original letters as much as possible, his help in deciphering the handwriting and his notes on the text have been invaluable. I have followed his practice of eliminating much of the underlining in the letters, a habit beloved by Queen Victoria and her children.

Finally, I must acknowledge with grief and infinite regret the death of my collaborator, Ladislas Farago. Without his inspiration and enthusiasm and hard work this book would not have been written. I hope that it may serve in some measure as a fitting tribute to the originality and energy of this exceptional man.

ANDREW SINCLAIR

Foreword

by
Wolfgang Prince of Hesse

This book is largely based on two collections of correspondence, one consisting of letters written by Queen Victoria and the Prince Consort, to my grandmother, the Empress Frederick, which are in the keeping of our family foundation at Kronberg, and the other of the counterpart letters from the Empress Frederick to her parents, which are in the Royal Archives at Windsor.

It is only through informed discussion of the problems raised by Dr. Sinclair that justice to the Empress's memory will be done in the long run, and no such discussion is possible without access to these papers. In furtherance of this aim I have not only released them to Dr. Sinclair, but also take this opportunity, with the author's kind consent, of joining in the debate, the more so as the interpretation that the book places upon the record of the Empress Frederick's aims and activities is in some respects far from my own.

It is not so much with the details of this book as with its general thesis that I take issue. The marriage of Queen Victoria's eldest daughter to the future King of Prussia is presented as an extraordinary event whose main purpose was to place a political agent and spy at the heart of the Prussian court. However, the Princess Royal's situation in Germany can not be seen as the result of some deep-laid conspiracy to subvert the independence of a foreign state.

The life of a sovereign's daughter who married a future foreign sovereign was never easy. Of course there were conflicting loyalties, but the line of duty was clear. Loyalty belonged first to the country of adoption. Everyone familiar with the life of the Empress Frederick would agree that she was a person of exceptionally high principles, and it would have been out of the question for her to have taken any action that conflicted with her duty to her adopted country. The Empress's correspondence with her mother may have been exceptionally voluminous, but nowhere can it be shown that anything in this correspondence actually led to consequences adverse to Prussia or Germany. We must also not overlook that the emphasis in it was on domestic and social matters rather than on politics. The moral integrity of the Empress is reflected in a letter written by her in 1888 shortly after the Emperor Frederick's death, outlining what was in reality the philosophy on which her political beliefs were based:

> Our patriotism wanted to see the greatness of the Fatherland linked with the noble sense for right, morality, for freedom and culture, for independence of the individual, uplifting of the single person as human being and as German, European and Citizen of the World. Improvement, progress, ennoblement were our motto. To this belong peace, tolerance and charity; those things, man's most precious possessions on earth, we saw trodden under foot. . . . One day there must and will come a reaction—they will praise the heroic deeds of the German Army, the ability, the readiness to sacrifice, the capacity for work and the health of the German people, also the cleverness, the sagacity, the genius, the luck of the great German statesmen of this time. But they will revolt against the poisonous spirit which is now spreading so widely. . . . Of course long before I shall rest next to Emperor Frederick in my grave and one will hardly know what we wanted, and how we loved our Fatherland for which we were permitted to do so little. . . . And yet our tragic fate belongs to German history.

> Ludwig Bamberger:
> *Bismarcks grosses Spiel*, 1932

FRIEDRICHSHOF, KRONBERG
AUGUST 1981

❧ *Introduction* ❧

The story of Victoria Adelaide Mary Louise and Frederick William is not only the story of a royal romance between the eldest child of Queen Victoria and the son of Emperor William Frederick III of Prussia; it is the story of two rival systems struggling for war or peace in Europe during one of the most climactic periods in modern European history—the period of German unification. Opposed to the marriage between the young English princess and the Prussian prince was the powerful Otto von Bismarck. Against Bismarck and his *realpolitik* stood Queen Victoria with her widespread sources of information through marriages and relations. The diplomacy of iron and blood was opposed by the diplomacy of gold band and blood royal. When nearly all the thrones of Europe were filled with the blood group of one Germanic line, kinship transcended frontiers. The extended royal family was greater than the national state.

This was a secret behind the long peaces and short wars that kept the great powers roughly in balance before the outbreak of the First World War. When ministers brought rival countries to the brink of battle over national interest, royal diplomacy would often find a compromise. A family quarrel rarely leads to bloodshed. A quarrel between nations too often does.

Queen Victoria herself knew nearly all the monarchs and aristocrats in politics who ran the affairs of the great powers during her long reign. A few hundred people with common backgrounds and assumptions ruled throughout the century. This was the legacy of the past, which the new nation-states inherited and destroyed in the massacres of the First World War. Then the aristocrats were decimated, the thrones toppled, and those who contacted their kinsfolk abroad were interned or shot.

In this twilight of the old system, the Princess Royal and Prince Frederick William played out their tragedy.

This is also the story of Bismarck, the minister of genius who proved that the *realpolitik* of the nation-state must triumph over the old manners and ceremonies and decencies of Court and international diplomacy. Based on thousands of papers in the royal archives, the book examines fully for the first time, the English Queen's sources of information and their role in international affairs—an importance exercised also by King Edward VII, but which died with him.

The book also opens a spyhole on the unwritten history of the rise of Bismarck's Germany through modern undercover methods of intelligence-gathering and press manipulation, distortions and intimidation, misinformation and surveillance. It is finally the tale of a princess who adored her father and her husband but was forced to divide her loyalty between her homeland and her adopted country.

❧ Contents ❧

Princess Victoria's Family Tree

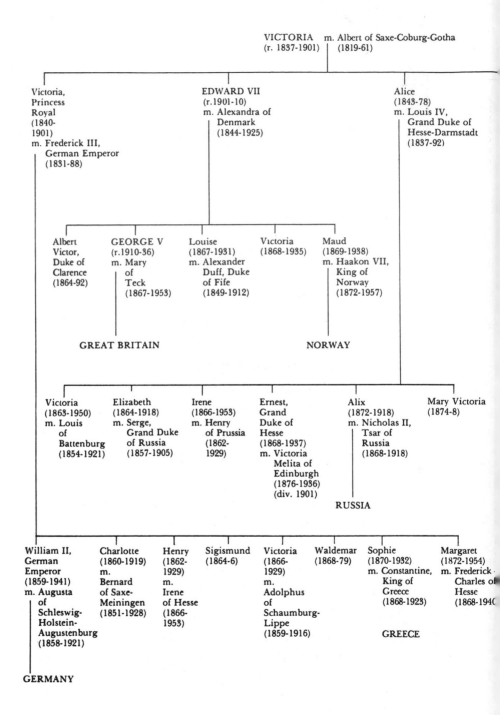

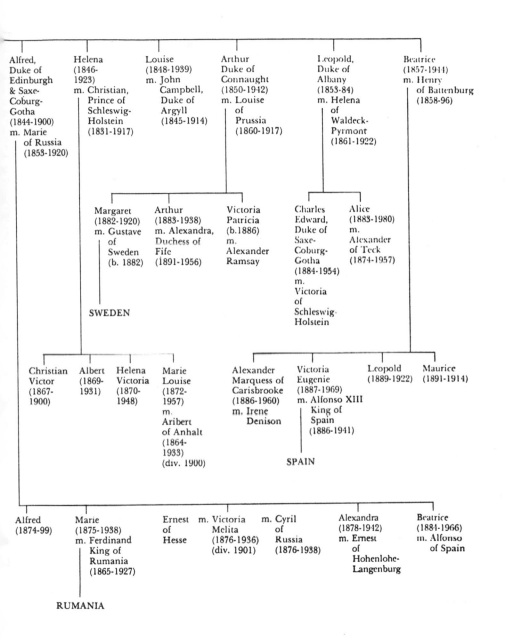

Alfred,
Duke of
Edinburgh
& Saxe-
Coburg-
Gotha
(1844-1900)
m. Marie
of Russia
(1853-1920)

Helena
(1846-
1923)
m. Christian,
Prince of
Schleswig-
Holstein
(1831-1917)

Louise
(1848-1939)
m. John
Campbell,
Duke of
Argyll
(1845-1914)

Arthur
Duke of
Connaught
(1850-1942)
m. Louise
of
Prussia
(1860-1917)

Leopold,
Duke of
Albany
(1853-84)
m. Helena
of
Waldeck-
Pyrmont
(1861-1922)

Beatrice
(1857-1944)
m. Henry
of Battenburg
(1858-96)

Margaret
(1882-1920)
m. Gustave
of
Sweden
(b. 1882)

SWEDEN

Arthur
(1883-1938)
m. Alexandra,
Duchess of
Fife
(1891-1956)

Victoria
Patricia
(b.1886)
m.
Alexander
Ramsay

Charles
Edward,
Duke of
Saxe-
Coburg-
Gotha
(1884-1954)
m.
Victoria
of
Schleswig-
Holstein

Alice
(1883-1980)
m.
Alexander
of Teck
(1874-1957)

Christian
Victor
(1867-
1900)

Albert
(1869-
1931)

Helena
Victoria
(1870-
1948)

Marie
Louise
(1872-
1957)
m.
Aribert
of Anhalt
(1864-
1933)
(div. 1900)

Alexander
Marquess of
Carisbrooke
(1886-1960)
m. Irene
Denison

Victoria
Eugenie
(1887-1969)
m. Alfonso XIII
King of
Spain
(1886-1941)

SPAIN

Leopold
(1889-1922)

Maurice
(1891-1914)

Alfred
(1874-99)

Marie
(1875-1938)
m. Ferdinand
King of
Rumania
(1865-1927)

RUMANIA

Ernest
of
Hesse

m. Victoria
Melita
(1876-1936)
(div. 1901)

m. Cyril
of
Russia
(1876-1938)

Alexandra
(1878-1942)
m. Ernest
of
Hohenlohe-
Langenburg

Beatrice
(1884-1966)
m. Alfonso
of Spain

Prince Frederick William's Family Tree

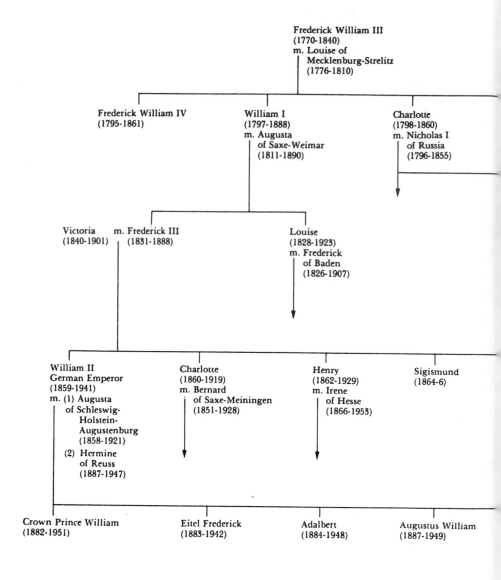

Frederick William III
(1770-1840)
m. Louise of
Mecklenburg-Strelitz
(1776-1810)

Frederick William IV
(1795-1861)

William I
(1797-1888)
m. Augusta
of Saxe-Weimar
(1811-1890)

Charlotte
(1798-1860)
m. Nicholas I
of Russia
(1796-1855)

Victoria   m. Frederick III
(1840-1901)   (1831-1888)

Louise
(1828-1923)
m. Frederick
of Baden
(1826-1907)

William II
German Emperor
(1859-1941)
m. (1) Augusta
of Schleswig-
Holstein-
Augustenburg
(1858-1921)
(2) Hermine
of Reuss
(1887-1947)

Charlotte
(1860-1919)
m. Bernard
of Saxe-Meiningen
(1851-1928)

Henry
(1862-1929)
m. Irene
of Hesse
(1866-1953)

Sigismund
(1864-6)

Crown Prince William
(1882-1951)

Eitel Frederick
(1883-1942)

Adalbert
(1884-1948)

Augustus William
(1887-1949)

3 sons 3 daughters

Alexander II
(1818-1881)
m. Marie
    of Hesse-Darmstadt
(1824-1880)

Victoria
(1866-1929)
m. Adolphus
    of Schaumburg-
    Lippe
(1859-1916)

Waldemar
(1868-79)

Sophie
(1870-1932)
m. Constantine,
    King of Greece
(1868-1923)

Margaret
(1872-1954)
m. Frederick Charles
    of Hesse
(1868-1940)

Alexander III
(1845-1894)
m. Dagmar
    of Denmark
(1847-1928)

Nicholas II
(1868-1918)
m. Alexandra
    of Hesse-Darmstadt
(1872-1918)

Oscar
(1888-1958)

Joachim
(1890-1920)

Victoria Louise
(b. 1892)

1

Minuet before a Wedding

"OH, MADAM," the doctor in attendance said, "it is a princess."

"Never mind," Queen Victoria said. "The next will be a prince."[1]

She had been in labor for twelve long hours before giving birth to the Princess Royal on November 21, 1840. Her husband, Prince Albert, had hardly left the bedroom in Buckingham Palace during the time of trial, only going behind a screen with the Queen's mother, the Duchess of Kent, during the actual birth. When he was brought the infant he was secretly delighted with it, but in the way of royal husbands he had to complain to his elder brother Ernest of Saxe-Coburg-Gotha: "Albert, father of a daughter, you will laugh at me."

Like all other babies, the baby had no choice about her sex or birth. In a way, her marriage and the waste of her qualities were already on the cards, for she was born a princess who, unlike her mother, would have brothers. Her father was a product of the great industry of the thirty-eight small German courts, which hoped to finance themselves by marrying their many offspring in the reigning houses of Europe. To be born a German prince or princess was the surest way of marrying a throne or being offered one by a new nation needing a king.

Prince Albert himself had been groomed by the chief adviser to the Coburgs, the wise and stealthy Baron Stockmar. There were too many candidates for too few thrones, but Prince Albert was successful. He was presented twice to his young cousin Victoria, once when he was fat and awkward at the age of sixteen, and again when he was handsome and blooming at nineteen, an angel with a glossy moustache and piercing blue eyes. *"Albert's beauty* is *most striking,"* Queen Victoria had confessed to her Coburg uncle Leopold, King of the Belgians, "and he is so amiable and unaffected—in short, very *fascinating."*[2] Within three days of their second meeting, the cousins had become engaged. Married at the age of twenty, they had their first child after nine happy months together.

Holding the little Princess in his arms, Prince Albert knew that he held a golden counter in the great game of royal marriages and European diplomacy. His own position was also changed. He was no longer the foreign husband of the youthful English Queen, he was now the father of the heiress to the throne. As if to confirm his new position, he had to leave the Queen's bedroom to attend for the first time a meeting of the Privy Council in her place. It was the mark of the importance of the first child. His name was also included in the liturgy. The nation would pray for him as well as for the new Princess.

Queen Victoria was too young and high-spirited and busy with affairs of state to devote herself to the baby. She refused to feed the infant herself; she did not think royal mothers should be milk cows. A wet-nurse was hired, while the sister-in-law of the poet Southey became Superintendant of the Nursery. The Queen saw the baby twice a day and called her "Pussy." The young parents found the infant "quite a little toy," but the Queen could not allow having children to dominate her life. This she called "the shadow-side" of marriage. The changes made to her body during pregnancy offended her feeling for her person. A queen should not need to endure the natural processes of birth.

Before the Princess Royal was christened and given the names Victoria Adelaide Mary Louise, her mother was pregnant again. She was angry about it, but there was nothing she could do. She had told her uncle King Leopold that he could not wish her to become the mamma of a large family. "Men never think, at least seldom think," she wrote, "what a hard task it is for us women to go through this *very often.*"[3] But she did go through it again the following November and she had to suffer the most severe of all her labors, to bear a son, the future Prince of Wales.

The child's birth started the first step in the marriage minuet around his elder sister, not yet one year old. After much anxious discussion, the Queen and Prince Albert chose the King of Prussia as a sponsor at the christening of the Prince of Wales. Frederick William IV, who was known to be eccentric and romantic, supported an alliance with Russia, which was becoming the chief opponent of the British Empire. It would be politic to draw the Prussian King closer to England. When he appeared at Windsor Castle, his fatness and his squeaky voice and his small head put off most of the court except for the infant Princess Royal, who sat on his knee and played with the gold watch-chain spread over his stomach.

The king had no children, and the heir to the Prussian throne was his brother William, the Prince of Prussia. Two years later, the Prince was chosen to act as a sponsor for Queen Victoria's second son, Alfred. William was unlike his brother, a handsome soldier of a man, who growled beneath the flowing locks and whiskers of a Teutonic Knight. He had little to say for himself, but listened politely as Prince Albert expounded to him a plan for Prussia to unite the many smaller states of Germany under its leadership. This was Baron Stockmar's plan, and Prince Albert had become its chief apostle.

This "Coburg" plan had many variations, but one central theme. In essence, Prussia would become a constitutional monarchy like England, instead of a semi-feudal military state thrust into prominence by Frederick the Great. It would serve as England's Protestant ally in Europe against France and despotic Russia. Its example and policy would cause the lesser Protestant states of North Germany to confederate with their powerful neighbor and protector. Eventually, the Catholic states of South Germany would see that the unity of a German nation was more important than the support of the Austrian Empire, which shared with Prussia a dominating role in the weak German Confederation set up after the defeat of Napoleon. Above all, Prussia must resist the temptation to unite Germany by conquest and war with Austria. It already dominated the German economy through the *Zollverein,* the customs union; now it must develop financially and liberalize its institutions. It must respect the smaller states of Germany, like Hanover and Saxe-Coburg, which were so closely tied to the English royal family. Gold, not iron, trade, not blood, example, not force, should create the new German nation with Prussia at its head. Finally, Prussia should merge into Germany, not Germany be made to join Prussia.

Prince Albert took every opportunity to put variations of the "Coburg" plan to the King and the Prince of Prussia. He lectured them when they visited England, and wrote them memoranda and position papers when they returned home. His ally was Augusta, Princess of Prussia, who came from Saxe-Weimar, the first German state to grant a modern constitution to its subjects. There, Goethe had once been the royal tutor and his liberal views were enshrined in various state policies. Augusta herself was as set as Prince Albert on an alliance with England and the "Coburg" plan. She even used the plan's originator, Baron Stockmar, as an educational adviser to her only son. What he had done for Prince Albert, he might do for Prince Frederick William of Prussia.

So the old Baron was given the chance to influence the

future of the heirs to the Prussian and the English thrones. Princess Augusta believed that a marriage between her son and the Princess Royal of England would support her hopes for the future of her country. She had thought of the Princess Royal as a most suitable daughter-in-law ever since the child's birth.[4] Even though she was a difficult woman, often vain and demanding, she took care to strike up a close friendship with Queen Victoria, and came to visit England herself in 1846 to further her plans.

Queen Victoria was much taken with the Princess of Prussia's show of respect and devotion. "There are whispers of her being *false*," she wrote to King Leopold, "but . . . I *cannot* and will not believe it. Her position is a very difficult one; she is too enlightened and liberal for the Prussian court not to have enemies; but I believe that she is a friend to us and our family, and I do believe that *I* have a friend in her, who may be most useful to us."[5]

Queen Victoria was right. Princess Augusta was suffering from the problems that any future English daughter-in-law would encounter at the Prussian court. While princely life in Weimar had been progressive, palace life in Prussia was formal and frugal, narrow and censored. A free spirit there was put in a corset of etiquette. To talk of change was to seem disloyal. To try to oppose the King's will was to seem treasonable. In a country that was still dominated by *Junkers* ruling peasants on their large estates, in a small power threatened with being crushed between the greater armies of France and Russia, liberal views could appear a betrayal of the monarchy and of national security.

Princess Augusta had other difficulties. She had little influence over her soldier husband, who had followed tradition and had become a lieutenant in the Prussian Guards at the age of ten. His wife had not even been his choice. As a young man, he had fallen helplessly in love with his second cousin Elise Radziwill, a beautiful Polish princess whose family was associated with the Prussian court. Unfortunately for him, the Radziwills were considered minor nobility, with blood that was not worthy to mix with that of the Hohenzollerns. Marriage into that family would have offended the Romanovs, who had blood ties with the Hohenzollerns and who would resent a relationship with nobles from a country subject to Russia. The King of Prussia had forbidden his son to marry his love, and the son had accepted his father's royal will, writing to him:

> With feelings of deepest reverence for you, but also with a broken heart, I reply to you, beloved Father. You have decided my fate in a way which I feared you would do, but tried nevertheless not to believe possible, so long as I saw a ray of hope on the horizon! But you have always found me an obedient son. This, I will continue to be in this decisive hour of my life![6]

He had made a loveless and arranged match with Princess Augusta. Elise Radziwill had not married and soon died of tuberculosis. After Augusta had given birth to her son "Fritz" and her daughter "Wiwy," she had refused to have any more children and had insisted on surrounding herself with the Radziwill family, as if to keep the wound bleeding in his heart. He could never forget, and became something of a tyrant to his son, who paid the price of his father's terrible obedience.

Prince Frederick William was born under a bright star, a frank and open child with a natural generosity. As a boy his health was frail but he soon strengthened with his military training, when he too became a Guards officer at the age of ten. His father had ridden by his grandfather's side during the defeats of Napoleon in Germany, and he wanted to ride out and defeat the French in his time. In contrast, his mother was careful to see that he had a liberal education. He was encouraged by her to admire England and its example of freedom, but he was also taught to carry out all the orders of the King and of his father, now a Prussian general. His duty was to do his duty without question. That was the mark of a Prussian prince.

Only a nature as generous and uncomplicated as Prince Frederick William's could have avoided warping by the conflict of values between his father and his mother. On one side, he was taught absolute obedience to a godlike figure, usually resplendent in uniform, only fulfilled in war. On the other side, a dominant mother taught him to probe at the old traditions, to think more freely, to look outside the confines of Prussia, to oppose the rigid system of the army and the *Junkers*. To get him to become what she wanted him to be, she had to set him against his father, but as a Prussian prince, he had to bow to his father's will. The contradictions remained dormant in the young man. Only later would they affect him psychologically.

There was no conflict between Queen Victoria and Prince Albert about the education of their children. The Prince had a great gift for management. He found chaos and extravagance at Buckingham Palace and Windsor Castle, where he soon instituted method and order. While the Queen looked after necessary affairs of state, he took control of his homes and his children. Baron Stockmar was asked for advice on running the royal nursery. It gave him more trouble, he complained, than the government of a kingdom would have done.[7] He produced some nursery regulations which provided for the constant care of the Princess Royal: whenever the child left the room, somebody had to go with her; she was never to be left alone.[8]

The Princess Royal was inquisitive and talkative by nature. She developed under her special supervision. Stockmar helped to choose her governness, Sarah, Lady Lyttelton, who was firm and kind and devoted, sacrificing herself to the lives of the royal children. She had her hands full with the Princess, whose fierce independence by the age of four convinced her mother that she was disobedient and not kind enough to her brother and sister.[9] This did not last. As the Princess Royal grew, she become close to Prince Edward and Princess Alice. The three elder children were to be particularly devoted to each other all their lives.

There was a fear that bad heredity might affect the Princess Royal, the Prince of Wales, Princess Alice and Prince Alfred, and the five brothers and sisters born after them. It was thought their natures would be warped if they were not always watched. Stockmar ignored the questionable history of Prince Albert's own mother, who had run away because of her husband's infidelity, leaving her son when he was only five. Stockmar merely damned Queen Victoria's predecessors, and the English royal dukes, who had either been badly educated or exposed to the wrong influences, often abroad. In Stockmar's opinion, the bad behavior of the royal dukes had done a great deal of harm to the influence of the Crown, but they had been tolerated because their faults were considered English faults. The lesson was plain. "The Education of the royal Infants ought to be from its earliest beginnings *a truly moral and a truly English one.*"[10]

So it was done. Queen Victoria and Prince Albert issued their own rules on how the children were to be taught. Before they were five, they must be started on the two principal foreign languages, French and German, as well as on speaking and reading and counting. After the age of five, they had to learn about religion: the Queen herself taught the Bible to the Princess Royal. Arithmetic, geography, history and grammar now had to find their place in the child's day. The morning began for the Princess Royal with a writing lesson at breakfast at eight o'clock.[11] Truthfulness at all times was an absolute rule and on one occasion, when the Princess Royal told a rare lie, she was punished by being shut up with her hands tied. This, Lady Lyttelton trusted, made her aware of her fault in the right way.[12]

This rigorous regimen was not as formal as it might seem.

Queen Victoria believed in fresh air more than the Germans did, and on weekdays, the children were taken out to play in the royal gardens for two hours in the morning and one in the afternoon. Sundays were to be "happy Play Days" with the children allowed to jump and run around with their dogs—an essential thing, in the Queen's opinion.[13] Prince Albert was also enormously fond of romping with his children before they went to bed. His particular favorite was the passionate and tempestuous Princess Royal, who insisted on being called "Vicky," and would often burst into tears of rage if she could not get her own way. While the Prince of Wales often seemed slow and dull, she was the child of her father's heart, and she doted on him in return. Prince Albert would sometimes dress his little "Vicky" in a sailor suit to watch her swagger about like a principal boy in a pantomime.

The royal children loved the seaside. It was no longer considered to bring certain death from exposure, after George IV had made Brighton fashionable and had built the fantastic Royal Pavilion there. At first, the children spent their summer holidays with Lady Lyttelton beneath Nash's curious domes and minarets. But whenever they went to the beach, they were mobbed, and when the pier was closed for their use for an hour, the public complained. The Princess Royal's first letter to her mother was written in Brighton. "I wish you very soon to come back," the child wrote to the Queen, "and I will give you a very good love. I have been *munching* very well."[14]

Wanting privacy for her family and a seaside estate for her husband, Queen Victoria purchased several hundred acres on the Isle of Wight. There Prince Albert designed Osborne House in the Italianate style with a pavilion and two differing towers—and a chalet, brought in segments from Switzerland and put in the grounds for the children. "The *greatest maxim* of *all* is—" the Queen wrote, "that the Children should be brought up as *simply* and in as domestic a way as possible;

that (not interfering with their lessons) they should be as *much as possible* with their Parents, share and place their *greatest confidence in them in all things.*"[15]

The Queen and Prince Albert began spending their summers at Osborne, even if public duties often called them away. Lady Lyttelton kept a diary to report on the royal children in her care. Once, when her mother was coming back two days later than promised, the Princess Royal boldly declared she would not do one good lesson and would be naughty during the whole remaining time. Happily she did not carry out her threat. On one Queen's Birthday, a military band played on the lawns in the afternoon, while all the royal children listened and ran about. But after the excitement the exhausted Princess Royal had one of her tantrums. "The evening of a festival is almost always disastrous," Lady Lyttelton wrote, "people grow naughty after much excitement—and accordingly the Princess Royal fell into a transport of rage on perceiving that the day was nearly over; and shrieked and roared in the open carriage, for no other reason. Luckily in a lonely part of the road . . ."[16]

With the number of her family increasing, and with a husband who she thought had a wonderful turn for architecture, Queen Victoria also decided to add to Buckingham Palace. The sale of the Brighton Pavilion provided the funds for a new east wing, built to add numerous small suites and rooms for the children and foreign guests. This matter of convenience became a style and a scale of rule. Queen Victoria was herself small, so as she could not make people look up to her, she made it hard for them to reach her. Even her children remembered having to proceed along endless corridors and through room after room, feeling more and more awestruck all the way, until they were finally admitted to see their royal mother.

Queen Victoria protected the mystery of her majesty by antechambers and anticipations. She reigned from the heart of a maze. In it, she read the state papers of British diplomacy and compared them with the intelligence she received from her European relations and advisers, whose letters told her of their fears of revolution and the threat of war.

⁂

"Old things are falling," Baron Stockmar wrote in 1847, "times are changing and a new life will come from the ruins."[17] His prophecies were only too true. The Holy Alliance of reactionary powers, which had tried to keep the peace of Europe since Napoleon's defeat, was crumbling internally. In 1848, revolutions overwhelmed some of the major cities of Europe. In Brussels, Marx and Engels had written *The Communist Manifesto*. In Milan and in Venice, in Vienna and in Paris, governments were toppled suddenly. Everywhere, monarchs and institutions were under attack from radicals and republicans. King Louis Philippe had to renounce the throne of France and flee with his Queen to England. He only escaped by wearing a humiliating disguise, hiding behind huge goggles and wrapped in a coarse overcoat. Queen Victoria gave the royal refugees houseroom at their son-in-law King Leopold's estate at Claremont. Yet she had to be careful not to mix her sympathy with the policy of her government, which would have to recognize a new French republic. "The public good and the peace of Europe go before one's feelings," the Queen wrote. "God knows what *one feels* towards the French. . . . All our poor relations have gone through is worthy only of a *dreadful romance.*"[18]

To the Princess Royal, the arrival of these royal exiles in disguise seemed very exciting. Their stories of mobs and flights, threat of death and loss of thrones, were worthy of a dreadful romance. To be born royal was to live dangerously. Her father had forbidden her to leave Buckingham Palace during the Chartist riots, and there had been more than one assassination attempt on her mother.

Soon an even more significant refugee arrived, the Prince of Prussia himself. He was hated for his military manners, and his association with the army and the reactionary *Junkers*. A revolution in Berlin made him flee for his life. He had to ask his shamed son Frederick William to bring scissors to cut off his beard, for without his imposing whiskers, he could run away undetected to England. His son had to watch his father escape shaven and disgraced.

This was the most humiliating time in the Prince of Prussia's life. No longer a commanding military figure, he had to beg asylum from the Coburg princeling who had married the Queen of England. In his opinion, the Berlin revolution might never have happened if the Queen had responded to his brother's appeal in February for a joint declaration by the sovereigns of Europe against the spreading principles of revolution.[19] As it was, the King of Prussia lost his nerve. He ordered his army to withdraw from Berlin rather than fight the citizens at the barricades. He rode out in the streets under the national colors of black, red and gold. He even agreed that the kingdom of Prussia should merge with a united Germany under an elected national assembly at Frankfurt— a solution in line with the "Coburg" plan. Prince Albert sent him another paper, advocating the revival of the Holy Roman Empire in a constitutional way. The King refused to take on an imperial role offered by the representatives of the German nation. He would rather be a certain monarch of Prussia by God's will than an uncertain German Emperor by the people's grant.

He soon recovered power in his own capital. The middle classes became frightened at the demands of the workers and radicals, and the ranks of the revolutionaries split. A secret group of *Junkers* advised the King to declare martial law and adjourn the new democratic national assembly. A royal decree gave limited powers to a reactionary government headed by the King's uncle, Count Brandenburg, and later by the archconservative Manteuffel. In fact, the Crown still ruled and the electorate was weighted in favor of those who had property. As the reactionary leader Stahl said, "Authority, not majority."

While the revolution in Germany took its course, the Prince of Prussia stayed at Windsor Castle, trying to recover his self-esteem. Every day he saw the Princess Royal and the Prince of Wales, speaking in German with them. He became fond of the children and was grateful for the kindness of the royal family. Prince Albert continued to hold up the virtues of the British Constitution as a model for Germany and the Prince of Prussia seemed to listen, but Prince Albert mistook his silence for assent.

After spending three months in England, the royal refugee was able to return to Berlin. He wrote to thank Queen Victoria for her tact and understanding during his time of humiliation. The support of England had helped to have him recalled to Prussia, where he was soon put at the head of the forces of reaction. In 1849, he commanded the troops of the German Confederation against the revolutionary forces from Baden. He revenged his exile by hanging most of the radical army's officers after their last stand at the fortress of Rastadt.

The Prince of Prussia would never forgive or forget the revolution. He had been made to flee by a conspiracy of radicals in Berlin, and his pride had been damaged publicly, in front of a foreign court. He became as determined as King Charles II never to go on his travels again, so he accepted his brother's restoration of a reactionary government and his refusal to look beyond the borders of Prussia. It was not only his duty to obey, it was also his will, even if his wife and son disapproved.

One event compelled all the neighbors of France to look toward an alliance with England: a Napoleon was elected to power in Paris. Prince Louis Napoleon became President and shortly after Emperor. The memory of French armies sweeping through Europe was enough to make even the Prussian reactionaries who hated England look to her for support against the French. The Princess Royal's hand seemed a good insurance against revolution at home and an attack from France. A royal marriage would involve England on the continent, even if her politicians tried to keep her free from entangling alliances. A joining of blood royal would compromise a policy of splendid isolation.

Prince Albert and Baron Stockmar were determined to prepare the Princess Royal for her future role in European diplomacy and the intensity of her education was increased. A brilliant teacher, Miss Hildyard, used the young girl's natural curiosity to stimulate her interest in science and literature, Latin and history. Her father encouraged her to begin thinking about politics and foreign affairs.

Her brother, the Prince of Wales, needed more pushing, for unfortunately he was lazy as well as intelligent, stubborn as well as tenacious, quick of temper but slow of speech. His father had a low opinion of his capacities, which his mother sometimes shared, although the Prince's faults were often a natural reaction to his parents' overwhelming expectations of him. "Other children are not always good," the Prince once complained to his German tutor. "Why should I always be good? Nobody is always good."[20]

He was straightforward, affectionate and loyal, especially to his elder sister. Although she outshone him and was closer to their father, he was close to her. She knew that he had displaced her and would become the King of England. He would often tell her so in their children's arguments about who was the better, yet she did not seem to resent it. It was she who basked in her parents' approval, although the Queen would sometimes scold her for her temper and willfulness.

Prince Albert was slowly emerging from the mere control of the affairs of the royal household and was engaged in his first great contribution to his adopted country, planning the Great Exhibition of 1851. Under his persistent and inspiring leadership, the extraordinary design by Paxton for a Crystal Palace in iron and glass was chosen and set up in Hyde Park. Under its curved transept, it enclosed some immemorial elms that were called "John Bull's Trees of Liberty" and were not cut down. Prince Albert was the business manager of the whole vast project, which was paid for by public subscription and rose as quickly as a mirage. The glittering exhibition hall was constructed in less than nine months, covering eighteen acres and extending for nearly a third of a mile. It was like a sudden Xanadu in the park, an instant marvel. Even the scoffing *Times* had to praise it as a splendid phantasm. And Thackeray wrote of it:

> . . . *By a wizard's rod*
> *A blazing arch of lucid glass*
> *Leaps like a fountain from the grass*
> *To meet the sun!*

The wizard's rod had been waved by the Prince Consort. The opening of the Great Exhibition was his supreme hour. The immense display of manufacturing power, housed in a triumph of new technology, proved that British craftsmanship only needed an organizing genius to dazzle the eyes of the world. Queen Victoria felt filled with devotion when she saw the gleaming edifice risen from her husband's imagination and thoroughness.

She wrote in her private journal:

> This is one of the greatest and most glorious days of our lives. The Park presented a wonderful spectacle, crowds streaming through it,—carriages and troops passing, quite like the Coronation, and for *me,* the same anxiety. The day was bright and all bustle and excitement. At half-past two the whole procession in nine State carriages was set in motion. Vicky and Bertie were in our carriage (the other children and Wiwy did not go). The Green Park and Hyde Park were one mass of densely crowded human beings, in the highest good humour and most enthusiastic. . . . The tremendous cheering, the joy expressed in every face,

the vastness of the building, with all its decorations and exhibits, the sound of the organ (with 200 instruments and 600 voices, which seemed nothing) and my beloved husband, the creator of this peace festival "uniting the industry and art of all nations of the earth," all this was indeed moving, and a day to live for ever.[21]

This was a far cry from 1848 with the crowds in the streets and on the barricades. All the crowned heads of Europe had been invited to the Great Exhibition, but few had accepted, either from jealousy or from fear that they might have no thrones left to occupy on their return. It was the only fly in the honey of Queen Victoria's joy. As she scathingly observed to Stockmar, "We regret for their own sakes that so few princes have come, here again dividing themselves from their people. Deeply will they repent it when it is too late."[22]

The Prince of Prussia and his family did come. At first, the King of Prussia had been deterred by the King of Hanover, Queen Victoria's uncle, from allowing his brother to go to the "rubbishy" event. He had written to Prince Albert that he had heard the Crystal Palace might collapse. And even worse, the Prince of Prussia might be assassinated, while the international crowds would probably cause another outbreak of the Black Death. Prince Albert had tartly reminded the King how glad he had been in 1848 to have his brother safe in England. If the refugee Prince did not return to visit the Exhibition, it would be taken as an insult by the British people.

So the Prince of Prussia arrived with his family and an entourage of twenty-nine. The visitors stayed for four weeks, spending the last few days at the seaside house of Osborne. While Prince Albert and Princess Augusta agreed on their private plans for a liberal and united Germany, her husband said little about his brother's reactionary government in Prussia. He might be impressed by the power of British technology, but he was not convinced by Prince Albert's claims that British institutions would work on the continent.

Disappointed, Prince Albert turned his attentions to Augusta's son, Prince Frederick William. The young man of twenty was handsome and fair-haired, impressionable and looking for a sympathetic father figure to help him form his opinions. He was already awed by the display of British power, surprised by the ease of manner and open affections of the royal family, and flattered by the attentions of Queen Victoria's husband. He was persuaded to look on Albert as a kind of intellectual father and adviser, while his own father remained a distant military tutor who demanded his total obedience. The struggle for the young man's mind was begun.

The Princess Royal was only ten, but she was allowed to show Prince Frederick William around the Great Exhibition. Although his English was imperfect, her German was excellent. She had been thoroughly briefed by her father on the technicalities of many of the innumerable exhibits, so she could tell the fascinated Prussian Prince about things he had hardly dreamed of.

Prince Frederick William was impressed with her. She knew who she was and who she was meant to be, even at so young an age. He had never been allowed to go abroad before, and his meeting with such an educated and loving royal family, so free from the rigidity and narrowness of the Prussian court, was both a shock and an inspiration. He could see that his mother's liberal views were not eccentric, but applied in the most powerful industrial nation in the world. By adopting them, he could assert himself against his father. And there was the Princess Royal, who was being steered toward him by her father and his mother. Allied to her, he might go his own way.

These visions of the future were no more substantial than the Crystal Palace itself. At the end of that enchanted summer of peace and display, it was to be taken down. Plans for putting it up again were not final. Tennyson's "Temple Made of Glass" seemed a season's wonder. The dreams of its visitors appeared to be doomed to a cold awakening. In answer to Princess

Augusta's letter of thanks for the visit, Queen Victoria warned her of the difficulties that lay ahead for her son because of the differences between his parents. She begged Augusta to put more confidence in him so that he could have more confidence in himself. She was afraid for the young man. She could see him torn apart if his father strongly recommended something and his mother warned him against it.[23]

Two years later, the Prince of Prussia and his wife and daughter visited England again, without their son. The ambitions of Louis Napoleon were causing worry to the Germans and to the British. Army maneuvers impressed the Prince of Prussia, while the Princess Royal impressed his wife. The twelve-year-old already wore her hair up like an adult, and spoke of art as if she were mature. Yet any progress toward a royal marriage between the two houses had to be delayed. The British government's relations with Prussia were worsening while they were improving with France.

By the end of the year, a crowd gathered outside Buckingham Palace, expecting to see Prince Albert taken to the Tower of London on a charge of treason for opposing war with Russia. In fact, Prince Albert had been urging military reforms for years, even making his brother Ernest smuggle a new Prussian needle-gun to London for examination. Parliament exonerated the Prince from the absurd charge of treachery, but Her Majesty's government decided on war with Russia in alliance with Louis Napoleon. At the last resort, England was not like Prussia. The crown could advise on peace, but not insist.

The reasons for the Crimean War were not convincing. France and Britain seemed to be sending their fleets and expeditionary forces to the Black Sea in order to prevent the collapse of Turkey, but in fact, the British were defending their Empire against its chief threat, while Louis Napoleon was avenging his predecessor's retreat from Moscow. The war cost half a million lives. One fortress fell at Sebastopol. No European conflict between Waterloo and the outbreak of the First World War would cost so many men and all for little gain. The Prince Consort had not been wrong.

The King of Prussia was terrified by the new alliance between England and France, which he feared might lead to another assault on his country by a Napoleon. Wooed by Austria to join the other western powers in the attack on Russia, he chose neutrality. Revolution was his bugbear, not Russia, and his family was linked to the Romanov dynasty by marriage, so he kept Prussia out of the war.

His brother, the Prince of Prussia, favored an alliance with England and France. He was stung by Queen Victoria's sending her declaration of war to his wife and adding, "For us it is extremely painful to see Prussia irresolute when we had hoped to proceed hand in hand."[24] He forced a political crisis on his brother and was exiled to Coblenz. Prince William's partial banishment was a prophecy of what would happen to his own son and heir if he were ever provoked to support an English alliance against the wishes of his father.

The Prince of Prussia's fall from grace was largely due to the rise of a new intelligence system created by an extraordinary spymaster, Wilhelm Stieber, who had first ingratiated himself with the King of Prussia in 1848. A criminal lawyer with many contacts among the radicals and the underworld, he was also an *agent provocateur* for the Berlin police. He became the spokesman for a group of rioters on a deputation to the King, and then revealed to His Majesty that he was a police agent who would protect the King from the rioters. The King was impressed by such artfulness. Stieber went on playing both sides of the law, advising his clients how to outwit it and telling the authorities how to entrap them.

In 1850, Stieber was appointed Commissioner of Police. The court was moved for safety to Potsdam, while Stieber was ordered to report on radical activity in Berlin and to put an end to it. The following year, he went to the Great Exhibition and to Paris to investigate German socialists and revolutionaries in exile. Among these were Marx and Engels. Stieber won the confidence of some of the exile groups and returned to Berlin with lists of sympathizers still in Germany. Dozens of radicals were now seized, and hundreds made to flee abroad as had once the Prince of Prussia. By the end of the Crimean War, Stieber had become the indispensable tool of Prussian security, a dangerous and ruthless schemer devoted to the Crown.

Outside France, Prussia and Austria, secret intelligence systems were not yet developed. Most intelligence came through diplomatic sources, particularly from military attachés whose position was known and agreed. Although they were expected to report back to their governments on the armed forces of foreign powers, these reports were considered more as deterrents than betrayals. A code of military honor was meant to bind these attachés. Their job was to observe and inform; spying meant dishonor and instant dismissal.[25] In Prussia, particularly, the British military attaché was often close to the Crown and was used as a direct channel of communication with Queen Victoria, who was constitutionally the head of her country's armed forces.

There were, in fact, five major sources of foreign intelligence: First, the secret services, elementary or developed; second, the normal channels of diplomacy, the information sent home by resident ambassadors or envoys; third, the special attachés at the legations or the foreign correspondents of good newspapers like *The Times;* fourth, the reports of nationals who had traveled abroad and had been briefed for a particular purpose; fifth, the proliferation of royal and aristocratic correspondence which ignored national frontiers—and seemed an international threat to Stieber and other agents of the state.

During Victorian times, the nation-states were rising to dominate European diplomacy. Although the Austrian Empire still existed, preventing the unification of Italy and Germany, like Turkey, it was ailing. Even in the Balkans, smaller nationalities were demanding their freedom. As each nation rose to demand control over its own destiny, it also demanded patriotism from its citizens and formed a new secret service answerable only to the state. These national loyalties conflicted with the wider loyalties of the aristocrats and the royal families which still ruled in Britain, Austria, Russia, Prussia and Spain.

The alliances of the well-born were formed through marriages. Cousins provided more certain information than spies; common blood was a surer source than secret service pay. The wide correspondence of European royalty and nobility made for an alternative diplomacy through connected families, usually carried on perfectly securely through diplomatic bags or private messengers. It relied on personal knowledge and shared values, not on the equivocal claims of double agents who had to manufacture information to earn their pay. It was more accurate and was usually meant to keep the peace, not to provoke a conflict.

The immense extended families of Victorian royalty and nobility did not want war. To them, it meant a father fighting a daughter's husband, a cousin at grips with a nephew. National quarrels led to ruptures among kin. A lost war might involve a lost throne and refugee princes. Although the new systems of secret intelligence might benefit republics and nations that practiced diplomacy by the deteriorating standards of Louis Napoleon, they stood against the old system of family diplomacy and international correspondence that depended upon common standards of accuracy and trust.

The decline in standards of international diplomacy after the Crimean War, and the rise of Stieber and the other spymasters of the nation-states, were to condemn the heirs of the old traditions. By being true to what she had been taught, the Princess Royal might seem disloyal to her second country.

※

Royalty follows the flag. Although Queen Victoria thought the French immoral and loathed the name of Napoleon, she had to invite the new Emperor and Empress of France to Windsor Castle as allies in April 1855. Unexpectedly, Napoleon III and his wife charmed Queen Victoria. Although the French Emperor was short and stout with long waxed moustaches, he had an air of mystery and dared to flirt with the Queen while the Empress Eugénie was elegant and wore the first crinoline ever seen in England. The Emperor had been threatening to go to the Crimea and lead the allied troops in person against Sebastopol. Queen Victoria, knowing her troops would not follow a Bonaparte, had the courage to ask him not to go. At a Council of War the following day, he seemed to accept her plea and invited her and her family to the Paris Exhibition in August. It would be the first time an English sovereign had set foot in the French capital since the Hundred Years' War.

Queen Victoria did not lose the opportunity of pointing out to her friend, the Princess of Prussia, how successful the French Emperor's visit had been. The return visit to Paris was another triumph, and a warning signal to Berlin. Queen Victoria and her husband took along the Princess Royal and the Prince of Wales, and the young people were delighted with their reception. They were treated as adults and were entertained as if their pleasure was more important than their duty. The Princess was almost fifteen, and found herself beautiful for the first time. In the Hall of Mirrors at Versailles, the French Emperor asked her to dance, and as she spun around catching reflection after reflection of herself, she saw a vision of what she would become. It was a heady experience for the young Princess.

At Versailles, Queen Victoria and her daughter met the heir of a *Junker* family whose sensitivity and political genius was masked by Otto von Bismarck, a ruthless and astute *Junker* with a reckless wit and demoniac energy. The heir of Teutonic Knights, with estates on the Elbe at Schönhausen, Bismarck had grown up with a wild reputation. Over six feet tall, imposing and red-haired, he had fought twenty-five duels in his first nine months at Gottingen University. He enjoyed being provocative, but only to prove his passionate commitment to the future of Prussia. A traditional conservative and royalist, he had armed his peasants in support of the King during the troubles of 1848, but had antagonized Princess Augusta by proposing a dangerous scheme for a regency under her young son. He was thought too rabid by the King, who noted against his name: "Red reactionary—smells of blood—to be used later."[26]

His connections with the King's military advisers such as Albrecht von Roon and his speeches against the liberals in the Prussian parliament made him known. His marriage to a Pomeranian, Johanna von Puttkamer, curbed his wilder side. He was duly sent to represent Prussia at the Federal Diet of the German Confederation at Frankfurt, where he developed his rough style of diplomacy, which he later said he had learned in the horse fairs of Pomerania. He resisted Austrian pressure to join in the Crimean War, and with the King he supported an understanding with the Tsar. For this, he was said to smell of Russian leather and to be a Berlin Cossack. When presented to the Prince Consort at Versailles, he thought the Coburg Prince handsome and cool in his black uniform, but full of malevolent curiosity beneath a surface courtesy. Queen Victoria herself found Bismarck reactionary and enigmatic and a supporter of England's enemies.

"Paris is beautiful," the Queen said to him.

"Even more beautiful than St. Petersburg," he said to her, although he had not yet visited the Russian capital.

Bismarck's reports of the growing Anglo-French understanding and the fact that their troops also seemed to be winning the war in the Crimea, caused panic in Prussia. Princess Augusta saw her hopes for her son's match with the Princess Royal begin to crumble, and the Crown Prince himself was in despair. Ever since his visit to England for the Great Exhibition, he had done everything to prepare himself for his marriage to the Princess. When he had been sent to St. Petersburg for a Russian imperial wedding, he criticized the barbaric luxury of the Tsar's court in his letters to Prince Albert. He studied English as much as he could, and his tutor, who found him eager for any information on England, made him compose imaginary letters to Cabinet ministers and society leaders. He attended the Anglican church services at Bonn, borrowing a prayer book and joining in the liturgy for Queen Victoria. He was also jealous of the Princess Royal's visit to Paris. There were imperial rivals there who might ask for her hand.

Prince Frederick William wanted to leave for England immediately to propose marriage to the Princess Royal, and his parents encouraged him, agreeing for once about the English alliance. Yet their son could not leave Prussia without the consent of his uncle the King, so he went to the palace to beg royal blessing for his suit. The King was uneasy about an heir to the throne trying to marry a foreign princess. This was not traditional. There were enough princesses of good German blood to make dozens of royal marriages. But he was even more uneasy about the Anglo-French alliance. At least a marriage between the Hohenzollerns and the English royal house would act as a counterbalance. So the King of Prussia gave his blessing. To disguise the reason for his trip, because a pro-Russian group at court had the ear of the Queen of Prussia, Prince Frederick William announced that he was setting off to go sea-bathing at Ostend. Incognito, he slipped across the Channel and took a train to Scotland. Unfortunately, the foreign visitor was seen at a station by the Duke of Cambridge, who told his mother he was astonished to see the young Prussian Prince on his way to Queen Victoria's estate at Balmoral. Evidently, the marriage was to be.[27]

This was more than Prince Frederick knew himself. He was nervous and uncertain by the time he arrived at Balmoral, where Prince Albert had just finished building a comfortable baronial schloss where everything was kept deliberately informal. Both Queen Victoria and her husband loved playing at Scots lairds and ladies. Prince Albert wore a kilt while the Queen draped the furniture and the beds and herself with Stuart tartans. They agreed with Lady Lyttelton, who thought the life of a country gentleman and his family, which the royal couple condescended to imitate, was about the richest in materials for happiness.[28]

The Princess Royal did not know the reason for Prince Frederick William's sudden arrival. Her parents did. Even if Queen Victoria had exaggerated her attachment to imperial France, the effect had been gratifying. Within a month of her return from Paris, the young heir to the Prussian throne had arrived with royal consent to offer his hand to Princess Victoria. Her acceptance was now essential for the success of the Coburg plan, which Prince Albert was already beginning to teach her. He did not reveal the part she might play in it by marrying the Prince of Prussia's son. He wanted her to choose what her father had chosen for her.

Prince Frederick William had come at a joyful time. Sebastopol had fallen and the ashes of the celebration bonfires were still hot on the heaths by the Dee. Princess Victoria sat next to him at dinner and hardly stopped talking to the silent and handsome young man, who looked down at her from large blue eyes above a sweeping blond moustache. Her own huge green eyes filled with pleasure at seeing the handsome prince again, but he could not tell if she felt anything more for him. The next day, he was taken off to hunt stags by Prince Albert, but his aim was poor; his mind was on the Princess. He thought her gaiety was girlish mockery of his chances. She was, after all, only fourteen. After four days at Balmoral, he was left alone with the Princess, who suddenly took his hand and squeezed it hard. It was her first contact with him, her innocent declaration. He slept well at last. After breakfast the following morning, he spoke privately to the Queen and Prince Albert. He told them that he wanted to belong to their family more than anything in the world. The Queen was full of emotion and clasped the young man's hand. He had her consent, but the Princess Royal was still too young to know. She must not be told until she was confirmed, the Queen said. The Prince could return in eighteen months' time to propose to her daughter.

Princess Victoria still seemed unconscious of the young man's desire. On their walks through the woods, she looked for some smoke-quartz to give him. "Oh," she said, "I would love to give you every beautiful thing I find." Yet he was still unsure of her. All he could report to his parents was that he was certain she liked him.

Prince Frederick William was too impatient to wait. On a morning of clear frost, he went out riding with the Princess in a party making for Craig-na Ban. She wore a large riding hat and a plaid over her long skirt. He made her lag behind the others until they were alone together. By the side of the track, he saw some white heather growing, dismounted and picked a sprig of it—for good luck—for life. He gave her the heather and swept her down from her pony and kissed her. Then he put her on her pony again and rode on beside her, telling her that he wanted her to stay in Prussia always, always. She blushed. He was afraid of having said something to annoy her, but she said, "Oh, no." She said she wanted to tell her parents. At Glen Girnoch, where the royal carriage was waiting, the Prince gave Queen Victoria a look full of meaning, and she knew the young man had declared himself. Her daughter would confide in her later.[29]

The Princess Royal was still half child, half woman, yet she had a mind of her own and had been brought up to be wiser than her years. She told the Queen that she had always loved Prince Frederick William. She had not had the chance to love any other young man, so the pure young Prussian Prince was given all the passion of her first love. He was four years older than her own father had been when he had married her mother at the age of twenty. Yet he still seemed so young, and her father so wise.

Prince Frederick William was allowed to give the Princess Royal a bracelet to confirm the engagement before he had to leave for Prussia. The secret could not be kept for long. Queen Victoria had to tell her Coburg uncle, King Leopold, of the success of their long planning. She confided to him that their wishes for her daughter's marriage were coming to pass in the most gratifying and satisfactory manner.[30] The Foreign Secretary, Lord Clarendon, also had to be told because

the marriage might affect British diplomacy. He replied that
he had heard of the admirable qualities of the young Prince,
also that the Princess of Prussia was set heart and soul on
the marriage.[31] Queen Victoria was glad of Clarendon's approval, especially as the Prime Minister, Lord Palmerston, was
thought to favor France and dislike reactionary Prussia. Behind
the love match lay something more essential. Politically, the
Queen wrote to the Foreign Secretary, the marriage alliance
was of great importance and might lead to a very different
state of things between England and Germany.[32]

The different state of things worried the editor of *The Times*
when he came to suspect the royal engagement. In an editorial,
he alleged that there had been a secret understanding as early
as 1851, when the Princess Royal was only ten. It was unfortunate for royalty that such private matters should have to be
made public, but they did affect the future of Britain. To
The Times, a royal marriage with the Hohenzollerns meant a
step toward an alliance with the Romanovs and Russia. "What
is His Prussian Majesty to us, or we to him? We never seem
to agree to do the same thing at the same time." The marriage
would divide the loyalties of the Princess Royal. Devotion
to her husband must be treason to her country.[33] This blast
from *The Times* caused great consternation at Balmoral and
at the Foreign Office. Lord Clarendon wrote to the Queen
that *The Times* was the worst enemy of his country. But there
was no way of stopping the nuisance. The complaints about
it were general, but nobody would give up reading it.[34] Unfortunately, it was read in Berlin as well, where the nature of
a free press was misunderstood because the Prussians did not
have one. The King himself thought that the editorial was
inspired by a Cabinet minister in London, although the British
envoy assured him that the newspaper was only a malignant
commercial speculation without politics or principles.[35] The
engagement was not broken off. The King of Prussia admitted
to a childish dream that a beautiful English princess would
sit on the Prussian throne, and Princess Augusta praised him

for standing alone in favor of her son's marriage at court.[36]

The Princess Royal was unconscious of the political furor, although her confirmation which would give a religious sanction to the engagement was hurried ahead in case worsening relations should make the match impossible. The service took place on March 20, 1856, in the Private Chapel at Windsor. The Princess Royal was wearing a rich white silk glacé gown with five pinked flounces, the body trimmed with white ribbons and Mecklin lace. The Chapel was filled with the royal family and its German relations, including the Princess's godfather, King Leopold of the Belgians. In front of the Archbishop of Canterbury she answered all the religious questions perfectly, her beauty and assurance convincing everyone that she was ready to accept marriage as well as God. This was precisely Queen Victoria's intention. She knew the Lord Chancellor considered the Princess Royal too young to know her own mind about a husband. This was not the case, the Queen wrote to Lord Palmerston. The Lord Chancellor was probably unaware that the Princess's choice had come entirely from her own heart, even though her parents had approved. "She is as solemnly engaged by *her* OWN free will and wish to Prince Frederick William as any one can be." She had pledged her word to him before God. She was old enough to know her own feelings, even if she was not yet old enough to consummate the marriage and leave her parents' home. Only that made the parents delay the wedding until after the Princess's seventeenth birthday.[37]

The Princess Royal had a great deal to learn. At Balmoral, she was enthralled to meet Florence Nightingale, and the great nurse's stories about the neglect of the wounded in the Crimean War gave the Princess a lifelong interest in looking after the wounded. For two hours every evening, her father taught her about Roman and recent European history. She had to produce essays for him, particularly on Prussian and German affairs. Prince Albert instructed her on the Coburg plan and also wrote to her future husband about it. Prince Frederick

William sent her his diary of the events of 1848, and came to see his betrothed in the May after her confirmation. He was now her "Fritz" and she his "Vicky."

This visit gave Prince Albert—soon to be created Prince Consort by his wife—the opportunity to catechize his future son-in-law on the virtues of constitutional monarchy and the English example, but the young man's mind was more full of the Princess. She was enjoying her first London Season and sometimes seemed almost frivolous with her new gowns and her dancing. One evening, a candle set her muslin dress on fire; she was quickly rolled in a rug to put out the flames, but her right arm was badly burned. At that moment of danger, the Prussian Prince knew that he would be devoted to her for life. "Through this accident," he told her, "you have really been given to me a second time."[38]

At the end of the Season, Queen Victoria confided her worries about her eldest daughter to her notebook. Her Dear Child did try her rather often with her wayward temper, her want of self-control and her sharp answers. She was contradictory and took criticism badly. But she had a very warm, affectionate and loving heart. Even though she was so clever and advanced for her age, she was still so simple, so childish, so inexperienced. She clung so passionately to her home and her father, her family and her country, that the Queen's heart bled to think of her daughter's future separation from her and isolation abroad. No doubt her Prussian Prince adored her and had the kindest and best of hearts—and the purest of minds. Yet his character was inferior to hers, and he would not be the support to her that he ought to be. "It makes me *very* anxious!" the Queen concluded. "*Every thing* for the *last* time—an *infant taking* leave, this is so dreadful for our poor dear Child!"[39]

Prince Frederick William made a more interesting impression on the imperial court in Paris, when he was ordered there on a visit. At a state ball, he thought that the Empress Eugénie looked like a true fairy queen in her tremendous crinoline and waterfalls of diamonds. She was intrigued by him and discovered hidden depths in his character. Although he looked like a Teuton straight from the pages of Tacitus, he was chivalrously polite and resembled Hamlet.[40]

In Berlin, a situation was developing which made him a Hamlet in reverse. His uncle the King was slipping into madness, and his father was taking over state affairs as the King's lieutenant. The Prince of Prussia had to tread warily and maintain the King's policies in case His Majesty recovered his lost wits. He was also surrounded by reactionary courtiers and spies for the Queen of Prussia. But at least his new power helped his son's marriage plans. There was a "state of fidget" in Berlin for a formal marriage treaty, but Prince Albert first wanted the question of his daughter's dowry settled. The British Parliament granted the Princess Royal £40,000 outright and an income of £8,000 a year—enough, but no fortune. Prince Albert insisted that she should keep control of her dowry. His principle was that while the Prussians were giving nothing to the Princess Royal, they ought not to take anything from her.[41]

There were further quarrels between the two families over her household. The young bride would be surrounded by elderly women, who would report back to her husband's mother and to the Queen of Prussia. Prince Albert insisted that two young women should join the household, Countess Marie zu Lynar and the brilliant Countess Walburga Hohenthal, who later became Lady Paget. He approved of the Count and Countess Perponcher to run the household with the Countess Blücher. Baron Stockmar's son Ernest must be appointed Treasurer. Prince Albert warned his future son-in-law that ill-natured people would say the young Stockmar was acting as a secret English political agent, but such people wanted the marriage to fail anyway.[42]

One last demand annoyed Queen Victoria. The Prussian court wished the marriage to take place in Berlin. Through Lord Clarendon, the Queen flatly refused. There was no possibility of the Princess Royal being married abroad. "The assumption of its being *too much* for a Prince Royal of Prussia to *come* over to marry *the Princess Royal of England* IN England is too *absurd,* to say the least," the Queen declared. "It is not *every* day that one marries the eldest daughter of the Queen of England. The question therefore must be considered as settled and closed."[43]

Otto von Bismarck was gloomy about the prospects which did not suit his view of Prussian politics. "If our future Queen," he wrote, "remains even only partly English, I can see our Court in danger of being surrounded by English influence." Bismarck distrusted the anglomania of sections of German society. Such servile admiration of a foreign country was unpatriotic.[44] He was already prepared to see the arrival of Queen Victoria's daughter as the intrusion of something alien and dangerous into the state.

As the wedding day approached, the Princess Royal grew more aware of all she would lose. Her letters to her brother, the Prince of Wales, show how much she loved and depended on him. From Balmoral, she wrote to tell him that she was always thinking of him and sometimes wished for a magic looking glass to see what he was doing. And when her "Fritz" left her for the last time before the marriage, she told her brother how sad she was to see him go—and yet she feared what was to happen. "The next time he comes," she wrote, "we shall not have to part; but then it will be good-bye to everybody—it is too dreadful—but we are always between two evils in this world."[45]

After her father and her future husband, her eldest brother would always remain the strongest influence on the Princess Royal. She did not share her parents' view of his defects. She knew how he had been driven and supervised more than she had because he was the heir to the throne. As his tutor admitted, the Prince of Wales had been forced early into life.

Too much was expected of him. The result was that he rebelled against his intensive education and his parents' excessive sense of morality. Once when he lied about smoking some tobacco, he was punished by three days' solitary confinement. He had to write to his father, begging forgiveness formally for the sin he had committed.[46]

The first two of the royal children particularly bore their parents' hopes and disappointments on their shoulders. Too much was desired for them, too much resistance was provoked in them. Queen Victoria could never see why her two eldest children had given her the most trouble. She thought the fault lay in their characters, not in her treatment of them. "A more insubordinate and unequal-tempered child and girl I think I never saw!" she wrote to her first child after her marriage. "The trouble you gave us all—was indeed very great. Comparatively speaking, we have none whatever with the others. You and Bertie (in very different ways) were indeed great difficulties."[47] The difficulties lay in being Victorian adolescents and heirs with most demanding parents. After she was married, the Princess Royal told her eldest brother that she had been neither fish nor flesh when she was younger. She had always felt shy and out of her element. She may have thought like a grown-up person, yet she knew she still had all the faults of childhood. But she had learned the lesson of creating harmony in the royal household. "Try and do what dear Papa wishes," she told her brother, "and you will see all will go right and dear Mama will be pleased and satisfied."[48]

She had done that herself. The Queen was pleased and satisfied at the marriage which Prince Albert had been so long making, but she could not accept the loss of her daughter. In the months before the wedding, her ambivalence became almost obsessive. Now that her daughter was an attractive young woman, the Queen was glad that this rival for her husband's love was leaving home, and yet she could not bear the thought that her child might be happy in marriage. The Queen was sure that the Princess Royal loved her father even more than her future husband. The child could not exist without Prince Albert. How different their two marriages were! The Queen had married an angel of a husband and did not have to leave her home. Although her daughter's choice was good, the Queen thought he did not have the strength to control his wife's temper and laziness. No marriage could compare with the Queen's, no happiness could be like hers; that would be a sacrilege.[49]

When a young French cousin died in childbirth, the Queen became even more anxious. She remembered Princess Charlotte dying during her labor forty years before—a death that had put her cousin Victoria on the throne. What then of Vicky, that beloved and difficult child? She might die herself, and never return from Prussia to see again the sweet sights of her childhood. On a last visit to Osborne, her daughter bade adieu to her pretty room, her favorite haunts, to her Swiss cottage and her garden. She would never again look at them in the same way. The girl in her would have vanished, and she would return only for a short time like a visitor. The thought filled the Queen with bitter sorrow. Then the Queen caught herself. She herself had a very unhappy childhood, quite alone and full of difficulties and trials. She ought not to be bitter. Fritz was only doing what he ought to do. He was good, straightforward and pure, and he adored Vicky. So be it, even if he was not the man of character her daughter needed. "None of our daughters will ever find *such* a Husband as Albert," the Queen told herself. "That is hopeless—and I know it."[50]

A fortnight before the wedding, the Queen began to think about the physical side of the marriage. The Princess Royal had been told nothing; the Queen would tell her nothing now, only that she must trust her husband and do what he said, however strange it might seem. The Queen did not dare think too much about it, it filled her with too much pity and anxiety. It was awful to give up a child to a stranger—and a man. But the child did love him tenderly and he loved her.[51]

In fear and concern, in turmoil and emotion, Queen Victoria waited for the marriage of the Princess Royal of England to Prince Frederick William of Prussia. It was what she and her husband had always wanted. Political duty must stand above personal feelings. That was what royalty was about.

2

Adieu to England

Deal kindly by her, noble man,
  She's but a child in years;
Cherish each hope, each new-found plan,
  And banish all her fears.

Deal kindly with her when afar
  From her sweet Island home;
Be thou to her a guiding star
  Through all her days to come. . . .

Deal kindly for her Mother's sake,
  So womanly and true.
Let not a fear her heart awake
  When she bids her child adieu.[1]

Deal kindly. She's her Country's Pride
  Who gives her for thine own.
And to thy keeping does confide
  A Jewel from her Crown.[1]

92-5812

DOLTON PUBLIC LIBRARY DISTRICT

O N NEW YEAR'S EVE 1857, the Princess Royal sent this poem from the magazine *John Bull* to her brother, the Prince of Wales. She was scared at leaving her home with a stranger for a foreign country she had never seen. She loved her noble Prince or thought she did, but she knew little of what was waiting for her in Prussia. Her mother and father had arranged for the members of her household to come to Buckingham Palace in the weeks before the wedding so that she could meet them and she was reassured by the competent Perponchers and found the young Countess "Wally" Hohenthal very good company. To the Countess, the Princess Royal seemed extraordinarily young:

> All the childish roundness still clung to her and made her look shorter than she really was. She was dressed in a fashion long disused on the Continent, in a plum-coloured silk dress fastened at the back. Her hair was drawn off her forehead. Her eyes were what struck me most; the iris was green like the sea on a sunny day, and the white had a peculiar shimmer which gave them the fascination that, together with a smile showing her small and beautiful teeth, bewitched those who approached her. The nose was unusually small and turned up slightly, and the complexion was ruddy, perhaps too much so for one thing, but it gave the idea of perfect health and strength.

If there were any fault to be found in the Princess Royal's face, it was in the look of determination about her chin, but her very gentle and almost timid manner disguised her willpower. Her voice was very delightful, never going up too high. It lent a peculiar charm to the slight foreign accent with which the Princess spoke both English and German. Countess Hohenthal also noticed the flaw which Queen Victoria knew well. The Princess Royal took violent fancies and dislikes to people, based on an intuition or their mannerisms. "She was no judge of character, and never became one, because her own point of view was the only one she could see."[2]

To the Princess Royal, the coming of her Hohenzollern

relatives-to-be was like an invasion. Everywhere, erect young princes with bristling moustaches, scarred cheeks and heels like castanets bowed stiffly and spoke sarcastically of England. They were surprised by the warmth of the crowds which cheered the Queen and her daughter, but they despised the lack of formality and ceremony at court. There were dinners for a hundred guests almost nightly in Buckingham Palace. The wedding presents were displayed at a state ball for a thousand guests, where there were great tables covered with jewels and candelabra and lace—and most magnificent of all the bridegroom's gift, a necklace of large matching pearls perfect in their whiteness. Queen Victoria glittered with all the diamonds of India, worn beside cornflowers and grasses on her silk and tulle costumes. Behind all the wealth, she had to show her love of a simple life.

Prince Frederick William arrived two days before the wedding. He had been preparing a home at the Babelsberg Palace, trying to make it less alien and cheerless for his bride. He had also been organizing their state entry into Berlin, testing their coach which swayed like a ship and looked like a gilded monkey-cage. He was nervous because his father was behaving ominously. The Prince of Prussia was now the effective regent in his brother's name. He had tried to refuse to come to the wedding in London because of state business and only gave way under great pressure from Prince Albert, who wanted to confide his daughter personally to the protection of another father figure in Berlin.

On the morning of the wedding, the Princess Royal went to see her mother, both still in their dressing-gowns. She was given a pretty book, *The Bridal Offering*, and dressed with the Queen. She wore white moiré silk trimmed with Honiton lace and white roses on her bridal veil. Her mother wore lilac and silver and a tiara. A daguerreotype was taken because Prince Albert wanted a memento of this last intimate occasion together. Father and daughter were composed, but the Queen was trembling and her likeness was blurred.

The marriage took place in the Chapel Royal of St. James's Palace. The Queen and her daughter drove alone in a carriage to the Royal Closet of the Palace, then made their way to the Throne Room, where the royal procession was assembling. Headed by drums and trumpets, the Poursuivants of Arms, Rouge Croix and Blue Mantle and Portcullis, and the heralds in their tabards led to the Chapel the Privy Councillors, the lords and ladies of the court, the royal dukes and the Queen with her two youngest sons in Highland dress. Once the Queen and the royal guests were settled in their places, the drummers and trumpeters returned to bring in the processions of the bridegroom and the bride.

Eight bridesmaids bore her train, "a cloud of maidens" who were all unmarried daughters of dukes or marquesses or earls. She stood by her Prince in front of the altar to say her vows before the Archbishop of Canterbury, her father at her back. The Princess Royal made no mistakes. Her mother thought that everything went off admirably, beautifully and most solemnly, with her daughter looking lovely and innocent, serene and calm. The service was like a dream to the Queen, as if she herself were being married again to her Prince Albert. He seemed as if he were renewing his vows to his wife, not giving a child away.

After the ceremony was over and the register had been signed and the organ had played Mendelssohn's "Wedding March," all the guests went to Buckingham Palace. Great crowds cheered the bride and groom when they appeared on the balcony. Soon it was time for the Princess to leave with her husband for a short honeymoon in the pretty rooms prepared for them in Windsor Castle. When she came in to see the Queen in her white épinglé dress and mantilla and bonnet to match, trimmed with orange flowers and a white lace veil, she was in tears. The Queen told her not to be distressed, she was as safe and happy with dear Fritz as if she were with her mother. She must not be frightened but should do whatever Fritz asked her. The Queen no longer felt any annoyance or alarm; after the holy scene of that day, all her fears seemed past.[3]

Yet the Queen knew her daughter was unprepared. Even the marriage sacrament made it no easier for her to surrender her child into the hands of a young man. She felt depressed and anxious until she received two letters from her daughter and her new son-in-law, both telling of their happiness together. Reading them brought on a fit of crying, but her tears were of gratitude and joy. She had struggled against these emotions all the time, and the reaction was sure to come.

Once she had overcome her fears and her prudishness, the Queen felt closer to her daughter than ever before. The court moved down to Windsor Castle, and the Princess Royal came to tell her mother about her feelings for her husband. "I am *not* shy," she declared. "Why should I be, if all is right?" The Queen was impressed. "What purity and simplicity and excellence there is in those words!" she wrote in her notebook. "How, just again, what I felt!" She praised her daughter's independence at last, and was glad that the trying little rubs of the past few weeks were over.[4] All she dreaded was her daughter's going away to Prussia and breaking up the family for the first time. She also feared the effect this might have on her husband, for she knew he was gloomy about losing his eldest child. He still thought her absolutely dependent on him.

The day of parting was overcast and gusty. Dark clouds threatened snow. At Buckingham Palace, the Princess Royal slept badly and then wept in her mother's bedroom. She could hardly control herself while she said "that dreadful word good-bye" to members of her family in the Audience Room. Nobody knew what she was suffering as she and her mother descended the staircase with an aching head and a far more aching heart.[5]

Snow was falling on the way to the dock at Gravesend. The enthusiasm of the enormous crowds in the City of London was indescribable as they cheered the royal carriage. It was

as if she were their own child.⁶ Girls had scattered flowers
before the gangway of the royal yacht *Victoria and Albert,* and
roses lay in the snow as the Princess Royal went aboard. But
the most dreadful good-bye was yet to come. She could bear
parting from her two eldest brothers, but in the ship's saloon
she clung to her father and wept on his breast. He could
not show the emotion he felt; his nature was undemonstrative.
He could only write to her saying that she could hardly know
how dear she had always been to him, and what a void she
had left behind in his heart and his life.⁷

She did not hide her feelings from him. She wrote to him
that she thought her heart would break when he shut the
cabin door and was gone—that cruel moment she had been
dreading for two-and-a-half years. She was weighed down
by grief. "I miss you so dreadfully, dear Papa, more than I
can say." She declared she owed him most in the world. Both
she and her husband still felt secure and happy that they
could rely on his precious advice.⁸ Prince Albert would not
fail them with that.

Slowly, the bride of seventeen, full of tears and grief, was
carried across the Channel through a blizzard and into thick
fog. The royal yacht reached Antwerp half a day late. The
assembled crowds could not even see the Princess for the
thick dull evening, although they could hear a military band
playing "God Save the Queen" in the muffled dark.⁹ This
was her uncertain introduction to a shrouded continent. Yet
that very evening, the Princess was universally admired at a
state ball given by her Coburg great-uncle, the King of the
Belgians who had always supported the policy behind her
marriage.

The fogs blew away, and the triumphal progress by train
to Potsdam began. Crowds gathered at all the stations in Belgium and in the smaller German states on the railway line.
The bride had to show herself at the compartment window
and smile through countless petty ceremonies, receiving bou-
quets from maidens in white, admiring garlanded arches and

listening to the speeches of local dignitaries. At Cologne Cathedral the mob was so great that the ladies were all nearly
crushed. Yet the feeling in the crowds was good. The British
envoy would have liked to have heard a good English cheer,
but he had to be content with the silent gasping of the Germans expressing satisfaction.[10] The tact and readiness of the
Princess Royal was a tribute to her training. She seemed to
have the right words and an enchanting smile for everybody.
She had, as her father said, a man's head and a child's heart.

If the journey was full of exhausting ceremony and lack
of privacy, the arrival in Prussia was even worse. It was an
affair of state, and royal dignity was second only to respect
for God. The Prince of Prussia with his full retinue was waiting
to meet his son and the bride (although the old Field-Marshal
Wrangel sat on a presentation meringue cake and had to be
cleaned up before the train reached its final destination). At
the first great reception in Potsdam, the young Stockmar reported that everyone praised the Princess Royal's kindness
of manner. The whole affair was brilliant with decorations,
illuminations, deputations, presents, music, and enthusiastic
crowds, hurrahing energetically.[11] The Princess was learning
the first lesson of the Prussian court: anything which could
be done on a larger scale always was.

Her ceremonial entry into Berlin the following day was
more like a war than a celebration. Eight black horses with
nodding plumes drew the gilt coach through the Brandenburg
Gate. Massed cannons thundered, flags waved in forests, and
the Prussian Guard stood rank on rank in glittering helmets
and cuirasses. Although the sun was shining, it was bitterly
cold, and the Princess Royal had to keep the coach windows
open throughout the drive and the loyal speeches. "It must
have been perishing work for her," Lady Churchill reported
back to Queen Victoria. The Princess herself said that she
felt like a bird perched in a gilt cage, petrified too. "I am all
one lump of ice," she told the Queen of Prussia when they
met. "My heart alone keeps warm."[12]

There was no respite for her. She had to meet all the court
and the German relations and the diplomatic corps. A huge
cercle was held, where she had to find something to say to
each ambassador and dance the polonaise with all the princes.
This meant she had to progress around the ballroom twenty-
one times, making low bows all the way and never tripping
over her long silver and pink train. Her style and grace were
enough to win over the watching Prince and Princess of Prussia. She was obviously an asset at the innumerable formal
occasions that made up court life. Her popularity with the
German crowds proved that she was also a political asset.
Her reception, far warmer than anyone could have expected,
was a spontaneous display of the true feelings of the nation.[13]
The personal triumph of the English Princess disconcerted
the reactionaries surrounding the Queen of Prussia. The country evidently approved of the new alliance. The eventual heir
to the throne was happy in his choice of a bride. Even though
she was staying in the dank and primitive wing of the Old
Schloss until the Babelsberg Palace would be ready, the Princess Royal enjoyed her success and did not see the snares
being set for her. She surprised everyone by taking her ground
so quickly and naturally.[14]

It could not last. Lady Churchill soon informed Queen
Victoria that she could only write about small matters because
all of her letters to England were being opened.[15] Stieber and
his state spies would not leave the foreign princess alone.
She was warned, and apologized to her mother for sending
her a letter by ordinary post. In future, she would always
wait for the royal messenger who brought her her mother's
letters or she would see that her messages home were put
in the diplomatic bag. She could not be too careful in Prussia.
The royal family there was the subject of perpetual stories
and criticisms; there was no respect for the princes—and there
could not be. This lack of respect hurt the Princess Royal
deeply. Things had been so different in England. Each prince
had spies in his household, and these people repeated all over

town what the princes and princesses said or did. The place
was a hotbed of gossip. The Princess Royal tried to be guarded
when speaking to her cousins and aunts and uncles by marriage. She would not open her lips on two topics—her husband
and her parents-in-law. In that way, and with God's help
and her mother's advice, she hoped to keep out of scrapes.[16]

The Princess Royal may have become disillusioned with
the intrigues and atmosphere of the Prussian court, yet she
could not have been happier in her relationship with her husband. In these early days of the marriage, he devoted himself
to her. She boasted of her happiness to her mother, who was
both pleased and annoyed. Queen Victoria did not like her
daughter appearing to compare her marriage with her mother's.
Prince Albert was obviously so superior to Prince Frederick
William that he should remain a Holy Grail to his daughter.
In only one way was the Princess Royal better off than the
Queen of England: her husband held the power in the marriage, while the Queen was in the "dreadful position of *sovereign*
and *wife!*"[17]

The nets began to close around the Princess Royal. The
Prince of Prussia ordered his son to undergo some intensive
military training, which took him away from his young wife.
Lady Churchill had to return home to Queen Victoria. She
had come to settle the Princess in her new country and had
stayed longer only because the Princess caught a bad cold
from the changes between the overheated rooms at court and
the chill air outside. In her last week in Berlin, she went on
a drive with the Princess and her husband to the Babelsberg.
It was a pretty little palace beautifully situated above the
river, but still not ready for them.

The waiting was sinister. The Princess's bedroom in the
Old Schloss was next door to the death chamber of her husband's grandfather. This room had been left untouched for
decades, as a mark of respect for King Frederick William III,
and the Princess had to go through the ghostly, musty room
every day to her dressing-room and boudoir. She thought it

was haunted. When a wind blew the door open, it brought
in the chill of death. There were not even any bathrooms in
the Old Schloss. This did not worry her husband, who had
always washed in cold water in the military way. The windows
were hardly ever opened, and were shrouded with thick curtains. Drafts blew up and down the gloomy corridors. The
Princess wanted light and air and hot water. These requests
seemed to the Prussian court a dreadful change, showing a
lack of respect for royal traditions. The mad King was in no
state to agree to such alterations. But the Princess was unwilling to wait, and let in light and freshness to the schloss, pulling
down the mourning drapes and pushing the windows open.
It was her first false move. Her English influences seemed to
be attacking Prussian dignity. Her young love of life was in
conflict with the state cult of death.

Her English influences remained strong. Her mother wrote
to her almost daily, her father once a week. They insisted
on a flood of letters home, spelling out the details of her
life and thoughts. They reminded her all the time of her duty
to her parents as well as to her adopted country. Although
most of the correspondence concerned social and domestic
matters, it still reflected their hopes that the young couple
might guide Prussian policy toward the English model and
the ideals of the Coburg relations. By maintaining their influence they were inducing the conflict of loyalties to which
their daughter was inevitably exposed. When the correspondence touched on political matters, she had to decide how
far she could reveal confidential information learned from her
husband. If she withheld it, her parents might feel that she
was not open with them.

The Princess Royal tried to remain English and become
Prussian. She was candid and open and attached to what she
had been and such discretion was foreign to her nature. What
her father said about her position was so right, she wrote
back to him. If she were to lose sight of her English title
and dignity, she would do herself and her husband much

harm. She was aware that there were people who would be only too happy if they could forget who she was. Her influence depended on being the Princess Royal of England, not just another Prussian princess; if she forgot her origins, she would lose the tools for doing good in Prussia. Her position was difficult. "I must take up my ground in this large family and then remain there. It must be completely neutral, if one can say so, and my extreme youth makes this only natural."[18]

Aside from her parents, the Princess Royal took only her mother-in-law into her confidence. Although the Princess of Prussia seemed a liberal and was very friendly with Queen Victoria, she wanted her son's wife to be her subordinate. She had done much to form her son's mind, and she was not going to lose her influence to the Princess Royal. They were also very different in their tastes. Princess Augusta loved expensive dresses and grand occasions, the formality and the glitter and the intrigue of court life. Her daughter-in-law hated the entire show, wanting privacy and close friends, honesty and plain talk. As yet, she was too young to assert herself, but she was soon disillusioned about the standards of her new society. "I cannot tell you, dear Papa," she wrote, "since I am married, how scales have fallen from my eyes on so many subjects."[19]

The Princess Royal knew her opinions mattered to her husband. She was able to influence his judgment but he was not to be led by the nose as Queen Victoria had thought. He was ten years older than his wife, who was still emotionally inexperienced and dependent on him, even if she were educated beyond her years. He cared about his military duties and excelled as a commander of men. Trained in obedience to his mother and father, he expected the same obedience from his wife. Although he frequently asked Prince Albert for advice, he rarely followed it. He was ever a Prussian first, and an Englishman only because of his admiration for his wife and her mother. His politeness and tact in public made him seem malleable, but in private, he was often stubborn and always held his ground. On one thing he was determined: he would replace his father-in-law as the leading man in his wife's eyes.

≫✦≪

Prince Albert could not let well alone. He sensed that his good advice made the Prince of Prussia evasive and his son-in-law reserved; a refugee or a suitor would listen, while a ruler or a husband would not. So Prince Albert decided to travel to Coburg at Easter and summon his eldest daughter to meet him there. He could show off his birthplace and recapture his dominance over her. He caught influenza and delayed his visit, while his daughter became pregnant and was forbidden to travel by her doctor, Wegner. She was angry, but her husband supported the doctor's decision. There was a quarrel between the young couple; its underlying cause was Prince Frederick William's suppressed jealousy of Prince Albert. But all was made well by the move to the Babelsberg Palace before Prince Albert's arrival in early June.

When the two fathers met, they seemed specters at the wedding feast. The Prince of Prussia was gaunt and sallow, while the Prince Consort was pale and puffy and nervous. Neither of them looked as if he would make old bones. The Prince of Prussia revealed that he would soon assume the official title of Regent, and Prince Albert tried to advise him on his future policy, but he was put off. There were to be no private conferences, no interference from England. The Prince of Prussia had not forgotten his humiliating months of exile. He distrusted the Coburg Prince's influence over his son who would soon become the direct heir to the throne.

Prince Albert's fears proved groundless. He found the relationship between his daughter and her husband good, and assured Queen Victoria that it was all that should be desired. He rehearsed them together and singly on the Coburg plan for Germany and a constitutional monarchy for Prussia. He did not seem to notice that the Prince of Prussia had been cold to the Princess Royal when her father made her ask that her husband be given more training in government and less in military maneuvers. Convinced he was right, Prince Albert could not see that his political influence on his daughter and son-in-law appeared to be meddling to the Prince of Prussia, and malign to Otto von Manteuffel's reactionary government. Prince Albert's agent in the Babelsberg household, Ernest von Stockmar, already thought that there was an official plot to get rid of him. Certainly the sudden visit of the Prince Consort had alarmed the powerful groups who suspected that English diplomacy stood too close to the Prussian crown.

Their fears were increased by Queen Victoria's decision to come to Prussia herself in August. She wanted to reassure herself about her daughter's pregnancy and check the way she was living. Although the Queen insisted that it was a private visit rather than a state occasion, she brought with her the Prince Consort and three of the most powerful men in England, Lord Clarendon, Lord Granville and Lord Malmesbury, the new Foreign Secretary. This diplomatic mission was in response to the unsettling policy of the French Emperor. He insisted on entertaining the Queen and the Prince Consort at Cherbourg before they went to Prussia, where he displayed huge harbor fortifications and menacing new ironclads, a warning to the English not to intervene in his plans for Italy. The sight made the Prince Consort's blood boil and forced the Queen to write to Lord Derby, insisting that he take immediate action in preparing the British Navy.

These were the war clouds massing behind the Queen's visit to her daughter. She had to undergo the same interminable railway journey from Antwerp to Potsdam, but her daughter was waiting to greet her at the Wildpark station, a nosegay in her hand. They fell into each other's arms. "So much to say, and to tell, and to ask," the Queen wrote, "yet so unaltered, looking well—quite the old Vicky still."

The Queen liked the Babelsberg, calling it a Gothic bijou. It was overcrowded with furniture and creepers, and had irregular towers like Osborne. In its intimacy, she grew very close to her daughter. She settled the pregnant girl on her day sofa and fed her with broth and good advice about the expected child. The Princess Royal was open with her mother. She broke through the barriers between them, not ashamed to talk about anything and everything. The Queen was touched and agonized about not being able to come back for the birth because she had to be in London for the opening of Parliament. Her daughter seemed so sensible about the pregnancy and felt so comfortable with her that they were now like sisters. The only fly in the ointment was Fritz's going away so much. He had foolishly Prussian ideas of his military duties.

The Queen marveled at her new ease with her daughter, whose marriage and delicate position in Prussia had given her a precocious maturity, even if she was still willful and lost control at times. Much as she disliked her present state and felt as if she were caught in a trap, the Princess Royal was sure that a child would be a great comfort to her. She hoped to educate the child differently from the previous princes and princesses of Prussia.[20] If she could not change her husband's country through him, she wanted to do it through their son.

Prince Albert was not so taken with the Babelsberg. He found it too small, and cluttered with Princess Augusta's hothouse taste. His daughter drove him to see Frederick the Great's Neue Palais in Potsdam, an enormous pillared block, now neglected and crumbling, a mere rest house for court pensioners. He suggested that she and her husband ask to move into it and decorate it in their own way. Their request was granted, and the Princess Royal was given a home which would make court life in Prussia more tolerable. Prince Albert was also pleased that his daughter was breaking out of the limited and backbiting court circle, discovering liberal intellectual friends who could continue her education. She had found two of her husband's old tutors, the natural scientist Professor Schellbach and Ernest Curtius, through whom she met the historians Ranke and Droysen, the classical scholar Brandis and the philosopher Werder. She was creating the first group of intellectuals seen around a royal princess in Prussia and, if it caused scandal, at least she was learning from such good company.

Although the royal visit was primarily a private one, ceremony could not be kept out of it. The Prince of Prussia and his wife arranged formal dinners and military reviews, and conducted tours of the royal palaces and tombs. The reactionaries who surrounded the Queen of Prussia did not hide their displeasure at this third invasion by English royalty within the year. Manteuffel himself was most unpleasant, cross and disagreeable to Queen Victoria. His anger had been excited by the Queen of England's unwise decision to invite her aged adviser, the old Baron Christian von Stockmar, to the Babelsberg. The Baron was the bugbear of the Prussian conservatives, the plotter for a liberal and constitutional Germany. His presence in Potsdam made Queen Victoria's visit look even more like a conspiracy to influence state policy.

Old Stockmar, however, caused less trouble between the visitors and their hosts than between mother and daughter. He thought that Queen Victoria was still trying to dominate her married child and make her feel inadequate. He complained to Lord Clarendon that the Princess Royal was becoming seriously ill because of her mother's incessant demands and rebukes. When Queen Victoria heard of his interference, she burst out into a towering passion.[21] She thought she was doing the right thing in showing her love and concern for a daughter who, for diplomatic reasons, had been allowed to marry too young.

Stockmar stuck to his guns, stressing the political consequences of such excessive mother love. In his opinion, the Prussian marriage was being wrongly treated by the Prince Consort and Queen Victoria and by England. They were proceeding much too actively, wanting much too much to control matters in Prussia to suit their opinions and feelings. They were meddling far too much in trivialities. He advised rather more consideration, moderation, calm and passivity.[22] He was absolutely right about the feelings of the Prussian court. The Prince of Prussia became Regent in October and King in all but name. This made his son the direct heir to the throne, and his son's wife might shortly be crowned beside her husband. She had now to put her second country before her homeland, to obey Prussian customs and traditions, and not accept contradictory advice from her parents.

The new Regent began by dismissing the Manteuffel government and installing a more liberal administration under Prince Karl Anton of Hohenzollern-Sigmaringen. The elections brought in a strong liberal majority to the Prussian lower house. Without pressure from England, the new régime in Prussia seemed to be reforming from within. It did not need the Prince Consort to send his congratulations a hundred times over. The Prince of Hohenzollern-Sigmaringen was friendly with Queen Victoria and praised the Princess Royal, saying that she saw through everything and understood things better than many people in Berlin. She was kind to those crushed by the court, and protected them.[23] She seemed to attract outcasts and dissidents.

Even more significantly, the Regent dismissed Stieber, the Berlin Chief of Police. He had suffered from the spymaster's attentions during his banishment to Coblenz when he had prematurely backed the alliance with England; now he could retaliate by removing Stieber from office and having him put on trial for his many secret crimes. While indictments were being prepared, Stieber filled in his time by advising the Tsar's government on how to organize a secret service. If his talents were not appreciated at home, they were abroad. He was devious enough to pass information on Russia back to Manteuffel and the reactionaries in case they returned to power. Old spies never go away, they simply wait for a change.

Yet another visit from the English court confirmed the Regent's search for a new alliance against the French. The

Prince of Wales came out to see his sister. Queen Victoria hoped that exposure to the social world of the Prussian court would improve his manners. His three weeks in Potsdam were a great success. He impressed everyone with his charm and ability to dance: as his father admitted, he had remarkable social talent. He renewed his close relationship with his elder sister, although she could not make him join in her intellectual activities. He preferred to hide his powers of thought. "Usually his intellect is of no more use," his father wrote, "than a pistol packed at the bottom of a trunk if one were attacked in the robber-infested Apennines."[24] His brother-in-law, however, became friendly with him, recognizing that considerable intelligence and tact lay beneath his surface laziness and boisterousness.

The Regent took particular care to invest the Prince of Wales with the Order of the Black Eagle and to make him an honorary colonel in the Prussian Guards. The awards of decorations and rank in Prussia were more than symbols, they were a form of diplomacy—in this case against Napoleon III's threats of war. When the Prince of Wales returned to England, he brought back not only better manners, but reports of Prussian fears of attack from France. Even the Prince Consort was impressed and said of his son, "The best school for him is the external stress of life."[25]

That was certainly the best school for the Princess Royal. Although six months' pregnant, she appeared on horseback at the Prussian army's deterrent maneuvers near the Rhine in November. Her mother might hope that her husband would be shocked at her sufferings, "for those very selfish men would not bear for a minute what we poor slaves have to endure."[26] But the Princess hid her condition and was a success with the soldiers, who were already devoted to her husband because of his concern for their welfare. Her husband's absence with his regiment made her heart grow passionate. She found life intolerable without him in the castle, missing him even more than she missed her father. She had become used to him near her. She began to write him loveletters, declaring that they were one and that the coming of the infant would bind them together. Once the child was born, Frederick William would displace her father as the natural source of love and authority.

With the New Year, Queen Victoria became very worried about her daughter's imminent confinement. She did not trust German medical training. The royal physician, Sir James Clark, was sent to Potsdam with her own midwife, Mrs. Innocent. When the Princess Royal began her labor a week sooner than expected, Dr. Wegner diagnosed a breech birth. Clark slowly administered two-thirds of a bottle of chloroform to the Princess to ease some of her pains. The labor lasted for four hours until half-past three in the morning. She suffered a great deal. "In truth I could not go through such another," Clark wrote back to Queen Victoria. "My close relation to the princess from her birth, and my affection for her made it more like the case of my own child."[27]

Two other Berlin doctors had been called in to help in the difficult birth. One of them, Professor Edouard Martin, shed tears to see the Princess's pain. As he had the most experience, he assisted the birth manually, which was a dangerous thing to do. Long ago, the old Stockmar had refused to help in the labor of the English Princess Charlotte, the heiress to the throne, in case she died during her difficult childbirth. He had known that the blame for her death would be put on him as the only foreign doctor present. When Wegner handed over responsibility to Martin and Clark, he was already despairing of the Princess's life, let alone a live birth. Martin's skilled hands brought out a boy, who took a long time to shake into breathing. He saved both mother and child, but he and Clark would take the blame for wrenching the baby's left arm and neck during the difficult birth. Wegner's incompetence would be ignored because he was a Prussian. The saviors Martin and Clark would be accused of ignorance and carelessness and harming the child. They were foreigners.

Throughout the long labor, Prince Frederick William rarely

left his post by the Princess's head, while the Countesses Perponcher and Blücher and Mrs. Innocent were always busy
in the room. The Princess was surrounded by care and devotion. There was general rejoicing, a state of perfect excitement
over the birth of a son. It was the best thing she could have
done for her husband and herself. Queen Victoria observed
that the son was an immense event for Prussia and would
cause ecstasy. She and the Prince Consort had become grandparents at the age of thirty-nine.[28]

The birth of the boy lessened the Queen's obsessive efforts
to run her daughter's life from England. It was as if the Princess
Royal, by becoming a mother, could really begin to take the
place of a younger sister as in the days of the Queen's visit
to the Babelsberg. The Queen could now concentrate more
on her unmarried daughters at home, which was a blessing
and politically wise. She had already made a New Year's resolution to let her eldest daughter go her own way. "Have I
improved as *much* as I ought?" she had asked herself in her
journal. "I fear *not*. . . . A married daughter! And *here—self*
is *still far* too *prominent!* I must crush it—must try and bear
patiently the utter change of position between Parents and
a married daughter! Several times *all* has been right—but there
have been relapses when I was wrong, and I *must* and *shall*
struggle against these feelings and many strange prejudices
and odd sensations I have."[29]

The Queen did, however, still warn her daughter against
baby-worship and spending too much time in the nursery.
She herself had never liked babies much and had found the
company of her children often tedious. The Princess Royal,
her mother knew, doted on babies, and, indeed, she had to
be stopped by her mother-in-law from breast-feeding her infant. That was not done by a Prussian princess nor by the
Queen of England. Instead, a wet nurse was found, whose
milk immediately irritated the baby's bowels.

By Prussian custom, the christening of the child had to
take place several weeks after its birth. The royal family filled

the private chapel of the Crown Prince's palace. The gold vessels for the baptism were covered by a silver brocade cloth on which the emblem of the Black Eagle was embossed, and above the altar hung a jeweled purple canopy embroidered with the golden crowns of Prussia. The baby was swathed in lace to hide his deformed arm. At the ceremony, he was christened Frederick William Victor Albert. He hardly cried, fascinated by the Regent's decorations and orders, while the proud grandfather held him in his arms for the holy rite.

Most of the forty sponsors were there, but not Queen Victoria and the Prince Consort. Although they had hoped to come, public duties kept them in England. The British envoy's wife wrote to the Queen, giving details of the grand occasion, but adding that the Princess Royal was still very tired and weak and needed great care. Even the joy at christening another heir to the throne could not dispel the ominous gloom in Berlin. It was as if a great black thick cloud were hanging which might burst at any moment.[30]

The day after the baptism, the Regent appointed Otto von Bismarck as the Prussian Ambassador to St. Petersburg. There Bismarck would get to know of the advantages of the Russian alliance and keep clear of the Regent's experiments in liberalism. As for the royal infant, there would be time to win him from the influence of his mother, *die Engländerin.*

So the year of 1859 began with a royal birth and a foreboding of war in Europe. If the succession to the Prussian throne was secure, the future of the country was less clear. The Princess Royal had grown closer to her husband and reached a new understanding of her mother. She was, as she wrote to Queen Victoria, so happy when she looked at her son and thought he was not a girl and could not suffer what she had suffered.

> I think if I had a daughter I could never bear the thought of her having to suffer so much! How much I can understand what a poor Mother must feel when her daughter

is going to be married; it must be a near torture to know all that she will have to go through, and not to be able to go with her and help her and be with her. It must be really a very hard trial; I can understand so well what you must have felt at my marriage now, but I could not then.[31]

3

Divided Loyalty

"**Y**OU AND YOUR CHILD must look like two babies together," Queen Victoria wrote to her daughter, "as you have such a child's face still."[1] The Princess Royal, who doted on her son, took three months to recover from the birth. When she was able to return to court circles, she found her father turning to her for intelligence during an international crisis. The King of Sardinia and his minister Cavour were intriguing with Emperor Napoleon III to drive the Austrians out of northern Italy. Prussia did not know whether to join Austria against the hated French, or to stand at a distance like England and try to profit after the event. In a way, Austria was the obstacle to a united Germany as well as to a united Italy, and the French goal of making a new nation by expelling Austria was an example for Prussia in the future.

Until the outbreak of war, the Prince Consort was like a *terrier* of personal diplomacy. Sometimes he seemed to be trying to keep the peace almost single-handedly for England. Queen Victoria complained that he worked too hard and wore himself out by all he did. His attempts to preserve the peace tried his nerves, while the endless contradictory telegrams coming in every hour raised and dashed his hopes continually.[2] Some of the disturbing news was coming from the Princess Royal. Although her letters home dealt mainly with her baby son and household arrangements, she was a good mirror of Prussian attitudes, reflecting them almost artlessly. She was also beginning to engage in her own sort of diplomacy, telling her mother that the Prussian situation was a very critical one. If Prussia stayed neutral and the Austrians won a war, it would damage the reputation of the country and its army. If Austria lost, the French could fall on Prussia alone. The Princess Royal suggested that an alliance be formed between Prussia and England that would help the security of both nations, deter the French, and stop Berlin from continually sniping at London for doing nothing to curb French ambitions.[3]

Such minor royal diplomacy could not stop Napoleon III from taking the field in Italy. The Princess Royal took the outbreak of war as a personal attack on her happiness, for she foresaw the moment when her husband would be called to join his regiment. She complained to her mother that it was all very fine for the men to talk of defending their country, of a soldier's life being the only one for a man, and of wanting death on the field of battle, but they did not think of their poor unhappy wives, taken from their homes and left behind alone.[4] As the Princess was married to a Prince who knew the plans of the Prussian general staff, she was in an impossible position. She was used to telling her father and mother of everything she thought was important. Her husband sometimes told her of the movements of the Prussian forces. There was no reason he should conceal such information from his wife. She had been trained by her parents to keep nothing of importance from them, and she was still too young and inexperienced to know when she should be silent. Her errors of judgment were still the faults of youth.

French victories in Italy scared the Prussian court, that

feared Napoleon III might defeat Austria and turn his armies on Prussia as his predecessor had done. Partial mobilization was ordered. The Princess Royal informed her parents immediately. "There is general consternation here!" she wrote to Queen Victoria on June 16, 1859. "All is preparing for war." The mobilization of six army corps had been ordered, she wrote, and her husband had been given command of a Guards Division. She herself was swept away by war fever. She hoped that the Prussian forces would soon cross the Rhine and make their country the leader of Germany by force of arms. She wished for once that she were a man, and that her son was a man, to fight the French. She could not help being savage.[5] Such bloody sentiments provoked her mother's worst rebuke. Her daughter was obviously suffering from enthusiasm. The Queen feared that they would diverge more and more, and to feel that her daughter's interests were so different was a sad trial.[6] Already the Queen could see that her married daughter, in time of war, would have to choose to follow her husband's sentiments. In a conflict of interest, Prussia must come before England. A daughter had been lost, no influence gained.

The Princess Royal went guilelessly on revealing Prussian military plans. Two days after her letter to her mother, she wrote to her father. She supposed he would have heard of all that was happening in Berlin, but in case he had not, she told him that eight army corps were not being called to the colors. Military organization had fallen apart. Full mobilization was proving impossible, although that was what was needed. "Please keep this to yourself, dearest Papa," the Princess added uneasily, "because I know this only from Fritz."[7] Her father's reply showed that his daughter was sending him better intelligence than the Foreign Office in London. He had known nothing of the partial mobilization. This confession startled his daughter, who wrote back that she found it strange he had not heard of the mobilization sooner. She was becoming more discreet—or else the Prussian government was beginning to withhold delicate information from her husband, and so from her and her parents in England. "We know as little as you do," she wrote on July 2, "and I think that they have no intention of keeping anything from you."[8]

The Prussian government almost certainly did have that intention. Together with his advisers, the Regent was suspicious of England's neutrality. They knew of the regular secret communications carried by royal messengers between Prince Frederick William's household and Windsor Castle. Unfortunately, the Prince Consort now chose to intervene, using the information sent by his daughter and suggesting its source. He wrote directly to the Regent in Berlin, counseling against military preparedness in face of the French. The Regent did not mention nor show this letter from England to his son. This omission provoked the Princess Royal into a disingenuous comment on the relationship between her husband and his father, who very rarely showed his son anything of importance. His daughter-in-law was convinced that it was from nothing but forgetfulness. She would question the Regent about a great many things. Then he would answer and tell her and her husband about everything—but then they could not always be asking.

She continued to reveal matters which might help her father keep the peace. She wrote home about the Austrian Empress coming to Berlin with the Prince of Windisch Grätz who had said, "If we did not help them now, they would *never* forgive us—and *not* help us if they made peace now and we were attacked." Prussia was still trying to prepare against a French assault. Two army corps had been moved towards the Rhine, while another corps was being kept back to defend Berlin; the rest of the reserves were still disorganized.[9] The Prussians were simply not ready to fight. Their army badly needed reform.

The military information which the Princess Royal was sending back to her father was secret, but she had been brought up to consider her father as a keeper of international peace, and he could not help to prevent conflict between other nations without accurate intelligence. As his daughter, she would have wished to keep him informed, while trying to make England side with Prussia in the probable war against France. As it was, she was under heavy pressure in Berlin because of the British government's policy of strict neutrality. Her husband was also under attack because of her: "Fritz says his peace of mind is gone."[10]

News of the sudden armistice between France and Austria after the Battle of Solferino was a thunderbolt in Berlin. Prussia was now isolated and vulnerable. It had lost credit in Germany and was exposed to France. Everyone was on the alert. "War is always thought of and talked of," the Princess Royal reported. "God avert this calamity from us, I say."[11] The calamity was averted because the French chose to digest their gains in Savoy and Nice and to defer their attack. The international crisis had proved that the Princess Royal's loyalty to her father had endured despite her marriage, that she could reconcile her duty as a daughter with her devotion to her husband. She hoped to combine the conflicting policies of her two countries through the two men she most loved. She was being disloyal only to the Regent's anti-English advisers, not to the policy which her father and her husband wanted for Prussia and Germany. The ministers were at fault; she was not. The future alone could judge her.

The Prince Consort aimed to influence European politics through his royal relations, and English diplomacy through his wife's right to advise on messages sent to foreign governments. Increasingly, he taught Queen Victoria to rewrite dispatches and letters to the other great powers. Her blue pencil became the terror and the delay of dozens of English administrations. On subjects such as Germany, the Queen and the Prince Consort knew far more and had far more influential contacts than their foreign secretaries, who came and went with the fall of governments. The most recent, Lord John Russell, was not in favor of an alliance with Prussia against France, but he had to reckon with the threat of the Emperor

Napoleon, and he was grateful to the Prince Consort for sending him private correspondence with the Prince of Prussia. No prime minister, even if he were as independent as Lord Palmerston, could ignore the power of the royal network across Europe. Often enough, a private letter from Queen Victoria to a royal cousin was the last trump to play, which might stop the outbreak of a war.

In March 1860, Russell asked the Prince Consort for a paper on the state of Germany and for advice on future policy there. It was the height of Prince Albert's influence. He used information collected from his daughter in Berlin to reply that the Regent of Prussia was very low and irritable. There were grave difficulties because more taxes were needed to pay for the reform of the army system. In general, the Prince Consort declared, the Italian and the German questions had been the same ever since Charlemagne. Through the old Holy Roman Empire, the Hapsburgs of Austria had held possessions in both Germany and Italy, preventing the unification of either nation. The German situation was further complicated because so many princes, such as an Elector of Hanover, had become the rulers of England, Denmark, Belgium or Poland. German politics had become international politics. England, for instance, was still interested in Hanover, not to mention Saxe-Coburg. Many foreign countries felt the right to interfere in German affairs. Austria's recent defeat had left it severely weakened, and if Prussia adopted a war policy like the Kingdom of Sardinia, it could unite Germany. The Prussian royal family, however, was too timid to play so bold a game, too honorable to play so false a one.[12]

Prince Albert's brilliant diagnosis ignored the factor which could unite Germany. If the Prussian royal family could not be ruthless enough, its Minister President could. The liberal administration of the Prince of Hohenzollern-Sigmaringen had already proved weak and indecisive, and as a replacement, one man was being mentioned to the Regent—the present Ambassador in St. Petersburg. Otto von Bismarck had been noted by British diplomats as a man of action, who wanted a war against Austria to unite Germany. "You have no notion how we hate them," he told one British Ambassador. The Prussian army looked on the Austrians as enemies.[13] He foresaw a major war, with Britain standing on the sidelines. Its army, outside India, was too small for it to interfere with the masses of men that Bismarck's war would put in motion, and the face of Europe could be changed without the British navy having much to do with it.[14]

The Regent hesitated about sending for Bismarck, even though the state of the army was driving him into depression and anger. His policies were contradictory. At times, he listened to the army leaders, who wanted a return to the military state, which would mean an alliance with Russia against France, and the stifling of reform. At other times, he seemed to favor liberal changes, and the English alliance championed by his wife and daughter-in-law. He was so sick of power that he often talked of abdicating in favor of his son, who was becoming more proud every day of being the commander of a regiment of Prussian Guards. Hopes were running high in the rococo Neue Palais, where the Princess Royal and her husband were now installed.

The prospect of coming to the throne may have made the Neue Palais seem more attractive to the Princess Royal. This palace of Frederick the Great's reminded Queen Victoria of Hampton Court, its grandeur the opposite of what the Princess Royal had learned from her mother. Most of its two hundred rooms were enormous. At first only a few were used, but as the court pensioners died off one by one, she took over more and more rooms until the whole place was hers. As a reminder of childhood intimacy, one small room was done up like the Blue Closet at Windsor Castle. The work of renewal was endless and daunting: the tapestries were rotting; the carpets eaten by mice; the chimneys full of bats; the silvered furniture black with age; the painted ceilings covered with grime. As usual, there were no bathrooms, only

an outside pump for water. Yet the fluted columns and carved
mantles, the classical proportions and the sense of space and
light, were worth all the efforts of restoration. The three graces,
after all, supported the crown above the main entrance. With
the Princess Royal in residence, they might return inside the
palace. There were also overgrown gardens outside which
could be rescued from neglect. Nurture would recreate the
careful nature beloved by Victorian ladies. Without a whole
state to remodel, the Neue Palais would do. That, and the
business of having more children, would pass the time while
her husband was sent away on his military duties.

Her second pregnancy did not stop her from paying a visit
to England with her husband. They had to leave their baby
son behind, because he was still too young to travel. The
visit was full of nostalgia and sentiment as the Princess Royal,
now the mother of a child herself, visited the places of her
childhood. Prince Albert was happy to be able to advise his
daughter and son-in-law in privacy. Even royal messengers
and diplomatic bags were not entirely safe. One of his letters
to the Regent of Prussia had fallen into the hands of Napoleon
III. His reaction was masterly. "If people have spies to open
and read letters," he said, "they must expect to see what they
may not like."[15]

He and Queen Victoria agreed to pay a return visit to
Coburg to see their grandson. In the interval, the Princess
Royal had an easy labor, giving birth to her first daughter,
Victoria Augusta Charlotte. It turned her even more from politics toward her home and her nursery, which was supervised
by a traditional English nanny, Mrs. Hobbs. Her household
did not run smoothly; royal households rarely did. The opportunities for intrigue and petty theft were too great. The English
princess was surrounded by the jealousies and judgments of
German ladies. She disliked her husband's chamberlain and
was suspicious of his military friends and advisers, who encouraged in him the warlike obstinacy that had led to their
first quarrel. Although her husband was being allowed to at-

tend councils of state, he was not allowed to comment. If he wanted to give orders, he could do so on the parade ground or at home. A war seemed his only way to distinguish himself.

In spite of the disapproval of *The Times,* Queen Victoria and the Prince Consort went to visit Coburg in September. There was a diplomatic reason behind the trip. The monarchs of Prussia, Austria and Russia were to meet. It was possible that they would try to form a new Holy Alliance against nationalism and the French, that would isolate Britain in Europe. So Lord John Russell accompanied the royal party in the usual mixture of royal family visits and foreign relations. The Foreign Secretary even went on a wild boar hunt with Prince Frederick William and the Prince Consort, who had survived a bad carriage accident. The Prince Consort bagged at least three boars and his guests one each. The wounded beasts were finished off with spears.

Queen Victoria was enchanted by the sight of her first grandson, who was always to keep a special place in her heart. He came walking up to his grandmother holding his nurse's hand "in a little white dress with black bows, and was so good. He is a fine, fat child, with a beautiful white soft skin, very fine shoulders and limbs, and a very dear face . . . He has Fritz's eyes and Vicky's mouth, and very fair curly hair. We felt so happy to see him at last."[16] In her description, Queen Victoria chose to ignore the damage done to the child's neck and left arm. Her daughter confessed to feeling guilty about tripping over a chair during her pregnancy and falling heavily on her back, perhaps damaging the infant within her. Her mother reassured her, saying that the little boy would grow out of it or respond to treatment.

More important than the trip to Coburg was the royal rendezvous at Coblenz. There the Prince Regent and Princess of Prussia went out of their way to welcome Queen Victoria and the Prince Consort. It was the highwater mark of Anglo-Prussian friendship and of the Coburg plan. Never again would the long policy behind the Princess Royal's marriage appear so convincing. Fear of a Russo-French entente had thrown the two Protestant powers together at a time when the Regent was still experimenting with a liberal government at home. The royal families shared their pleasure in their grandchildren and their heirs. Diplomacy and kinship walked hand in hand.

The Regent was so swayed toward the English alliance that he chose to stalemate the meeting with the Austrian and Russian Emperors at Warsaw. More earth was piled on the grave of the Holy Alliance. Prussia could not support Austria when they were rivals in Germany, while Russia always feared an Austrian attack in the Balkans supported by Turkey and Britain. For the time being, the Regent of Prussia preferred to trust in the known commitment of the British royal family. This was soon strengthened by the engagement of Queen Victoria's second daughter, Alice, to Prince Louis of Hesse. Once more, the British crown seemed to be the treasure house of German princes. Its heartland lay across the Rhine.

❦

Prince Frederick William was heir to the throne, and he was behaving as heirs to the throne normally behave. He did not believe that the father was ruling as well as the son could. He set up two groups of advisers in opposition to the reactionary court group which increasingly had his father's ear. One group consisted of five military men who rose to be generals in time: Mischke, Winterfeldt, Blumenthal, Stosch and Winterfeld. The first two had great loyalty to the Prince and a loathing of people with a court bend in their backs. Blumenthal was a clever strategist and rose to be Chief of Staff, while Stosch became chief of the Admiralty for a decade. He was an intimate enemy of Bismarck, who distrusted his influence with the Crown Princess and suspected him of wanting to become chief minister.[17] Winterfeld was to prove the Judas among them.

The other group of liberals and counselors was led by Prince Frederick William's brother-in-law, Grand Duke Frederick of Baden. His chief minister and adviser was Baron Roggenbach, the creator of Strasbourg University. A great raconteur, he was trusted by the Empress Augusta as well as Queen Victoria and the Crown Princess. The lawyer, Heinrich von Friedberg, was an intimate of the household along with Professor Geffcken, who had been a fellow student of the Prince. Baron George von Bunsen, the historian and politician Max Duncker, and Count Usedom completed the group. On the fringes of the circle were Baron Walter von Loë and the novelist and poet, Gustav Freytag, whose words were bolder than his character.

One fat Englishman, who was to become Bismarck's *bête noire,* was the courier. He was Robert Morier, an elephantine and wily and brilliant and self-important man, who understood German affairs as well as did the Prince Consort. When he was serving as a paid attaché at Berlin, his reports were among the few valued by Prince Albert. He ingratiated himself with the Princess Royal and helped her try to influence Prussian policy through her husband's advisers.

From the outside, these military and civilian consultants to the heir to the throne looked like an opposition group, and could be represented as a conspiracy by spymasters such as Stieber. Fortunately, he had offended the Prince Regent by spying on him during his own period of opposition to his brother the King, and found himself on trial for misusing his police powers. Morier wrote a long and foreboding memorandum on the trial. Stieber's organization and methods had not ended just because their master was accused. The new administration of the Prince Regent had announced that it would not break violently with the past, but would better the previous system. Unless there were to be a housecleaning, the past bureaucracy would prove too strong for the present government. The new wine would not burst the old bottles, but the old bottles would unfailingly taint the new wine.

Only Stieber had been removed. The Minister of Justice, the President of Police and his hated underlings had been kept on, which seemed weakness rather than generosity. Stieber was merely the scapegoat for the sins of the Prussian police state. The press was still gagged, individual liberties were still uncertain, and the doings of the political police shrouded in mystery. Even at Stieber's trial, a decent veil was drawn over the illegal acts of the Manteuffel government, including the theft of secret papers from the King's own secretary. Stieber himself was only accused of a minor offense, while Morier called him "the life and soul" of the police spy system.[18] Stieber pleaded that all the illegal acts committed by him were on the orders of ministers still in the Cabinet. He had royal authority for his work. If he fell, many powerful people would fall with him. His threat of more revelations secured his acquittal. To convict him would be to convict Prussian aristocrats, perhaps even point a finger too near the person of the mad and dying King.

Although Stieber was temporarily put out to grass and to advising the Tsar, his men were still working for the reactionary circles around the Prince Regent, who was waiting to become king. The Regent was, as Lord Clarendon found him later, surrounded by retrogressive relations and advisers and in the meshes of a villainous police.[19] With or without Stieber, nothing changed overmuch in the police state of Prussia. Worse than with Hamlet's father, the Regent daily had poison poured into his ear. As the Princess Royal reported, spies and police informers inflamed his fears of another revolution like that of 1848 in Berlin, and pushed him into the hands of the reactionaries. He thought that he had the best police in the world and was better informed than his ministers, and he became suspicious, irritable and nervous. He would believe the truth was told by those who played upon his fears.[20]

᠊᠊

It was a year of significant deaths. After 1861, nothing could be the same again. The first was that of the King of

Prussia, who finally died in Potsdam on New Year's Day. His passing brought out the excessive melancholia of Prussian royal observances. The Princess Royal and her husband were awakened in the middle of the night to witness his death throes. The Queen of Prussia was sitting at the head of the bed, her arm underneath the King's head, her other hand wiping the sweat off his forehead. The Princess Royal described the scene to her mother:

> You might have heard a pin drop—no sound was heard, but the crackling of the fire and the death rattle—that dreadful sound which goes to one's heart and which tells plainly that life is ebbing. This rattling in the throat lasted about an hour longer and then the King lay motionless. The Doctors bent their heads low to hear whether he still breathed and we stood, not even daring to sit down, watching the death struggle, every now and then the King breathed very fast and loud, but never unclosed his eyes— he was very red in the face, and the cold perspiration pouring from his forehead. I never spent such an awful time, and to see the poor Queen sitting there quite rent my heart—3, 4, 5, 6, 7 struck and we were still standing there— one member of the Royal Family came in after the other and remained motionless in the room, sobs only breaking the stillness. Oh it is dreadful to see a person die![21]

With the morning, all the watchers went to the next room. The Princess Royal, exhausted, fell asleep on a sofa, while the others walked up and down. During the following day of waiting and waiting she was sent home by her husband, only to be called out again at one in the morning. The old King had finally gone. She had to pay homage to the new King and Queen before visiting the deathbed. The dead monarch looked like a sleeping child to her; every moment she expected to see him move or breathe. She kissed both his hands which were quite cold by then, for the last time. At the formal filing past the corpse, the dead King's sister, the Grand Duchess of Mecklenburg-Schwerin, pushed the Princess Royal close up to the pillow, so that her cheek almost touched the face of the dead man. It gave her a great shudder.[22]

At the lying in state, the obsessive cult of the dead continued. The King's body was laid out in the room, all hung with black, where Frederick the Great had died. The coffin was covered with a mantle of violet velvet and ermine, set in a niche beneath the same canopy that had overshadowed the christening of the Princess Royal's children. Born to inherit— born to die. The King was dead—long live his heirs. The embroidered crowns of Prussia topped all.

The funeral was held in a freezing Berlin with the temperature seventeen degrees below zero. The royal and diplomatic guests were as cold as icicles outside, while inside the palace was like a Turkish bath. The crown and scepter and orb were carried into the royal chapel, while the pall was borne on the shoulders of eight generals; a field marshal, carrying the royal standard, brought up the rear. The new King and the Queen Dowager sat at the foot of the coffin, the Prussian princes and foreign royal mourners standing nearby. The service was chanted, the address was short.[23] The King, already sixty-four years old, seemed frail and ready to follow his brother. The ceremonies continued beyond the grave. Every evening there was a reception for all the German princes who had gathered to pay their respects and see one another. The Princess Royal found a room full of them humiliating, but funny, rather like the collection of Scots earls she had seen with her mother four years before. A death in the family had assembled a vast congregation of pomp, power and tedium. "Half Europe was together," the Princess Royal informed her father, "and I had the pleasure of doing the honours *all alone* for all these Princes every evening here!" She found that the Prince of Bavaria looked like a telegraphist, while another prince was an Ostrogoth.[24]

Prince Frederick William was now the Crown Prince and his wife Victoria the Crown Princess of Prussia, a title superior even to that of Princess Royal of England. She might now hope to sit beside her husband on a throne. Her brothers would always keep her from that in her home country. His new position involved the Crown Prince increasingly in state affairs. He was rarely in the Neue Palais and now slept at the other end of the vast building, so far from his wife that she complained she might just as well not be married at all. Yet she was delighted at his new responsibilities and their effect on his character. As she told her mother, he was so good and so courageous and so useful to the ministers and the Queen that it made up for her hardly ever seeing him.[25]

One gift from England pleased the new king; Queen Victoria sent him the Order of the Garter. This honor mattered to a military monarch who valued decorations and orders and court ceremonial as the emblems of a rightly ordered country. However, he resented the flood of good advice from the Prince Consort, who still treated him as a refugee from Berlin rather than a ruler there. So he put the letters from the Crown Princess's father on the fire and scolded her, when she approached him on some liberal errand at Prince Albert's or Queen Augusta's dictate. She kept on burning her fingers for the Queen of Prussia, who used her as a catspaw to tell the King things she did not choose to say herself. Then, the Queen spoiled the whole thing by throwing out hints in advance. The result was that the King always interrupted his daughter-in-law by saying: "I am sure Mama told you that."[26]

The friction between the King and the Queen was made worse because the liberal majority in the Prussian lower house blocked the necessary reform of the army. The King saw this refusal to increase his country's military strength as a deliberate plot against the nation's security, and began listening more and more to the reactionaries. A swing to the right seemed inevitable as early as March 1861. "Heaven knows what is to become of us, if the Old Régime is to begin again," the Crown Princess told her father by letter. She would have liked to pour out her heart and her fears of a repressive future, but that would have to wait until they met again.[27]

The meeting was to be unexpectedly soon. There was a second significant death that year. Queen Victoria's mother, the Duchess of Kent, died of erysipelas. Although her childhood had been made unhappy by her mother, the Queen collapsed. Her own motherhood was sacred to her. Her mother's death seemed the violation of a holy state, an intimation of her own mortality. "You, my darling, have seen a death bed," she wrote to the Crown Princess , "—I never."[28] The shock of watching a long expiring through a night and a morning prostrated the Queen. There were false rumors in Berlin that she had to be confined to a padded room in Windsor Castle. "To lose a beloved mother is always terrible," she confided to Queen Augusta, "and the blank can never be filled, that you know."[29]

The Crown Princess hurried over to England to console her, and in June she again visited her homeland, with her two children and her husband. She wanted to relive the happiness of her childhood at Osborne, where she could watch her small boy and girl playing as she once had. The King of Prussia had been reluctant to let them leave the country, and his reasons were given a brutal point. A radical student tried to assassinate him at Baden and he was wounded in the neck just below the ear. The Crown Prince had to hurry back to Germany in case he might have to take over from his father. Although the King recovered, he was so shocked by this murder attempt that he was ready to welcome any protective measures. Bismarck profited from the occasion to send in a memorandum advising the use of repression and force, and the creation of a national assembly. His time was near.

≫≪

The Prince of Wales needed to marry. The Crown Princess and her mother had gone through all the possibilities. The next Queen of England had to be a princess and a Protestant. The best and the most beautiful seemed to be the Danish Princess Alexandra, whose father was next in line to inherit the throne. So the Crown Princess artlessly arranged for the two to meet, when they were both sightseeing in the gothic cathedral at Speyer. She left them alone together, while she went off with the bishop to admire the frescoes. "May God bless this budding romance," she wrote to her parents, "as He has done in our case."

Her brother had told her that he had never seen a young lady who pleased him so much. Although Princess Alexandra was only sixteen, the Crown Princess thought her forward for her age, not shy at all. Yet there was no fault in the way she behaved. She was simple and unaffected and quite unaware of her charms. She was bound to grow upon the Prince of Wales, even though he would not commit himself to his sister "in his own funny undemonstrative way."[30]

The Crown Princess could not have done a more reckless or more loving act. She should not have been involved. She may have helped to find her brother a wife, but she had provoked the King of Prussia. The Danes were at daggers drawn with Prussia and the German Confederation over the border provinces of Schleswig and Holstein, where they controlled a majority of German subjects. If the Prince of Wales married Alexandra, it would suggest an alliance of England and Denmark against Germany. By arranging the rendezvous, the Crown Princess seemed deliberately to flout the interests of her new country. Her concern for her brother's happiness turned out to be poor diplomacy.

The rift between England and Prussia grew with the approach of the King's coronation. He reacted against the English model and would not be crowned, as his son suggested, at a popular ceremony in Berlin. He would go to the ancient capital of Königsberg, where the old Prussian kings had exercised their divine right. There, with his full regalia, he insisted on putting the crowns on his own head and on the Queen's head. His speech stressed that he was crowned by the grace of God, not by the church or by men. He held up his sword and scepter to show off his earthly powers. He made this declaration in the presence of half of the sovereigns of Europe, who looked like a happy family shut up in a cage.

The Crown Princess's description of the ceremony was kinder. She found it a touching and magnificent spectacle. Outside, the diamonds of the ladies glittered in the sunlight as they moved in procession in front of the massed uniforms of the Guards and the five bands playing "God Save the Queen." Inside, the royal chapel was all hung with red velvet and gold. The Knights of the Black Eagle wore red velvet cloaks, the Queen's four young ladies wore white and gold, while the *Oberhofmeister* was in gold and white brocade with green velvet. The Crown Princess herself wore gold with ermine and white satin, with one of her ladies in blue velvet, the other in red velvet. The sun poured in through the high windows and tinged them magically. The music was very fine and the chorales were sung loudly and strongly. The King and Queen—and even the Crown Princess—were cheered loudly wherever they appeared.[31]

In pomp and rejoicing, the new King was crowned by his own hand. He then dissolved the liberal parliament that had opposed his army measures put forward by his Minister of War, Albrecht von Roon. The King felt that any reforms proposed by the liberals threatened the lawful powers of the throne. In the Crown Princess's opinion, the government rested on a false basis and would not last. She and her husband were fully aware of the dangers that surrounded them. There seemed to be an impasse, which must lead to the King's abdication or a social upheaval.[32]

In November, two Coburg cousins, the King of Portugal and his younger brother, died of typhoid. It was the prelude to the most significant death of that fatal year. The bad news depressed the Prince Consort, who was already sickening of typhoid himself, probably contracted from germs breeding in the unsanitary drains of Windsor Castle. Agitated by the news that the Prince of Wales had been having a brief affair with an actress while stationed at the Curragh camp in Ireland, he hastened to Cambridge to reprimand his son for causing terrible pain and sorrow to his parents. On his return to Windsor, he fell ill, lingering for a fortnight at the mercy of doctors who, Lord Clarendon thought, were not fit to attend a sick cat. On December 14, he died "from want of what they call pluck."[33] He seemed to have had little will to live, no strength to fight off the fever. His last political act had been to tone down a bellicose dispatch which might have involved England in the American Civil War. He had exhausted himself by caring too much and working too hard for a country that was never quite his own.

Widowed at forty-two, with eight unmarried children, Queen Victoria was overcome by grief. Her eldest daughter was ill and pregnant again. Her doctor forbade her to travel to England to console her mother, but the Crown Prince came in her place. Irrationally, the Queen at first blamed the Prince of Wales, as though his wild oats rather than bad plumbing had caused his father's death. She had so worshipped her husband that his loss seemed too much to bear, both for herself and for the elaborate network of influence he had built up for the crown. She asked her eldest daughter:

> What is to become of us all? Of the unhappy country, of Europe, of all? For you all, the loss of such a father is totally irreparable! I will do all I can to follow out all his wishes—to live for you all and for my duties. But how I, who leant on him for all and everything—without whom I did nothing, moved not a finger, arranged not a print or photograph, didn't put on a gown or bonnet if he didn't approve it shall be able to go on, to live, to move, to help myself in difficult moments? How shall I long to ask his advice! Oh, it is too, too weary! The day—the night (above all the night) is too sad and weary.[34]

The Crown Princess was afflicted almost as much as her mother. She had depended on her father for advice. Now she was left alone, totally dependent on a Prussian prince and husband. Earlier in the year, she had written to her mother that there was not a thing that she heard or saw or did, which did not make her consider what would her dear Papa say— what would he think. Now he could not say or think anything, only leave his ideas and his Coburg plan behind him. She, also, abandoned herself to grief. "He was too great," she wrote to her mother, "too perfect for Earth, that adored father whom she ever worshipped with more than a daughter's affection."[35]

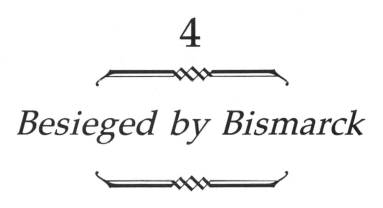

4

Besieged by Bismarck

"HERE DO I SEE crumble before my eyes," the old Baron Stockmar wrote, "that edifice which I have devoted twenty years to construct, prompted by a desire to accomplish something great and good."[1] He had trained Prince Albert to carry through the Coburg plan, but Albert was dead. His heirs and pupils, the Queen of England and his eldest daughter Princess Victoria, had withdrawn from public affairs. Their inspiration and guide was gone, and their will to act seemed buried with him.

For two months, Queen Victoria hibernated at Osborne. Her ministers hardly dared approach her over Christmas. But in the new year, her sense of duty revived. Devoted to her dead husband's plans and to her family, she began to exercise her influence from her seclusion. She knew how the projected marriages of her children might affect her country's diplomacy. The royal family already had too many relations with duchies across the Rhine. If Princess Alice married Prince Louis of Hesse, there would be yet another English connection with minor German states such as Saxe-Coburg and Hanover that Prussia would have to sweep away in order to unify Germany. And if the Prince of Wales married Princess Alexandra, the Danish crown would be strengthened in its efforts to hang on to the disputed duchies of Schleswig and Holstein.

So Queen Victoria went back to her match-making, anxious to prevent quarrels in her family developing from quarrels between nations. She also needed to occupy her weary days and nights. Within a month of her husband's death, she was tartly reminding Lord John Russell that no letters should be sent to foreign ambassadors until she had seen the final draft. As the final revisions made by the stricken Prince Consort had led to the peaceful outcome of the quarrel with America, she wanted to continue his peacemaking from his example and with her eldest daughter's help. She was encouraged in this duty by her uncle, the King of the Belgians, who would not give up the Coburg plan just because Albert was dead. He wrote to the widowed Queen:

> There is but one CONNECTED with your DEAR ANGEL . . . to follow up his plans, his wishes, to give to him, who I trust is not cut off in the spirit from this earth, the *satisfaction* that the good he wished, the plans for every thing good and useful which he had so much at heart, *are followed up* as much as our diminished means permit; that in *that way you will* MORE THAN *ever be* WORTHY OF HIS AFFEC-TION. When once united, he will tell you how much he was *pleased with your devoted effort.*[2]

This devoted effort was continued by the two women who had most loved him. On the thorny subject of Schleswig and Holstein, the Queen of England asked her daughter's opinion of what would satisfy Prussia. She assured her own ministers that Prussia did not contemplate a war against Denmark. She could not tolerate the thought that her beloved Prussian son-in-law might be fighting against the family of her future Danish daughter-in-law. She sent on to Lord John Russell her daughter's pacific proposals, which, the Crown Prince thought, might be acceptable to the Prussian foreign office. Prussia might well be prepared to recognize the Kingdom of Italy, which Lord Palmerston's government desired, if the British would support the partition of Schleswig between Prussia and Denmark. This partition, Queen Victoria added, had also been an idea of the Prince Consort's, but Palmerston rejected the deal. He said that only three men understood the thorny problem. He was one of them, and had forgotten about it. As for the other two, one was mad and the Prince Consort was dead. The trouble was that too many Germans lived in the Danish part of Schleswig and too many Danes in the German part. Anyway, the Danes did not want to give up Holstein, although it was mainly German-speaking. Palmerston resisted the efforts of the Queen and her eldest daughter to influence the government. He told Lord John Russell that Prussia had no shadow of a right to demand such an agreement.[3] That was the end of that piece of royal diplomacy.

The rejection of the Crown Princess as a go-between confirmed the King of Prussia's belief that his family alliance with the British crown had no effect on British policy. That was the trouble with a constitutional monarchy; autocracy was better. The wearing of the Prussian crown seemed to have changed his nature. Instead of being weak and vacillating, as when he was Regent, he now appeared stubborn and overbearing as Monarch. He had the unfortunate quality which had proved the ruin of others, the British Ambassador reported back to Lord John Russell. The King never yielded until it was too late. Being born and bred a soldier, he was always leaning on his sword.[4] As his Minister President, the King replaced the ineffectual Prince of Hohenzollern-Sigmaringen by Prince Adolf of Hohenlohe-Ingelfingen. He was not much better. The Crown Princess thought him frightened of his own shadow. Reactionary and pliant ministers were also put into the Cabinet, which was responsible only to the King, not to the newly elected Prussian parliament. This was soon dissolved again, because the deputies refused to vote for a larger military budget. As early as April 1862, there was talk of recalling Bismarck to head the government, but instead he was transferred from St. Petersburg to Paris. The King wanted him nearer at hand in case he was needed to advise or to take over the administration and change its policy.

The crisis was making things impossible for the Crown Prince and Princess. They could not oppose the King without seeming disobedient, while they could not support him without denying their principles and their friends and supporters. Government in Prussia was in such a mess that it made the Crown Princess ashamed, angry and depressed by turns. She began to speak her mind to both the King and Queen of Prussia, which only increased their displeasure with her. Except for her mother and her husband, she confessed that there was no one she now cared to please.[5]

She was no longer passing information to Queen Victoria about Prussian military planning. These secrets were being reported to the Queen by Major General Hamilton, who relied on the military attaché in Berlin and on observers at the Prussian annual maneuvers. Queen Victoria had specifically asked for a breakdown on the increased army estimates, and she received one, that showed the Prussian army had grown by 60,000 men in the past five years. With the mobilization of a reformed *Landwehr* it would total 357,000 men in time of war.[6] Queen Victoria now knew what the Prussians could put in the field against the Danes and the French. She was better informed than her daughter in Berlin.

Her son-in-law, of course, did not tell her of the new Prussian military arrangements. He was discreet about them now even when alone with his wife. Queen Victoria, however, was flattering him by asking him to take her dead husband's place at public ceremonies. She had ordered a full year of mourning for her children, so that the Prince of Wales could not stand in for his father at the opening of the second Great Exhibition. She begged for the loan of the Crown Prince for a second time in 1862. He had already agreed to come to Princess Alice's wedding to Prince Louis of Hesse. "I cannot demand the sacrifice of yet another journey in the same year," she wrote to the King of Prussia. "On the other hand, you will understand how important it is to me that this Exhibition in which my dearly-beloved angel took such a keen interest, should pass off brilliantly in every way. . . . Fritz's presence, both as your son and ours, will have a most important effect on the Exhibition at such a gloomy time."[7] The King of Prussia felt obliged to agree to the widow's plea. His son was obviously being made to stand in for the Prince Consort in the flesh and in his ideas about Germany. Although the Crown Prince was nine years older than his wife and did not accept all her views, the Prince Consort had been the first person to recognize his political sense. Now that the Queen of England continued this recognition and treated him as if he were her support, Prince Frederick William found it hard not to hold to the English example. He was gratified to find himself popular and widely praised in London, which was scarcely the case in Berlin.

After the magnificent opening of the Exhibition, the Crown Prince stayed on in England to give away Princess Alice at her marriage to Prince Louis of Hesse. The Crown Princess could not travel to join him because she was expecting her third child. Again he was being used in place of the dead Prince Consort, as if Queen Victoria needed to take over her daughter's husband in recompense for her own. In her letters to the Crown Princess, there was sometimes a note of envy at her daughter having a good husband, even if he could never match up to her angel Albert. A woman in her position and of her nature could not stand alone.

Although Queen Victoria's grief seems extravagant now, it was the fashion of the time to mourn publicly and too long. The Queen spent as much time and care in the building of a mausoleum for Prince Albert at Frogmore near Windsor as he had on building country houses for her. His bedroom was kept always aired and ready as if he would drop in. His evening clothes were laid out each night with a towel and hot water in a basin. His habits were not allowed to die. Daily reminded of him, the Queen in her widow's weeds kept his memory alive by the display of her sorrow.

When she looked at her daughter Alice's trousseau before the wedding, she found it sad to see nothing but black gowns. The Victorian cult of death affected the royal wedding ceremony. Not only had the Prince Consort died recently, but also the Grand Duchess of Hesse. The ceremony was more like a funeral than a wedding. The Queen wore a widow's cap and sat hunched on a chair near the altar with her four sons at her side. One of them, Prince Alfred, sobbed dreadfully all through the service. So did the Archbishop of York, who had just lost his own wife, and whose cheeks ran with tears. Princess Alice herself was serious and melancholy, conscious of how unbearable her wedding must seem to her bereaved mother remembering her own betrothal. "A dagger is plunged in my bleeding, desolate heart. . . ." the Queen confessed. "I feel what I had, what I hoped to have for at least twenty years more and what I can only have in another world again."[8]

In August, the Crown Princess gave birth to her second son, Prince Henry. The labor was easy this time, and she recovered quickly. Within ten days, she was walking around the redesigned gardens of the Neue Palais among the plants and trees which her father had sent to her. She felt as if the renewal of life had overcome the loss of her father. She had everything to hope for in the near future.

❧

It was as a dream. The King threatened to abdicate rather than turn to Bismarck as his last resort. He sent for the Crown Prince, who was at Coburg with his wife. Queen Victoria had gone there on a visit of sad remembrance. God and conscience, the King told his son, had made him decide to give up the throne. It only needed one signature to hand over the crown. Already the announcement of the abdication had been drawn up, and the King gave it to the Crown Prince to read. He could not give in any more to parliament, he said—although he had hardly given in to anything as Regent or King. His son urged him to stay on the throne, for the good of the country and the dynasty. The power of the crown would be diminished if a parliament were able to get rid of a King. Even so, the King declared that he had made up his mind. The Crown Prince was told to stay in Berlin and prepare to take over from his father.

The Crown Prince informed his wife in Coburg. With the throne so near, she did not know what to advise. Unfortunately, the offer of abdication had come at the worst possible time. She and Queen Victoria were together at Coburg, when the engagement of her brother, the Prince of Wales, to the Danish Princess had just been announced. The proposed marriage seemed to the reactionaries near the King to line up England with Denmark against Prussia. How then could the King give up his throne to a son with an English wife?

Aware of the risk, the Crown Princess decided to advise her husband to take the throne from his father. The offer of abdication might be a ploy by the King to discredit his son. It would make the Crown Prince seem to be plotting to take over too soon. It might also be a trick to prove that the King was so desperate he had to send for the dangerous Bismarck. Yet the Crown Princess wanted the influence and responsibility of power. Even though she was only twenty-one, she had stood by five long years waiting to become the Queen of Prussia. "I see no way out," she wrote to her husband in Berlin, "and consider you should make this sacrifice for the country. If you do not accept, I believe that you will regret it one day." She did not wish to have the responsibility of advising him against it. The alternative would be much worse for the King. "To take Bismarck is equivalent to a man, who cannot swim, jumping into the water where it is deepest!"[9]

As the King hesitated, his Minister of War, Albrecht von Roon, appealed to his royal conscience. How could a soldier king give up his command when the battle was going against him? It was a battle to develop the Prussian army and defend the country. Bismarck must be summoned from Paris. The King appeared to agree, and Roon had the vital telegram sent to Bismarck. It was written in Latin and French and signed with a pseudonym. The message was: *"Periculum in mora. Dépêchez-vous."* There was danger in delay. The Crown Prince might become King.

Bismarck took the next express train to Berlin.

The Crown Prince heard of his adversary's arrival and summoned him to his presence. Bismarck said little at the meeting and made no commitments. He had already compromised himself with the King, who complained to Roon that Bismarck was no good. He had first been to see the Crown Prince. Two days later, he was ordered to Babelsberg to see the King. There he was shown the letter of abdication, but he did not notice whether it had been signed or not. He assured the King that he could form a Cabinet and would force through the reorganization of the army against the opposition of the liberal majority in parliament. This was what the King had been waiting to hear. He may have promised his wife and the Crown Prince not to appoint Bismarck as his Minister President, but now he said it was his duty, with Bismarck's help, to try to continue the battle. "I shall not abdicate," he declared. Bismarck promised his absolute loyalty in making the King supreme above parliament. He would give the King the army he wanted, and he would also defend the royal prerogative that had elevated him to power. He did not, however, promise to carry out the King's ideas on foreign policy.[10] The King, delighted to be promised the army he wanted, suppressed his own doubts about Bismarck's known recklessness and double-dealing in diplomacy. Within the week, Bismarck had told the parliamentary budget commission that Prussia's might would resolve the future of Germany, not its example of liberalism. "The great questions of the day will not be decided by speeches and majority resolutions—that was the great mistake from 1848 to 1849—but by iron and blood."

The King knew that he had misled and offended his son. He feared open opposition from the Crown Prince, but Frederick William had also been trained in the virtues of a Prussian officer. He gave his father his obedience and kept silent in public. He only declared that any breach of the constitution would be disastrous. He would not tolerate a royal tyranny. The King said that he was tired of hearing sermons and dismissed his son. It was the beginning of the long breach between them. Knowing that any show of opposition would play into Bismarck's hands, the Crown Prince decided to leave with his wife on an extended tour of the Mediterranean. They would sail with the Prince of Wales on Queen Victoria's borrowed yacht, the *Osborne.* This dutiful act of withdrawal may have been politic, but it appeared cowardly. The liberals were left without their royal figurehead to halt Bismarck and the reactionaries. If the Crown Prince's discretion was the better part of valor, it was the worse for his cause.

The King of Prussia also feared that Queen Victoria would feel betrayed and turn against him, supporting Denmark on the question of the two border duchies. He went to Coburg to meet her in the dead Prince Consort's homeland. He would not talk to her about politics except to complain about the heavy weight of affairs on him. She was too tactful to reproach him with Bismarck's appointment or the reasons behind the temporary exile of the Crown Prince and Princess. The Queen felt it wise to keep her lines of communication open to the King of Prussia. In the near future, she might need to protect her daughter over there.

For the Crown Princess and Prince, the Mediterranean voyage was a time of rest and peace. It was also a time for the Crown Princess to bring her husband closer to her adored brother, the Prince of Wales. They sailed together from Marseilles to Palermo and to Malta, where there was a review of

British troops in their honor. It was the first time the Crown Princess had ever seen "our dear troops without beloved Papa." She was overcome particularly when the riflemen marched past.[11] They sailed across to Tunis, where the Bey presented the two Princes with Orders studded with diamonds, but wrapped in brown paper. The Crown Princess was seasick for two days in Malta, because of a storm on their way back, but she revived on the passage on to Naples.

There the Prince of Wales celebrated his coming of age. He had endeared himself to his brother-in-law, who had become almost as fond of him as the Prince's sister was, in spite of his proposed Danish wife. "Bertie is extremely amiable, accommodating and good natured," the Crown Princess reported from Naples to their mother, "and we are as happy as possible together." He seemed to be enjoying himself very much and making progress. He was taking much more notice of what he saw and heard. The Crown Princess begged her mother not to worry about him, there was so much good to come out of him yet. His consideration and tact attracted everyone. Now that they had no father, it was doubly important that the scattered brothers and sisters should hold together in perfect love and confidence.[12]

The Pope received the royal party in Rome. They found him a good-natured and jocose old gentleman, not without dignity, but then as Protestants they had no great respect for the Supreme Pontiff. The Prince of Wales now had to return to England. Both his sister and his brother-in-law had plenty of time to put the Prussian point of view on Schleswig and Holstein before his marriage to Princess Alexandra. They did not want him at daggers drawn in case of hostilities with Denmark. War had to be kept out of happy families. Queen Victoria hoped that the Crown Princess had "germanized" her brother as much as possible, for it was most necessary.

Returning to Potsdam by way of the Austrian Emperor's court in Vienna, the Crown Princess met the American histo-

rian and diplomat John Lothrop Motley, an old student friend
of Bismarck's at Göttingen. He was attracted by her appearance. "She is rather *petite*," he wrote, "has a fresh young face
with pretty features, fine teeth and a frank and agreeable smile
and an interested, earnest and intelligent manner. Nothing
could be simpler or more natural than her style, which I should
say was the perfection of good breeding."[13]

Her grace and good manners did not save her when she
returned "behind the bars" of Berlin. During the six weeks
she had been away, Bismarck seemed to have transformed
the feeling of the city. It was charged with nervous energy.
When her husband went to the barracks, he found morale
high and a sense of purpose and urgency. The King was revital-
ized from spending so much time with his troops. He considered the new spirit of the forces as a triumph engineered by
his chief minister, although the man was a mere civilian. Bismarck had persuaded the army command that he would drive
the reorganization and the military budget through parliament
whether approved or not. He was preparing schemes to raise
money unofficially, to govern without reference to the elected
deputies, to muzzle and direct the press even more, and to
develop the spy system which Stieber had created. With a
strong army and the Prussian state under his control, there
was no telling how far he could go in his pursuit of a greater
nation.

The Crown Princess was disturbed by her husband's unwilling approval of what Bismarck and the King were achiev-
ing with the army. He shared the ambivalence toward
Bismarck which was to emasculate the liberal opposition to
the Minister President. He approved of Bismarck's measures
to strengthen Prussia and make her powerful abroad, although
he hated the suppression of rights at home. He wanted to
have the power without paying the price of loss of liberty.
His wife saw his dilemma and made one of her rare complaints
about her husband to her mother. "He is not born a free

Englishman," she wrote, "and all Prussians have NOT the feeling of independence and love of justice and constitutional liberty they ought to have."[14]

With the rest of Prussia, liberal and conservative, the Crown Prince would respond to the ha-ha of the trumpets and the neighing of the war horses. He waited for Bismarck to start the war.

※

Bismarck was only forty-seven and not trained to lead Prussia. He was known to be forceful and opportunistic, solitary, devious, ruthless and quick to move. Yet he could charm as well as bully, persuade as well as command. To keep power, he depended wholly on the King, but his remarks about iron and blood had made his master doubt him. He was summoned to explain himself to the King on a train journey back to Berlin, and was accused of being another Strafford, who would be executed together with his monarch who was playing King Charles I of England. "They will cut off your head," the King said sadly, "and a little later mine." Like Strafford, Bismarck ended by asking what death could be better than in the struggle for the King's rights granted by the grace of God.[15]

By a bold piece of trickery, Bismarck did secure the King the budget for his reorganized army. He influenced the upper house to pass the budget, although the Chamber had rejected it. The state, however, collected taxes directly without depending on annual grants from parliament. In an impasse between the upper house and the Chamber, Bismarck claimed the King had the duty to use the tax money on the army and to defend the state. Through this hole in the constitution, Bismarck could give the King what he wanted and govern without reference to the liberals.

This was not the coup d'état that the Crown Princess had feared; it was an intolerable state of dangling and indecision with Bismarck holding the strings and the power of the executive. "We live with a sword hanging over our heads," the

Crown Princess wrote to her mother in England, "and it will fall when we least expect it and on the innocent ones."[16] She herself thought a radical solution very possible, another explosion as in 1848. Her husband began to look even more ill than his father, who now seemed to flourish even in the dreadfully hot rooms and crushes of courtiers of the Berlin winter season. As the Crown Prince became more pallid, his aged father seemed to become infused with the desperate energy of his new minister and the growing force of his new model army. Berlin was very much of a city of uniforms, investitures and parades. Everywhere there were spiked helmets and flat caps, white tunics and dark blue field dress, epaulettes and iron crosses, swords in long scabbards, racket of drum and trumpet and fife. If society did not change much, the guard was changed daily and loudly and ceremonially. Berlin often seemed like a barracks in a country that was an armed camp. With such a military presence, peace seemed a mere truce standing sentry on the next war.

During this time of trial and waiting, the Crown Prince and Princess and their eldest son William went to England again for the wedding of the Prince of Wales to the Danish Princess Alexandra, whose charms had grown on the Prince until he had proposed to her. Court protocol and family feeling decreed that they should go, but it was a political mistake in their silent struggle against Bismarck. He could represent the journey as disloyalty to Prussia, an indication that the Crown Prince took the Danish side on the vexed question of Schleswig and Holstein. The Crown Princess's frequent trips to her home country had begun to worry her liberal supporters. "She has nothing to do there and nothing to seek," one of them complained.[17] Even their close adviser Max Duncker thought that their English parliamentary ideas could not be applied in Prussia.

When her eldest daughter arrived for her brother's wedding, Queen Victoria found her very pretty, so young and fresh and slim.[18] The English Queen knew perfectly well that she was playing with German politics by asking for the Prussian Crown Prince to attend her eldest son. "On account of the Danes," she confessed to her daughter, "I am so anxious that he should be there."[19] She hoped to prevent a war between Denmark and Prussia by having the Crown Prince attend the wedding of the heir to the English throne. This obvious diplomacy through royal marriage aroused great suspicion in Bismarck and in other Prussian nationalists, who saw it as another extension of Queen Victoria's influence. She might seem to remain secluded in widow's weeds, but the letters with their suggestions for shaping policy were still pouring out to her royal relations. As Lord Rowton pointed out, the Queen selected all over Europe the most intelligent member of each royal family. "On any question, domestic or foreign, which arose, she obtained by letter an opinion."[20] No international statesman could hope to have better information.

The marriage of Queen Victoria's heir into the Danish royal family had spread the network still further. The Greeks were looking for a king who would bring with him an English connection and the friendship of the British navy. Their first choice was Queen Victoria's second son, Alfred, but she wanted him to become Duke of Coburg on the death of her brother-in-law Ernst. The second choice of the Greeks was Duke Ernst himself, but eventually he decided to stay in his German duchy rather than risk the violent politics of Athens. Finally, Prince William of Denmark, the seventeen-year-old brother of Princess Alexandra, was chosen. Through the marriage of her eldest son to Alexandra, Queen Victoria had now cast the meshes of her relations over the royal families of two maritime nations with excellent ports for the British fleet.

Bismarck was not wrong to be suspicious. A royal wedding was a form of alliance and part of an intelligence system. A royal death could still cause a war of succession. The King of Denmark, whose ancestry tenuously sustained the claims to rule Schleswig and Holstein, would not live forever and had no direct heir. If Bismarck wanted to make Prussia's future by iron and blood, Queen Victoria wanted to preserve England's security by gold ring and blood royal. To her, marriage—not war—was diplomacy by other means.

※

Bismarck's first crisis in foreign affairs found him wanting and fortunate. The Poles rose against their Russian occupiers and, although he knew of French and English sympathy for Polish liberty, Bismarck decided to help Russia put down the rebellion which menaced East Prussia and his own estates. He was anyway a *Junker* and thought the Poles unfit to be much more than peasants. He had four army corps set to seal off the frontier. He described this extreme act as a simple police measure. He also allowed the Russian troops the right of hot pursuit of the rebels over Prussian territory.

The Russians were grateful, and began to put down the insurrection brutally. The French Emperor, however, threatened a war on the Rhine, and Lord Palmerston in England blustered about helping the Poles. There was another crisis in Berlin, with rumors of Bismarck's fall. Queen Victoria was so alarmed that there might be war on the Rhine that she would not allow her second daughter, Alice, to return to Hesse-Darmstadt and have her first child there. "We *must*, on NO account," she declared, "let ourselves be dragged into what *may* be a war with Germany! The Queen shudders at the very thought of *what*, if we are not *very* careful, and very guarded in our expressions to France, we may find ourselves plunged into!"[21]

The Queen's intervention played its part in keeping her divided Cabinet neutral. The government adopted a policy of keeping its hands off, refusing to join with the French in another Crimean War. Bismarck survived in Berlin. So Queen Victoria indirectly helped her daughter's adversary in Prussia to weather his first diplomatic blunder. England had also set a precedent for not intervening. Perhaps the British fleet might not assist Denmark, despite the Prince of Wales's marriage to Princess Alexandra. It was common knowledge that Queen Victoria preferred her eldest daughter to her eldest son. If she wanted to avoid war with Germany at all costs, she might hamper Lord Palmerston enough to stop him sending the navy to Copenhagen.

The constant worries of the political situation did not lessen the Crown Princess's anxiety over the condition of her firstborn's neck and arm, damaged at his birth. Prince William's left arm was bluish and useless, while his neck was angled due to constricted muscles. The German doctors wanted him put in a machine to straighten the neck. A belt at his waist would hold an iron rod up his back to support something like a horse's bridle. The boy's head would be strapped into that and turned as required by a screw. Seeing her child treated as if he were deformed was very hard for the Crown Princess, though of course she would submit to all that was necessary for his good. But she found doctors very odd sometimes.[22] They were odd and the treatment was odder. It made the child odd and angry. Prince William hated the torments inflicted on him and reacted savagely to them. Slowly, he learnt to deny his deformity, but he never learnt to live with it. Obscurely in his heart he blamed his mother, who was blameless and suffered for him. Although she tried to hide her pain, her heart bled to see him tortured. When writing about his early life, he accused her of having been wrapped up in the husband she adored. She was the wife rather than the mother, and her three elder children had a stern upbringing. She only turned to the nursery with her younger children, who enjoyed her tender heart and care.

So it seemed to the eldest child. The truth was that the Crown Princess was devoted to all her children, but while she was still young and her husband was engaged in immediate politics, she had to devote herself to him and his affairs. The boy William gave his affection to his father, who was religious and good of heart, so tender that he was almost soft. The huge military figure had a genuine sympathy for any form of suffering. He was friendly, full of jokes and a great tease, but he was taught to respect authority and would tolerate no opposition. He was subject to fits of depression, a *Weltschmerz* that was a presentiment of the long-drawn tragedy to come.[23]

The curtains were being raised on the first act of that tragedy. The members of the lower house of parliament remained intransigent about the military budget. In an address to the King, they went so far as to threaten him with a revolution. A chasm separated the advisers to the crown from the country, they warned. The chasm could be bridged only by a change of Cabinet and by a change of system.[24] If the King would not abdicate and allow the Crown Prince to succeed him, then the liberals wanted the Crown Prince to challenge Bismarck before he turned the government into a tyranny. The King and his Minister President had their reply: parliament was dissolved again.

Bound by the duty of obedience to his father, the Crown Prince remained silent. His wife, Queen Victoria and the British government urged him to speak out and assert his liberal principles. "We want a Frederick the Great now!" the Crown Princess declared. "When will there be another?" There was a regular pitched battle going on between the Chambers and the government, she informed her mother. Many believed there would be a revolution, though she did not share this opinion. The King was determined to uphold Bismarck, the author of all the mischief.[25] Pressure at home and from abroad forced the Crown Prince to speak his mind too soon. On May 19, 1863, the Crown Princess told Queen Victoria that her husband would protest in writing, if the government did anything unconstitutional. Queen Victoria passed on this information to her Cabinet. In a significant reply to the Queen, Lord Palmerston praised the Crown Prince's intention to protest as wise and satisfactory. The Prime Minister found it painful to see the unconstitutional course taken by the King of Prussia and his advisers, and echoed the King in comparing it to the career of Charles I of England, who had lost his head for it. If persevered in, it must be ruinous to the King.[26]

Bismarck knew of the English and liberal pressure on the Crown Prince to declare himself as leader of the opposition. He had already placed his agents in the Prince's household, and the Crown Princess was fairly sure that their letters were intercepted and read before being passed on. She warned her mother to keep all details for the royal messenger who came to the Neue Palais twice a week.[27] With Bismarck as the adversary, nothing was safe.

Bismarck believed that the outspoken liberal opposition menaced the security and reputation of Prussia. It showed a divided and ungovernable nation. He asked the King to use his emergency powers to silence all the opposition newspapers by royal edict. Such a strong measure would smoke out the Crown Prince, who would have to declare himself against the acts done in his father's name if he wanted to keep his supporters. He had already been ordered to leave the capital and proceed through East Prussia and Poland, which would divorce him from his liberal advisers and the Berliners. It would also associate him with the reactionary *Junkers* and the army garrisons he was being sent to inspect. In this crisis, the Crown Prince depended chiefly on the advice of his English wife and her counselors. Bismarck's suspicion of foreign influence was correct. The Crown Princess was working all the time for her husband, copying out drafts and letters because nobody could be completely trusted. Before he left on his tour of the eastern marches, the Crown Prince wrote a long letter to his father the King, saying that he had no intention of meddling in things which did not concern him. Yet he could not see the danger the King was in without warning and imploring him never to give his consent to any unconstitutional measure as the only way out of present difficulties. Such a measure would endanger the dynasty and the peace of Prussia. Nothing could possibly be improved by it. If this were done, it would be the Crown Prince's painful duty to protest. He could have nothing whatever to do with it. He hoped it would not come, but could not share in the responsibility.[28]

That same day, the press edict was issued in the name of the King. The Crown Prince immediately wrote to Bismarck, stating that the edict was a disaster for the crown and the country. He would not be a party to it. He failed to see that Bismarck had provoked his response, causing a rift between father and son, between Prussian nationalism and English example. The Crown Prince's courage and obstinacy would make him blunder further into the trap. Two days later, he wrote to his father the King: "I owe it to you as your son and your first subject to tell you frankly when I differ from you, and when my views disagree with those of your Government." This was hardly what the King wanted to read. He remembered his own painful obedience to his father and the sacrifice of his first Radziwill love to his sense of obligation. Filial duty was the primary duty of royal sons. The King was even more angered by receiving another letter from the Crown Prince the following day, again opposing the press edict. Then, on June 5, the Crown Prince ignored a warning from his father. He repudiated the edict at a reception in the town hall of Danzig, following a parade of its garrison. He told the mayor and the guests that he was astonished at the edict, which had been issued in his absence from Berlin. He had nothing to do with it. Yet he urged everyone to have confidence in the excellent intentions of the King.

He had fallen for Bismarck's provocations. He had declared himself publicly in opposition to the King's will. Taking Bismarck's advice, the King now accused his son in harsh terms. "You have now spoken quite frankly that you are opposed to my system of government. What therefore will be your attitude towards me and my Government in the future? . . . Anyone who does not wish this disgraceful press to be kept within bounds also desires the downfall of the Monarchy."[29] The King then ordered his son never to make any such indiscreet statement on any occasion in the future. Supported in his defiance by his wife, the Crown Prince replied that he could not take back the words he had spoken in Danzig. He offered to resign his commission in the army and his place in the King's Councils. He said he would retire and live apart from politics, and he begged his beloved father's forgiveness for the pain caused by his disobedience and convictions. He was, as the Crown Princess told her mother, in a state of perfect misery. She hoped Queen Victoria would make his conduct known to her ministers and all their friends in England. They felt dreadfully alone, without a soul to give them advice. But her husband's necessity and duty was so plain that it required no explaining or advising.[30]

So the Crown Princess owned up to her responsibility in her husband's brave charge at the guns, like the charge of the Light Brigade at Balaclava. It was magnificent but it was not war against Bismarck. She persisted in thinking the liberals more powerful in Prussia than they were. The Chambers were not the same as the House of Commons and the House of Lords; their powers were more limited and recent. Traditional authority in Prussia was still vested in the King ruling through his chosen ministers—Stuart England rather than Victorian. The Crown Prince was fettered by tradition and training, kept from any major act of defiance. His independence and pride had been molded and controlled since his childhood. Whatever his mother or his wife urged, his father would deny and make him suppress. Resistance only increased his psychological turmoil and prolonged melancholies.

Prussia was still Prussia. It would not change for the English Crown Princess. As she was alone with her husband in the east during his repeated acts of defiance, she had to take the responsibility for aiding and abetting him. Certainly, her mother and the English ministers egged him on to further opposition. "Let Fritz be firm!" Queen Victoria wrote. He must not shrink from separating himself from all his father's unhappy acts. "I know Papa would have said the same." During the crisis she praised her daughter more than she had ever done, saying that the Crown Princess was taking the Prince Consort's place—his child in mind and genius.[31]

Her daughter's error was to expose herself as the present influence on the rebellion of the Crown Prince. She had been used as the go-between to carry angry letters from the King to his son. Bismarck had succeeded in making the Crown Prince and Princess rebel in the wrong place at the wrong time. They were surrounded by spies, who were watching all they were doing, the Crown Princess reported from Königsberg on June 11. All was fed back to Berlin to checkmate everything they were attempting. They had no final answer from the King.[32]

Their fate was being settled in Berlin. There was no one close to the throne to help them except the Queen of Prussia— and the King would not listen to her. The old Field Marshal Wrangel wanted the Crown Prince put in a fortress and the Crown Princess exiled. Bismarck was too clever for that. He knew the political mistake of making martyrs and proposed a merciless clemency. The King should not accept his son's offer to resign from the army and the Councils; he should let the Crown Prince's resistance wear itself out in minor duties. Bismarck knew the Crown Prince's weakness, instilled in him rigorously since his boyhood: his absolute belief that he should obey his father the King. Only the thought of his father made him feel powerless, the Crown Princess wrote of him to her mother. "Think if it was your father," he asked her, "would you like to disobey him and make him unhappy?"[33] That was the crucial question. In obedience to her dead father's training of her beliefs, the Crown Princess had encouraged her husband's rebellion. Her mother and her mother's government had stood behind her while the Crown Prince charged toward his defeat. "You are the best and wisest adviser he could have," Queen Victoria assured her daughter, "and the worthy child of your beloved father who will look down approvingly on you."[34]

᠀

As with many a crisis, there was no solution—only a definition of attitudes, the search for a small common ground of truce and compromise. The heir to the throne could not be replaced. He was only kept from power by the good health of the King, who had now gone to Karlsbad for a cure. Bismarck moved quickly to increase the isolation of the two rebels, to let them know that he had saved them from prison and exile—his political genius made him thwart his opponents' plans while making them grateful for his personal forbearance. Acting on Bismarck's advice, the King sent his son a severe reprimand, but did not strip him of his offices of state. He made it plain that the English influence was to blame for the Crown Prince's public indiscretions. "You inform me," he wrote to his son, "that those statements were made intentionally and, as Vicky writes to Mama, after due deliberation with her."[35] The Crown Princess was guilty together with the Crown Prince.

Their chief supporter, Queen Augusta of Prussia, was encouraged to pay a long visit to her friend, Queen Victoria, in order to explain the King's position on the reform of his army, but her visit to England compromised her as another part of the great game played from Windsor Castle and the Foreign Office. Bismarck was reckless enough to assert to the British Ambassador in Berlin that the Crown Prince's speech would encourage an assassination attempt on the King by radical exiles given asylum in London. Moreover, Bismarck added, the Prussian court believed that the Crown Prince had been acting on advice from abroad, channeled though young Stockmar.[36] Bismarck was not entirely wrong. "Be quite easy about Fritz," the Crown Princess was writing to her mother. "He will do all he should, he will let himself be guided by Stockmar and you will see that all will go right."[37] As Bismarck told one of his agents, the sly Moritz Busch, the trouble with having foreign princesses at the Prussian court was that they brought their nationality with them and retained it, preserving their foreign interests.[38]

The indiscretion of some of the Crown Prince's liberal German advisers and the intervention of *The Times* played further into Bismarck's hands. Gustav Freytag had versions of the correspondence between the King of Prussia and his son published in two liberal German papers, and *The Times* also received copies of the important letters from an unknown source. As the Crown Princess herself could not be accused of the leak, Ernest von Stockmar was held guilty, and was pressed to resign from the Crown Prince's household. Bismarck was determined to eradicate the Coburg influence as far as possible.

The Times' articles stoked the King of Prussia's rage against his son and daughter-in-law. *The Times* pointed out that the King was at Karlsbad in Austria, while Queen Augusta was at Windsor and the Crown Prince touring the far frontiers of the kingdom. All three were separated, intent on different policies. Fuel was added to the flames by *The Times'* praising the Crown Princess for her liberal views and support of her husband's protests. Nothing could have caused her more embarrassment. She was thought now, she told her mother, the *genius of evil.* With the Stockmars and Robert Morier, she seemed the head of the Anglo-Coburg influence near the Crown Prince. It hurt her, of course, to be thought so powerful and dangerous. She felt she had to give advice as positively as she could, yet it was disagreeable to be thought meddling and intriguing. Mixing in politics was not a ladies' profession. She would have liked to live in peace with everyone, but that would mean having no opinion or policy of her own. She could not be a freeborn Englishwoman and Queen Victoria's child if she were silent. She was very ambitious for the country, for her husband and the children, so she was determined to brave all the rest.[39]

Of course, the Crown Prince and Princess had their chosen advisers and sources of information, just as Bismarck had his own growing network of financial and secret agents. He treated

as an intimate Gerson Bleichröder, the Rothschild's representative in Berlin. He needed the shrewd and capable banker
to finance the state and the army when parliament would
not authorize funds for Prussian expansion. He also knew
that Bleichröder would pass on information immediately to
the Rothschilds in Paris and London, and so it would reach
the French Emperor and the English City and Cabinet. It was
a method of unofficial diplomacy, of information and disinfor-
mation. As Bleichröder's distinguished biographer says, the
banker was supplied with bits of selected truths. The full
truth, as always, Bismarck kept to himself.[40]

For secret operations necessary to his policy, Bismarck was
again using the spymaster Stieber despite the King's distrust
of the man. A newspaper proprietor, August Brass, a fiery
democrat who had fought the authorities in 1848, had founded
the radical *Norddeutsche Allgemeine Zeitung* with the socialist William Liebknecht as his chief assistant. Bismarck decided to
use the paper rather than suppress it. Brass became one of
his chief supporters, the mouthpiece of many of Bismarck's
planted stories and insinuations. He also introduced Bismarck
to Stieber as a reliable counterforce to conspirators at home
and enemies abroad. Stieber would be used against the new
Crown Prince as he had been against the old one.

Badly advised, the Crown Prince decided to continue his
attack on the Minister President. He sent Bismarck a memorandum on government that questioned his honesty. People
who advised breaches of the constitution were the most dangerous advisers to crown and country. "Youth is hasty with
words," Bismarck scribbled in the margin. His comment on
the Crown Prince's justification of his defiance of his father
was even more pointed—the one word "Absalom!"[41] He sent
on the annotated document to the King, making him even
more angry against his son.

In retaliation, Bismarck encouraged the King to start a
witch-hunt over the leaks to *The Times.* He loosed Stieber and
his police agents. All leading liberals were under suspicion,

particularly the circle around the Crown Prince. Young Stockmar's health gave way under the pressure, and he had to retire
to a spa. Max Duncker was turned slowly until he believed
Bismarck and agreed to act as his informer. The Crown Princess was scared enough to feel guilty about sending Queen
Victoria copies of the correspondence between her husband
and his father. Perhaps, without meaning it, her mother had
been the source of the leak to *The Times* which now threatened
their future. "There has been a regular inquisition about it
which has caused us the greatest annoyance," she wrote to
her mother. The King said he would not rest until he had
found out the guilty people.[42] Queen Victoria replied that
the letters had been absolutely safe with her. What the Crown
Prince had done and said had been no secret. As for the leak,
the King should look nearer home.[43]

The death of the old Baron Stockmar in July was an unexpected help to Bismarck and a sad blow to Queen Victoria.
The Prince Consort had depended on his advice. With Stockmar's son now separated from her daughter, the Queen felt
bound to try and fill the breach herself. She traveled to Coburg,
officially to visit old Stockmar's grave and see her dead husband's birthplace, but unofficially, she wanted to intercede
with the King of Prussia on behalf of her daughter and the
Crown Prince. If they were to be forced into retirement, she
wished them to join her in England. A married daughter and
grandchildren would keep her company.

Two of the wiser members of the Anglo-Coburg group
did not support the Crown Prince's defiance of his father.
Robert Morier thought that this was no way to fight Bismarck.
The Crown Prince had already been enmeshed before being
provoked into playing Absalom. Every kind of calumny had
been spread about the Prince's friends. Spies had been placed
over him in the shape of aides-de-camp and chamberlains.
Conversations had been distorted and imagined until the Danzig episode had brought matters to a climax.[44] In Morier's
opinion, Bismarck had caught the Crown Prince in a snare,

and could now remove the heir to the throne from all policy-making.

The oldest Coburger of them all, King Leopold of the Belgians, took Queen Victoria gently to task for her interventions. "I think that you have a sort of *right* to *interfere in an amicable way*," he wrote to her. The King of Prussia was more likely to forgive his son at her request than for any other reason, but there was the Fifth Commandment, "Honor Thy Father and Thy Mother." Queen Victoria's daughter could not alter the law or the traditions in a foreign land. In her own position, the Queen of England could not promote the disobedience of her children.[45] As King Leopold knew well, she had her problems with the Prince of Wales.

When she arrived in Coburg in August, Queen Victoria's intercession with the King of Prussia did clear the air. The King respected her as a widow and a monarch more powerful than he was. Without hesitation, he gave her what she chiefly wanted. He allowed a visit to Balmoral by the Crown Prince and Princess. But the policy which she had hatched with her daughter was not successful. She asked the King to attend the current Congress of German Sovereigns at Frankfurt. It had been called by the Austrian Emperor, who came personally to invite the King to attend, but the King still would not go, and the reason was Bismarck. The Minister President had to argue half the night with his master until the King was sobbing uncontrollably and Bismarck was smashing glass bowls to relieve his feelings. But the point was won. The King did not go to the Frankfurt Congress, which was stillborn without his presence.

Bismarck was not wrong in aborting the Congress. Queen Victoria's observer, the urbane Lord Clarendon, likened it to a team of thirty horses, some half-bred and shambling and vicious, some Shetland ponies, with two great dray horses always kicking and biting at each other. The German Confederation did not work and reform would not make it work.[46] There had to be another solution. Bismarck hinted as much to Lord Granville, saying that a civil war between Germans would be a relief. Good with terror was better than terror without good.[47]

At Coburg yet another solution was urged on the King of Prussia by Queen Victoria. With her two married daughters and their children living in Germany, she did not want war there. She asked the king whether he would accept what the Crown Prince and Princess had suggested he might accept—equality with Austria in managing German affairs. "But how?" the King asked, then listed a series of slights by and disagreements with Austria. Queen Victoria would soon be meeting the Hapsburg Emperor. She asked if she might tell him of Prussia's wish for a good understanding in Germany on the basis of complete parity. The King took his leave, saying, "I recommend my interests to your care."[48] The meeting was a personal triumph for Queen Victoria and threw Bismarck into a fury. The King of Prussia was allowing the Queen of England to represent him with the Austrians. It was too much. Bismarck hid his anger and returned to Berlin with the King, who was very kind to the Crown Princess and "as jolly as possible." Her mother met the Austrian Emperor three days later, feeling like a child—unprotected, unsupported. "I took care *to say what you wished,*" she wrote later to the Crown Princess. She kept on telling the Emperor that Prussia had to be treated as an equal by Austria. He assured her that this was his wish and that there was no other wish anywhere in Germany, that she might repeat this to the Crown Princess. He only regretted that the King of Prussia had not come to the Frankfurt Congress, but laid the blame at Bismarck's door.[49] The Crown Princess was delighted to be able to tell the King of her mother's diplomacy. "How kind and good of you to say what I begged to the Emperor of Austria . . ." she wrote to her mother, "I am sure it will have done some good." The King of Prussia was touched and grateful that Queen Victoria had spoken in the way she did.[50] He did recognize the occasional value of the English relationship and influence—something

Bismarck wished to destroy for the good of Prussia and Germany.

The opportunity to retaliate came with another paper from the Crown Prince, protesting against another quick dissolution of the new parliament. Bismarck enjoyed mocking the Crown Prince about what was constitutional and what was not, saying that he had sworn to observe the constitution conscientiously—but what if his conscience told him not to observe it?[51] In his comments on the Prince's paper, Bismarck played on the King's fears and suspicions. The witch-hunt over the leaks of the royal letters to *The Times* was still continuing. The King went on blaming foreign influence for his son's opposition to him. He had threatened the Crown Prince, saying: "I shall deal very severely with whoever it is who puts these ideas into your head."[52] If the Crown Prince were invulnerable because he was the heir to the throne, his advisers were not, nor his wife entirely.

Bismarck struck swiftly at the heart of the matter. At one stroke he could discredit the Crown Prince and destroy the King's respect for Queen Victoria's meddling in international diplomacy. He inserted a comment on the Crown Prince's paper, accusing him of being too indiscreet through his marriage and his English relatives. He knew too many state secrets and told them to his wife, who could pass the information to her mother and so to the British government. It would be wise, Bismarck wrote, not to trust the Crown Prince and Princess in confidential matters until they realized that in reigning houses their nearest relatives were not always their fellow countrymen, but had to represent *other* interests than those of Prussia. It was hard when a country's frontier was the boundary of interests between mother and daughter, between brother and sister, but to forget that spelled danger to the state.[53]

The accusation was true. The question of Schleswig and Holstein was already dividing mother and son and sister in Queen Victoria's family. Bismarck was also firing the opening salvo in his war to subordinate the international royal intelligence system to the security needs of the new nation-state. He could never allow Prussian interests to be represented by a foreign Queen, even if she called the King of Prussia her "brother." Equally, he had to stop official secrets reaching the wife of the heir to the throne, because she had been born in an alien land where half her heart still was. So Bismarck worked on the King's fears, and won an easy victory. The Crown Prince had been indiscreet and was in opposition to his father's wishes. It was simpler to blame foreign influences than German liberals, although they too were blamed. At the end of September, the Crown Prince and his whole family were packed off to Balmoral for a long stay. This would give Bismarck time to turn the King finally against his son and convince him that the Crown Prince should be excluded from the councils of state for fear that he might betray his country's secrets to his mother-in-law in England.

What Bismarck had predicted occurred at Balmoral in November. The problem of Schleswig and Holstein split the family. The Danish King was trying to incorporate Schleswig into Denmark through a new constitution. The Crown Prince and Princess were dead set against this. The duchies lay across Prussia's access to the North Sea and were essential to its future strength. There was bickering among Queen Victoria's children with some on the side of Prussia and others on the side of Denmark. Open quarrels broke out on the sudden death of the Danish King in mid-November. It was a major international crisis. The King had no direct heir. Princess Alexandra's father was proclaimed King Christian IX and immediately signed the new constitution incorporating Schleswig into Denmark. The local assembly in Holstein appealed to the German Confederation to send as their ruler Frederick of Augustenburg, a liberal duke. The conflict was fought over at Balmoral, where the Crown Prince stood up to Queen Victoria for the first time. Prussian interests could not be reconciled with Danish or English ones.

Queen Victoria complained to her uncle King Leopold that her son-in-law was very violent on the subject. She trembled at what he might say to the Prince of Wales and his Danish wife. She was miserable, wretched, almost frantic without the Prince Consort to stand by her and put the others down and in their right place. No respect was paid to her opinion now. This helplessness almost drove her wild. In the family, his loss was more dreadfully felt than anywhere. "It makes visits like Fritz and Vicky's *very painful* and *trying.* Oh! God, why, oh! Why was *all* this permitted?" And now that everything that the Prince Consort understood so well was taking place, he was not there to help them and write those admirable papers which were gospel now.[54]

With the Queen's family divided among itself and the Anglo-Coburg group in disarray, Bismarck continued to widen the rift between the Crown Prince and the King. The Prince was recalled to Berlin and told that he should keep away from all state councils. He must give up any sign of opposition in public, and he must be careful not to disclose official or army secrets to anyone at all. This last warning was obviously directed against the Crown Princess, who was still in Scotland.

So Bismarck ended the year triumphant. He was preparing to unite Prussia by a short sharp war against the Danes. A glorious victory would change the mind of parliament about the need to strengthen the army. It would even change the mind of the Crown Prince, who was first and foremost a soldier. In one year of office, Bismarck had confused and scattered his opponents at home and abroad. The Crown Princess and Queen Victoria's efforts at diplomacy in Germany seemed futile. In fact, Bismarck could be grateful for the English Queen's interference. She had also advocated a good understanding between Prussia and Austria. Why not? At least, until the Danes were beaten and the duchies taken. Then the victors could fight over the spoils.

The Princess Royal is two years old. 1842.
(Winterhalter)

Queen Victoria, Prince Albert, and their children
[LEFT TO RIGHT] Prince Alfred, Prince Edward, Princess Alice,
Princess Helena, and Victoria, the Princess Royal. 1846.
(Winterhalter)

The Princess Royal and Prince Arthur as "Summer" in the Tableaux of the Seasons, Windsor Castle, February 10, 1854. (Roger Fenton)

Prince Frederick William of Prussia,
September 29, 1855.   (G. W. Wilson)

Prince and Princess Frederick
William of Prussia,
December 1860.   (Haase)

Crown Prince of Prussia and his son Prince William, Balmoral, October 1863. (G. W. Wilson)

Queen Victoria and Prince William of Prussia, 1864. (Hughes)

Crown Princess of Prussia,
November 1865.   (Hills and Saunders)

The Crown Prince and Princess of Prussia
with Prince William, Princess Charlotte,
Prince Henry and Prince Sigismund,
November 1865.   (Hills and Saunders)

The Prince of Prussia, later the
German Emperor, William I.   (Von Angeli)

The Crown Prince of Germany
with Prince William and Prince Henry,
June 1874.   (H. Graf)

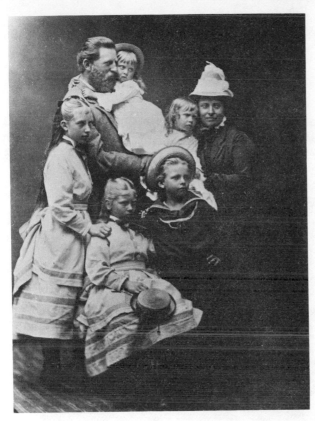

Group, August 1874,
with the Crown Prince
and Princess of Germany
and some of their children,
Princesses Charlotte, Victoria,
Sophie, and Margaret,
and Prince Waldemar.
(Hills and Saunders)

The Crown Princess of Germany
and Prince William, February 1876. (Prümm)

LEFT TO RIGHT: *Princesses Sophie, Victoria and Margaret of Prussia, August, 1879. (Selle)*

5

To Us Germans

THE CROWN PRINCESS stood on her balcony in Berlin. Below her, the grey and blue soldiers were marching away, rank on rank, to Schleswig. The Crown Prince was going with them to join the forces under the old Field Marshal Wrangel. Parades had always excited the Crown Princess, and the prospect of war overwhelmed her. "Our dear troops" she called the Prussians now. Until the war against Denmark, "our soldiers" had always been British ones, but the sound of boots and drums in Berlin made the Crown Princess identify herself with her adopted country at last. There was no problem about Schleswig and Holstein for her. It was "to us Germans plain and simple as daylight and one for which we would gladly bring *any* sacrifice!"[1]

Bismarck had provoked the war. Technically, the Danes were in the wrong. The new constitution signed by King Christian IX broke the terms of the London treaty which had defined the extent of Danish power in Schleswig and Holstein. When Bismarck's ultimatum was rejected, Prussia and Austria could claim the right to intervene on behalf of the German Confeder-

ation. While the smaller German states wanted a new independent duchy set up on the borders under Frederick of Augustenburg, Bismarck wanted Prussia to annex enough territory to
secure its access to the North Sea. At a Crown Council, he
reminded the King that each of the recent rulers of Prussia
had increased its size. The King thought Bismarck had been
drinking, the Crown Prince raised his hands to heaven as if
Bismarck were mad, and the other ministers did not know
what to say.

The invasion was a bitter blow to Queen Victoria, who
had to struggle for six months to keep her government from
helping the Danes. Lord Palmerston told the Queen that the
Germans were acting like bullies, but in real life, as in romance,
the wicked giant sometimes found that his intended victim
met with unexpected support.[2] The Queen replied that England had to play a passive role. She lobbied other Cabinet
ministers to keep her country out of the war, and in fact,
the Cabinet was divided on the issue and came to no decision.

The conflict in the royal family was bad enough. The
Queen's eldest daughter and the Crown Prince had supported
the King in wanting to go to war. Both of her German sons-
in-law were army officers and had left for the front. "I had
hoped that this dreadful war might be prevented," she wrote
to the Crown Princess, "but you all (God forgive you for it)
would have it!"[3] Her heart and her sympathy were all German,
but she had to think of all the family. The Prince of Wales
was frantic, thinking that everybody wanted to crush Denmark. His young wife Alexandra was in a terrible state of
post-natal depression after the birth of her first child. Her
father and brothers were fighting against their German cousins. "Oh! If Bertie's wife was only a good German and not
a Dane!" the Queen wailed. It was not so much the politics,
but the peace and harmony of the family were being destroyed.
It was terrible to have the Prince of Wales supporting the
wrong side. It aggravated her sufferings greatly.[4]

The Crown Princess had no special reports on what was

happening in the war. Bismarck kept most confidential information from the Crown Prince, and the King had warned
his son not to reveal state matters to his wife. Bismarck did
not even tell the King much of what he was planning or doing.
As he admitted later, with the risks he was taking, he was
beginning to live as close to the gallows as to the throne.
He was chiefly fretting about having to pay for the war ille-
gally from Prussian treasury reserves. He was not getting the
quick cheap victory he needed, for the outnumbered Danes
fought well, withdrawing slowly. Not until April 18, 1864,
did the German troops storm the trenches of Düppel and provide a glorious action, which forced the Danes to accept an
armistice. The action had been preceded by the bombardment
of the town of Sonderburg, which caused an outcry against
Prussian brutality in *The Times* and in the British Parliament.
Inspired by growing Prussian patriotism, the Crown Princess
was indignant. The bombardment of the town had been necessary in order to take Düppel. The constant meddling and interfering by England in other people's affairs had become
ridiculous abroad. They made her own position in Prussia
intolerable.[5]

Attacks on Queen Victoria began appearing in British
newspapers. She was accused of embarrassing the government
through her pro-German views. Lord Palmerston sent her a
critical editorial and accused persons near her of being indiscreet about her opinions. Queen Victoria referred to him as
Pilgerstein and complained that he was gouty and extremely
impertinent. Yet when Lord Ellenborough attacked her in the
Lords for her German sympathies, she was grateful for Lord
John's, (now Earl Russell's) defense of her, and for his claim
that the government alone took the responsibility for British
foreign policy.

The same sort of thing was happening to the Crown Princess in Berlin. People there said she was unhappy at the success
of Prussian arms, and court circles regretted having an Englishwoman in the royal family. New rumors spread that she had

discovered secrets from a Crown Council meeting and had telegraphed them to Lord Palmerston, who had immediately threatened Prussia. "I feel as if I could smash the idiots," the Crown Princess declared, "it is so spiteful and untrue. I am sure that I would almost quarrel with my real and best friends in dear England rather than forget that I belong to this country."[6]

On the advice of her foreign minister, Queen Victoria wrote twice to her "Dear Brother," the King of Prussia. In her first letter, she congratulated him on his victorious army. Her son-in-law the Crown Prince was soon to be given command of the Second Army Corps. The agitation in England was only because people wrongly believed that Prussia wanted to annex Schleswig and Holstein. She did not believe this, and could not believe it of the King. In her second letter, she begged him to show generosity to the weaker party and not ask too much of the Danes. Her letters had little effect on the King. Victory had made him stubborn. He wanted ports and fortresses on the Baltic and the North Sea, also the larger part of Schleswig. The armistice negotiations were broken off and the war was resumed. Because of Field Marshal Wrangel's advanced age, the Crown Prince was becoming the effective commander of the Allied army, and his tact and leadership saved many lives in the inexorable progress through Denmark. If there were any credit to be had from such a one-sided contest, it went to him.

Feeling for brave little Denmark was so strong in England that the sending of the fleet to help it seemed probable. Earl Russell proposed to do this, but was opposed by the Queen. At two critical Cabinet meetings in June, the peace party just prevailed. The navy would not be sent to help the Danes unless Copenhagen were threatened or Denmark in danger of being destroyed. It was a close thing. The Queen's unwavering support for Germany, her insistence that she would not agree to a war in which English interests were not directly menaced, had just prevented intervention. "After a week of the greatest anxiety," she wrote to her uncle, King Leopold, "the only wise and reasonable course *has* been pursued; and *this* country is safe." She felt that Prince Albert had blessed and guided her. His ideas still worked on for everybody after his death. "*It* IS satisfactory to see that my *efforts* were not unavailing."[7]

The King of Prussia thought so too. Although he was exasperated by the threats coming from Palmerston and Russell, he was conscious of the Queen's role in helping to keep England out of the war. He never missed an opportunity of telling the Crown Princess how much he owed her mother for keeping the peace. What tormented the Crown Princess was the feeling of animosity between her two countries. It was dangerous and harmful; it was kept up by foolish trifles and could be avoided. Aware her soldier husband and Prussia were becoming more important to her life, she warned her mother: "Now dear Papa is no longer here I live in constant dread that the bonds which united our two countries for their mutual good are being so loosened that they may be in time quite severed!"[8] Queen Victoria would not admit to that possibility. She would not permit any break in relationships, as long as the Crown Princess could keep open her sources of intelligence from Prussia. She would use that special knowledge to prevent a rupture between the two countries. Unfortunately, at the moment public opinion in England was ungovernable, because it was thought that Prussia wanted to seize both the duchies. The Queen, however, had taken to heart Lord Palmerston's accusation about the indiscretions of those close to her. She told her daughter never to say that the Queen's opinions were in opposition to her government's—which they often were, which she sometimes told her daughter they were, and which her daughter used to excuse England's behavior to the King of Prussia. It was only a constitutional hypocrisy to say they never were.

The resumed war against Denmark did not last long. The Prussians and Austrians pressed forward in Jutland, there was a change of government in Copenhagen, and the Danes sued for peace. They were ready to concede both Schleswig and Holstein to the German powers. When the Prussian and Austrian representatives met to agree to a division of the spoils, Bismarck demanded the two duchies for Prussia. The Austrian Foreign Minister was prepared to accept this, if Prussia would guarantee to help Austria reconquer Lombardy. Bismarck agreed, only to find that the King of Prussia's sense of honor would not allow him to seize the duchies. He had no right to them, he said. So Bismarck had to accept a joint occupation of the duchies by Prussia and Austria. It was not an alliance, but an increase of opportunities for misunderstanding. It was the prelude to a civil war in Germany.

≥≪

During the war, the love between the Crown Prince and his wife grew deeper and stronger. Although the fighting took her husband away, the Crown Princess recognized that it brought out the best qualities in him. She envied him because he won the love of his troops. Only when he was away did she realize how she was disliked in Prussia. His love and presence usually protected her; now she felt she could do nothing right. Her husband reassured her that they were made for each other. He also joked that he did not understand how a gifted woman like her could put up with an inferior fellow like him.[9] The Crown Princess had become pregnant again. Her mother did not approve. She ought to have had two good years' rest before she began again, Queen Victoria declared. Her own example could not be cited against her: she had begun three years later than her daughter had, and she had never suffered in the same way, even if it had done her nerves terrible harm.[10]

Of course, with her nine children Queen Victoria was in no position to complain about her daughters' having too many children themselves. The offspring would actually increase her family and her influence. Now that Alice was also pregnant again in Hesse-Darmstadt, the Queen could look forward to having enough grandchildren to fill the thrones of many more kingdoms and principalities.

Although the Crown Princess was not allowed to travel to England because of her condition, she wanted her eldest son Willy to go. The sea air at Osborne would do him good, and English doctors could look at his bad arm. The King was reluctant to give permission for his grandson to visit England. As the Crown Princess herself admitted, feelings in Prussia were so violent that anything which seemed to point to her English sympathies could damage her and her husband's position very much. Yet she could not help thinking how natural it was to send a little child away for the good of his health and to see his grandmother, who personally was most popular in Germany.

The trouble with her son Willy was that, in a sense, he was public property, the heir to the throne after his father. "We have to consider all these things," she told her mother, "particularly as there is such a jealousy about me as a stranger—and such a fear that I have a bad influence and would wish to bring up the *children* as foreigners."[11] She did not wish to give useless offense to good, if prejudiced, people, yet she ended by doing so. Willy was sent over to see his grandmother, all because the King was grateful to Queen Victoria for having helped to keep England out of the war. The Queen of England immediately wrote to her friend, the Queen of Prussia, to say how pleased she was at her grandson's arrival. He felt quite at home and was a dear, sweet child, affectionate to her and, more important, tactful enough to remember his grandfather. She herself felt terribly sad. It reminded her so vividly of the happy summer three years before, when the Prince Consort had been alive and had doted on his grandson at Osborne. "Now everything is as it was then—and everything in ruins!!!"[12]

During that summer holiday, with her Prussian grandson to herself, Queen Victoria formed a special relationship with him. He felt so certain of her affection that he would turn to her all his life, even when he was warring with his mother. This special feeling between the aged Queen and her grandson who was to become Kaiser, was a factor in keeping the peace between the British and German Empires at the turn of the century. He could never quite ignore his awe and love of her, while she could never quite forget her care of him when his mother was away.

Willy's education worried the Crown Princess. As he would probably inherit the throne from his father, he must be influenced in the right way. She wished him to become a great man, a second Frederick the Great or Prince Albert. With his father, he would have so much to do in rebuilding what was being destroyed by the "powers of darkness" presently ruling Prussia.[13] She wanted to bring him up with a British feeling of independence and common sense. Her mother agreed with her. "Bring him up simply, plainly," she stressed, "not with that terrible Prussian pride and ambition, which grieved dear Papa so much."[14]

Hopes were one thing, practice another. Steps were being taken to select a tutor who would be right for Willy. Trusting Robert Morier too much, the Crown Princess soon interviewed Georg Hinzpeter as the man who would instruct her son. He was a pedant and a bore, who believed in discipline and high principles at the cost of compassion and understanding. Unfortunately, Morier had praised Hinzpeter's morals and political principles—not exactly the qualities needed to deal with a willful and difficult child like Willy, who was being even more tormented by electric shock treatment for his withered arm. Young Stockmar, still an occasional adviser in the Crown Prince's household, distrusted Hinzpeter, finding him heartless and too hard a Spartan. Still, Hinzpeter was to have the job for thirteen years, in spite of Willy's mother's wishing to study her child as he was and judge what was best for him.

In September, the Crown Princess gave birth to her third son, Sigismund, whom she particularly adored for his sweet and loving nature. She seemed to delight more and more in domesticity, seeing in it a private blessing, a compensation for her public misfortune. As distrust of *die Engländerin* grew, and as Bismarck managed to keep her husband more and more in quarantine, she concentrated on making a happy home and a large family for him. She looked for a quiet country house near Potsdam where she and the children could retire from the suspicious atmosphere of court circles. In the little village of Bornstadt, she found a deserted house in an overgrown orchard. Surrounding it was a broken-down village where poor peasants slept like their own beasts on straw beds. The place would be a haven and an experiment in reform, where the family could be happy and live simply.

The playwright Gustav Zu Putlitz, for a time a chamberlain to the Crown Princess, drew an illuminating portrait of her in the first summer of her quarantine by Bismarck. He found her wonderfully well read, more cultivated than any other woman of her years. She debated like a historian, with judgment and discrimination. Above all, with her candor and simplicity, she had the gift of putting people at their ease. Sometimes she wore a plain woolen dress and sang songs as she sat at a spinning wheel. She devoted herself to making a home for the Crown Prince, where all might feel secure from intrigue, and where frankness and clear intelligence were prized.[15]

Robert Morier found the Crown Princess's island of security and straightforwardness more at risk. He saw the couple soon after Bismarck had finally forced young Stockmar to leave their service. This ended all direct Coburg influence and eliminated one of Queen Victoria's two main sources of intelligence. Bismarck's diplomatic victories had not affected the Crown Prince or his wife. They told Morier that they were disgusted at such successful brilliance. They stood like a dead wall against the cynical sophistries of Bismarck. Morier thought that the Crown Prince's defiant speech at Danzig had made Bismarck hesitate to attack the constitution again. The continuing passive opposition of the heir to the throne was paralyzing Bismarck's illegal activities. The fact that the two young people had remained unscathed was a credit to them. Now that Stockmar was gone, there was not a single person in their entourage who was not a devoted Bismarckian. The two men closest to the Prince were Bismarck's creatures body and soul.[15]

Beset and marked out, the Crown Prince and Princess stood firm. Bismarck kept up the slights upon the Crown Prince in the hope of eroding the dead wall of his resistance, while the King's displeasure at his son's persistent opposition was shown in the most public way. The Crown Prince was forbidden to be in Berlin to take the salute of the victorious troops returning from Denmark. This made him sad, but left him stubborn. The hardest thing, his wife admitted, was not an open struggle, but coping with the constant little annoyances and persecutions. They were allowed to meet the Prince and Princess of Wales at Cologne, but it was a stiff and awkward encounter. The Prussian prince could not hide his pride at his recent victories in Schleswig; he flaunted a very objectionable campaign ribbon—Queen Victoria was told by her son—which he had received for his deeds of valor against the unhappy Danes.

The only refuge from the pinpricks of the reactionary court and the attentions of Bismarck and his spies was in the family. The great success of Queen Victoria in the rearing of her children had been to keep them close-knit and loyal to her—they would tell her everything without much discrimination. The special quality in her huge correspondence with her daughters in Germany lay in the mixture of the personal and the political, the trivial and the secret, as if all matters were equally important. Babies teething and rumors of war, difficulties with nannies and Bismarck's intrigues, gossip about relations and possible royal marriages, all were given the same space and weight—a ragbag of inside information which the Queen of England could pick from at her leisure, sending

on selected paragraphs to her Foreign Secretaries for the good
of her country, and reserving the rest to treasure as a mother
and as the center of her powerful family.

The flow of political information from Berlin diminished
with the new year of 1865. Bismarck's quarantine was working. Little important news, no secrets of state, were reaching
the Crown Princess. She had to make do with stories about
her children to amuse her mother, now reverting to seclusion
and detachment after her six-month burst of activity in helping to prevent her country from going to war with Germany.
The Crown Princess wrote to her mother about an argument
between her Willy and Charlotte on the nature of the divine.
Charlotte had thought that God was in her heart. Willy had
disagreed, saying that she was sometimes naughty, so God
had come into him. "Yes, but I am not naughty now," Charlotte had replied, "and God will not fly away to you." Yet
Willy would not give up. If his sister had God, he had Jesus
in him. When his governess had tried to point out that God
was powerful enough to be in the hearts of both the children
at the same time, and that He was really the same as Jesus,
Willy had protested: "Oh no, *mademoiselle*, Jesus and God are
not the same thing. Jesus Christ has some whiskers, I saw it
in my book, and I am sure *der liebe Gott* has no whiskers."[17]

><

"Now you are head of all the family," Princess Alice wrote
to her mother Queen Victoria. "It seems incredible, and that
dear Papa should not be by your side."[18] With the terminal
illness of her uncle and father figure King Leopold, the Queen
of England found herself the elder statesman of them all. Bismarck was maneuvering to swallow up the two duchies and
provoke Austria into a losing war. Queen Victoria and the
Crown Princess were set on a collision course with Bismarck
on the best way of uniting Germany. It was to be the last
year of the long Coburg dream, for Germany would be united
soon by iron and blood, the quicker and more certain way.

To Bismarck, the English Queen's trump cards, the marriages of her children, seemed to be played as deliberate provocations. Her third daughter, Princess Helena, now needed a husband, and the Queen chose Prince Christian of Schleswig-Holstein, an intimate of her eldest daughter and the Crown Prince. He was the younger brother of Frederick of Augustenburg, the pretender to the two duchies who was backed by the smaller German states. Bismarck had deprived both brothers of their army commissions and their property at the end of the Danish war, because he was furious that they would not give up their rights. And at the convention of Gastein in August, he arranged that Holstein should be administered by Austria and Schleswig by Prussia. The Augustenburg claims were ignored. This agreement with Austria, Bismarck sneered, was papering over the cracks. He took Queen Victoria's choice of a husband for her third daughter as a slap in the face and a reminder that she did not expect Prussia to gobble up smaller German states and eliminate their rightful rulers. The fact that both the Crown Prince and Princess supported Prince Christian as Helena's husband, calling him the best creature in the world, made them greater offenders in Bismarck's eyes. They seemed to enjoy thwarting him.

Queen Victoria's visit to Coburg that summer also seemed to be a demonstration of her support of the lesser German states against Prussian aggrandizement. Officially, the Queen went to Coburg to unveil a statue of her beloved dead husband, but she was joined by all her nine children and fifteen of her princely German relatives at the "beautiful, touching and solemn ceremony." It was an impressive display of the Queen's influence—a reminder that the Queen was deeply concerned with the future of Germany. At Coburg she was showing that she would do her best to carry out her husband's policies, which Bismarck was determined to deny.

For the first time, Queen Victoria's letters began to take on a bias against Prussia. "Prussia seems inclined to behave as atrociously as possible, and as she *always has done*," she de-

clared. "Odious people the Prussians are, *that* I *must* say."[19]
Bismarck's policy of making his country larger had changed
Queen Victoria's belief in the necessary alliance of the two
great Protestant powers. She did not even want to meet the
King of Prussia during her visit to Germany, but she felt she
had to see him after a plea from his wife, who claimed the
King's personal feelings for Queen Victoria were what they
always had been, but he sadly was under the influence of a
clever, unprincipled man who had completely changed him.
When Queen Victoria did meet the King, he had clearly been
told to remain as silent as possible. He talked about the
weather and left after half an hour.

The Queen could do nothing to help her eldest daughter
against the ascendancy of Bismarck, who was created a count
by the grateful King after the Convention of Gastein. The
Crown Princess continued to send her mother stray pieces
of political information, but nothing of great importance. Surrounded by Bismarck's spies, she knew the danger of criticizing
the Minister President in writing. From Schleswig in August,
she dared to send a letter by ordinary mail instead of waiting
for the royal messenger. In it, she declared to her mother
that Bismarck was a reckless adventurer. She added that if
the letter were opened by the postal officials, she would be
accused of high treason—but that she was as loyal as anyone."[20]

Bismarck took pleasure in having the Crown Prince
shunted aside to become the honorary Protector of Public
Museums. The new realpolitik was consigning the antique
decency of the Crown Prince and his Coburg friends to a
repository of the past. "The Crown Prince occupies himself
with politics he does not understand," Bismarck jeered to a
French diplomat, "talks of things of which he knows nothing,
and opens books which he does not read."[21] He was almost
irrelevant to Bismarck's unfolding plans to make Prussia into
Germany—unimportant as long as he could not rally the liberal
opposition and did not inherit the throne. The Prince still
performed his military duties and visited the great Krupp

works at Essen, where ten thousand workers were turning out the breech-loading needle-guns for the Prussian army. But he had effectively been put out to grass. Only if Bismarck were to get the war he wanted against Austria would the Crown Prince have his opportunity to command.

The fact that the army reforms were being carried out and paid for increased Bismarck's dominance over the King. The Chambers went on refusing to vote funds for the military budget, and they went on being dissolved by Bismarck. He preferred ruling without the nuisance of having to consult a pack of deputies. Yet he found the money to pay for more troops and munitions, also preparing a war chest for the coming conflict against Austria. His financier was still Bleichröder, who arranged for the illegal sale of the Prussian state interest in the Cologne-Minden railway for thirty million *talers*. This would pay for the mobilization of nine army corps, and would keep them in the field for a month without touching the reserves in the state treasury.

So Bismarck acquired the sinews of war, but he was not sure about its outcome. Financing was one thing, fighting another. The leading strategist Moltke continually reminded him that war was uncertain. Austria was held to be more powerful than Prussia. What had to be avoided was a war on two fronts, with the French attacking across the Rhine. Bismarck went to Biarritz and saw the French Emperor, who alone in Europe was as enigmatic and secretive as himself. He hinted that if Napoleon III stayed on his side of the Rhine during the coming German war, France might be compensated with parts of Belgium or Luxembourg. Also, Italy would be able to seize Venetia from Austria and round off her kingdom below the Alps. The Prussians would do the fighting, the French and their allies would reap some of the harvest. When Bismarck left, he had promised nothing definite, yet he had neutralized Prussia's western flank. "Napoleon will dance a cotillion with us," he boasted, "without being clear in his mind when it will begin or what figures it will include."[22]

Bismarck's brilliance at this time even seduced the new British Ambassador to Berlin, Lord Napier, who reported that Bismarck had some great and generous qualities even if he were indiscreet and unscrupulous in pursuing his aims. The Prussian minister intended to quell all opposition at home by his success abroad. Finally, Napier confessed to a peculiar sympathy for Bismarck's strange, impetuous, desultory, domineering, aspiring, humorous character. He was a man who should not be in government in Berlin, but should live in London with free spirits and men of letters.[23] To have a British Ambassador being as cynical and realistic as Bismarck was too much. Napier was replaced by a previous Ambassador to Berlin, Lord Augustus Loftus. Queen Victoria would not have as her representative in Prussia somebody who seemed to side with Bismarck against her daughter. The Crown Princess still thought that Bismarck and a small reactionary clique were the villains who perverted and misrepresented all. Like Lord Napier, the King of Prussia had been turned. He had agreed to take over Schleswig and the naval base at Kiel. He had put aside his deep beliefs in the sanctity of hereditary right in order to gain more land and power for Prussia. His honor now seemed to consist in accepting what Bismarck achieved for him without inquiring too closely into how it was done. The Minister President's most dangerous quality was his ability to attach people to the tail of his comet. Where he blazed, they were dazzled and drawn on. By admiring his successes and his genius at diplomacy, they stifled their doubts about his morality and methods.

The Crown Prince and Princess seemed old-fashioned. Their liberalism, once a revolutionary force in Europe, appeared dated and futile beside the new thrust of national diplomacy. Their pious judgments were irrelevant and insupportable, an intrusion on what had to be. Even their moral rock, the values and example of Queen Victoria, was slippery beneath their feet, for she was becoming involved in the only scandal of her private life. She had taken to herself a permanent Highland servant, John Brown. She had been alone too long, and needed the comforting and devoted support of a strong man. Brown cleaned the Queen's things and did odd jobs, put her on her pony and took her off, fussed over her welfare and shielded her privacy, and even put his body between her and attempted assassins. The Queen's Highland servant was five years younger than she, a handsome brawny man with a curly beard and a bright blue gaze. He had a trenchant manner which could offend. He was liable to call the Queen "wumman" and tell her how to behave outdoors. The Prince of Wales thought him a boor and an intruder, yet Brown could be so tender, particularly about the Queen's grief for her dead husband, that she was touched to the heart. In her most illuminating story about her new relationship, she told the Crown Princess about Brown's first visit to the Frogmore Mausoleum near Windsor.

When he came to her room later, he was much affected. He looked at the Queen with pity, while the tears rolled down his cheeks. In his simple, expressive way, he said: "I didn't like to see ye at Frogmore this morning. I felt for ye—to see ye coming there with your daughters and your husband lying there—marriage on one side and death on the other. No, I didn't like to see it. I felt sorry for ye. I know so well what your feeling must be—ye who had been so happy. There is no more pleasure for you, poor Queen, and I feel for ye but what can I do for ye? I could die for ye."[24] The Queen was deeply moved by this emotional speech from her strong hardy man, her child of the mountains. She grew to depend on his care and judgment. His constant presence by her and her continuing refusal to make public appearances led to rumors and jokes that she was "Mrs. John Brown." She would try to dismiss these insinuations as ill-natured gossip among the aristocracy, because she could not be forced out of her seclusion.[25] Yet she could not stop the deterioration abroad of her image of strict morality, particularly where viperous tongues were stinging the King of Prussia's ear.

Queen Victoria's character and dignity made it unbelieva-
ble that she could be John Brown's mistress or his secret wife.
She wanted security and devotion, no more than that. But
her fierce defense of Brown's position so close to her person,
her refusal to listen to the wise advice to shed him for the
sake of her reputation, damned her in the eyes of the gossips
and intriguers against the Coburg influence and the English
alliance. What Queen of England could complain of immoral
behavior by foreign diplomats when she was so close to a
body servant? Those who lived in glass palaces could not
throw stones.

6

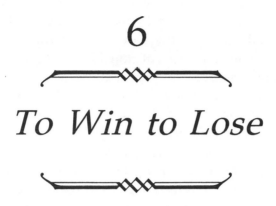

To Win to Lose

"**Y**OU ARE AMBITIOUS to be a king," the Crown Princess mocked Bismarck in 1866, "or at least president of a republic."

She was half-joking, half-serious. She had that touch of ironical superiority which Bismarck remembered from his one meeting with Queen Victoria at Versailles. Such an amiable and condescending manner irritated the Prussian minister. The English Queen and her daughter seemed unwilling to be unfriendly to a man they found unsympathetic and eccentric. So Bismarck replied in the same semi-jocular tone. He was more confident now, and even more powerful, for he had provoked the war with Austria which the Crown Prince had helped to win. Yet he still feared the potential influence of the alien Crown Princess, who was so intelligent and provocative that she dared to fence with him.

"I am personally spoilt for a republican," Bismarck answered her. He had need of a monarchy for his well-being on earth. He thanked God he did not have to live like a king, constantly on show: until his death, he was fated to be the King's faithful subject.

As he protested his loyalty, the Crown Princess still looked mockingly at him. He had to change his tack. He said that not everybody thought the monarchy would last as he did. Royalists would not give out, but kings might: "To make a stew, a hare is needed. To make a monarchy, a king." If there was not a king who wanted to be king, the next generation might be republican. The heir to the throne made him anxious; he did not seem to respect monarchical traditions.

The English princess refused to be drawn. She kept up her ironies and her pleasantries, and gave Bismarck the impression that she wished to tease a political opponent. She seemed to like provoking his patriotism by playful criticism.[1] It was a policy that she had learned from Bismarck, who had taunted the opposition at home and tormented Austria until it had been driven into mobilization. He had provoked the war he wanted. Now he had become too strong for the Crown Princess to do more than taunt him.

The Crown Prince had been the leading supporter of peace with Austria and fair dealing over the independence of Schleswig and Holstein, so Bismarck had put his motives under attack through his wife's relations. When the betrothed Prince Christian and Princess Helena had proposed to spend part of their honeymoon in the Augustenburg family castle of Gravenstein, they were forbidden to do so by the King of Prussia on Bismarck's advice. The castle was in occupied Schleswig, where Prussian troops held the ground. Might displaced right. Queen Victoria could think the King's behavior a gross insult, and the Crown Princess could be dreadfully hurt and shocked, calling it monstrous for the King to forbid a prince to go to his private property. But politics came before property. When Queen Victoria insisted that the Crown Prince show his father an outraged letter from her, it merely made the Prince seem more in the wrong and under his mother-in-law's thumb.

Bismarck knew his worth to the monarchy, yet he knew

he might be dismissed when the Crown Prince became King. He told Count Robert von der Goltz, his Ambassador in Paris: *"Après moi le déluge.* The Crown Prince can never govern the country."[2] In a Cabinet council, he accused the Crown Prince of being personally antagonistic to him and pernicious to Prussia. He had the Crown Prince called to the deathbed of a leading *Junker,* who used his last breaths on a paean of praise to Bismarck as the ablest pilot of the state, worthy of all support. Similar sentiments poured from the lips of the Burgomaster of Berlin, who cut across a business interview with the Crown Prince to laud and magnify Bismarck's name. These did not convince the Crown Prince, who also resisted veiled threats. When the Burgomaster of Magdeburg pointed out that Bismarck's hold on power would be gone when the Crown Prince took the throne, Bismarck replied that he would succeed in annihilating that opposition before it became dangerous to him. The previous Minister President, Manteuffel, repeated much the same menaces.[3] The Crown Prince was kept in a state of siege and alarm. "I am the only one who is not told even an iota about political affairs," he wrote in his diary. "Everyone is thinking of war with Austria which Bismarck wants at all costs."[4]

Bismarck intended to drive the Crown Prince into declaring his open opposition to the coming war. On February 24, Bismarck once again had the Chambers closed, after they refused to vote for an expanded military and naval budget. He wanted no elected deputies present to criticize his orchestration of the conflict with Austria. "Look what a lamentable pitiable spectacle we are," the Crown Princess complained to her mother, "with worse than no constitution, a prey to the caprices of a bad and dangerous man! One feels so sad—so ashamed and so helpless."[5] Four days after the closure of parliament, the Crown Prince was summoned to a vital Crown Council, where all were bound to an oath of secrecy. There Moltke and the General Staff were seated with the court's military advisers; the War Minister Roon and the Finance

Minister von Bodelschwingh and Bismarck were also present; so were Goltz and the King. All the generals favored a war with Austria that spring. Bismarck recited a catalog of Austrian perfidies and insults over the past fifty years and claimed that it was Prussia's mission to unite Germany. He also agreed with Moltke on the need for an alliance with Italy to involve Austria in a war on two fronts.

Not everyone agreed. Knowing that the Prussian treasury could not support a campaign of more than a few weeks, the Finance Minister was hesitant and favored a last attempt at peace. The Crown Prince stood firmly against a war, declaring that when brother fought brother in Germany, only the French would profit on the Rhine. He did not know of Bismarck's dealings with Napoleon III to neutralize him. All he had done was to expose himself as a pacifist, although he might well be given the command of a Prussian army in the event of war.

The King listened and finally spoke. He said that his conscience and his God demanded justice for Prussia even at the price of a war with Austria. But he would not allow an unjust war against fellow Germans, so peace with honor would still be preferable. He approved of Bismarck's working for French neutrality and a military alliance with Italy. Accepting a conflict was inevitable sooner or later, the King left its timing to the generals. They and Bismarck thought he meant to fight, but they could not be sure. So secret was the meeting that even the Crown Princess did not hear of it from her husband. The new British Ambassador, Lord Augustus Loftus, could only report back that it had taken place and that a campaign had been planned to annex the Danish border duchies.[6]

In early April, Bismarck achieved a military alliance with Italy. If war were to break out within the following three months, Italy would attack Austria in Venetia. While Italy committed itself, Napoleon pursued his ambiguous neutrality, negotiating with Austria so as to become the arbiter of a struggle in Germany. The winner would have to pay him off in the Rhineland as the price for keeping the French out.

The Austrians were provoked enough to take elementary military preparations against a surprise attack. Their army needed seven weeks to mobilize, the Prussians only three weeks after the King's military reforms. Forced to play Bismarck's game, the Austrians felt obliged to reinforce their fortresses in Bohemia and Moravia. With intelligence sources reporting every detail of these troop movements, Bismarck could represent defensive measures as aggressive ones. Strengthening a fort against a sneak attack seemed a menace to the Prussian borders. The King of Prussia was persuaded to send troops and munitions to the southern frontier, yet he still would not call up the reserves.

While Bismarck pursued his policies, the Crown Prince and Princess tried, along with Queen Augusta of Prussia, to prevent the war. At a reception given by Bismarck in the middle of March, the new British Ambassador managed to have a long conversation with the King. Unexpectedly, the King responded to an offer of British arbitration between Prussia and Austria, and declared that he did not want to push things to the extreme. He then, for the first time, spoke to his son on the political crisis, asking him to write to Queen Victoria and offer her the agreeable task of mediating between the two German powers. This was a strange turnabout and a blow to Bismarck's methods of diplomacy. As the British Ambassador said, the question for Bismarck was: "Will he carry the King with him?" If the British could get the wedge in, Bismarck would find it more difficult.[7] "You again, dearest Mama," the Crown Princess wrote in elation, "may be the means of averting a European conflagration." England's interference had often been untimely and unlucky, but this time it had every chance of success. Bismarck probably knew nothing of this new policy of the King's. He was bent on war for his own "wild, mad purposes." It was in Austria's interests not to fight. All now looked to Queen Victoria as their good genius.[8]

When he heard of it, Bismarck was appalled by such direct royal diplomacy. He immediately protested through the Prussian Minister in London, Count Albrecht von Bernstorff. The Crown Prince should not have sent the King's message to Queen Victoria, it should have gone through the Prussian embassy. Lord Clarendon, now the Queen's Foreign Secretary, was himself annoyed at rival royal negotiations. Yet he defended the Crown Prince, saying that if he had not sent on the message, or had modified it, he would have been blamed by the King.[9]

"The wicked man" Bismarck was frantic, the Crown Princess wrote to her mother. He said that the alternative royal diplomacy would not do. It crossed his plans. It was a useless interference. In short, he was very angry. He would now do all he could to pin the King to his policies and paralyze any intervention. She thought Queen Victoria should know this without delay, even though it might appear like an intrigue, which she hated.[10]

The Crown Princess knew the risk she was taking. If Bismarck laid hands on any of her messages to her mother that revealed a state secret, he could utterly destroy her and her husband. *"Please pray* do not betray me," she implored her mother in early April. "I am not supposed to know anything contained in the Despatches, but as I *did* hear this I thought I would tell you."[11] She had to protect herself against Bismarck's increasing surveillance, so she asked her mother for more secure and quicker methods of communication. She did not even want the British Foreign Office to know what she was telling Queen Victoria. Her mother would not betray her, where an ambassador might. "Will you not arrange a cypher between *me* and *you?*" she asked her mother in England. "When I want to use it, I can send the figures to Lord Augustus Loftus. Nobody here will know that he is not telegraphing something of his own. The Foreign Office can pass on the figures to you without knowing what they are. I think this might be very useful, and if you approve, no time ought to be lost about it."[12]

Queen Victoria knew the limits of royal diplomacy far bet-

ter than her daughter did. She told her Prime Minister immediately of the information in her daughter's last letter, but she
did not think an offer from her to mediate between the two
German powers would work. It was made superfluous by Bismarck, who had already sent a long letter to Count Bernstorff
saying that such an attempt would all end in smoke. Her
own Foreign Secretary, Lord Clarendon, was being disagreeable and unmanageable, resenting her efforts to intervene, but
Earl Russell was still anxious that she should do all she could.[13]
Bismarck's insistence, however, that all the faults lay on Austria's side meant that her good offices would mean persuading
the Hapsburg Empire to surrender to Bismarck's demands.

Bismarck followed up his instructions to Bernstorff by
making it clear to Lord Augustus Loftus that Prussia meant
to fight unless it was delivered Holstein on a plate and the
control of the whole of north Germany. He declared that Prussia was only responding to Austrian military preparations.
"What would you do," he asked Loftus, "if you found a violent man in the street threatening the public security and
peace?" Loftus replied that he would call for the police, which
were in this case the great powers of Europe. "But if it was
the case of a gentleman," Bismarck countered, "you would
give him your card"—and fight a duel to the death. The truth,
Loftus stated, was that Bismarck had fully made up his mind
for war. He had gone so far that he must either carry out
his hazardous policy or resign.[14] This bleak assessment stunned
Queen Victoria, although it struck a chord in Earl Russell.
As the Crown Princess admitted to her mother, trying to stop
a war without the Prince Consort's help was a nervous business. Queen Victoria was prostrated by one of her worst headaches when she heard from Queen Augusta that there was
no time to lose. She must reply to the King of Prussia's offer
to accept her mediation. He seemed a good deal hurt at not
having a response from her.[15] She could not tell him that
because of the reactions of Bismarck and of her own Foreign
Secretary her mediation was unacceptable and foredoomed.

She was forced to agree with Earl Russell's diagnosis. There was but one remedy, one certain path of preserving peace: It was the dismissal of Bismarck by the King. If that could be achieved by any patriotic Prussians near the throne, all might go right.[16]

So began the "Coburg intrigue," the last-ditch effort of the surviving believers in old Stockmar's plan to unite Germany. Not entirely in jest, Princess Helena had asked her eldest sister, the Crown Princess, to send her as a wedding present—Bismarck's head on a charger. He had to go, or sister would be set against sister in Germany, brother would fight brother in Bismarck's civil war.

Queen Victoria began the Coburg intrigue by suggesting that Bismarck was treacherous. In response to the King's offer to accept her arbitration, she wrote to the Crown Prince that the course pursued by the Prussian government made it difficult, if not impossible, for England to intervene. The annexation of both duchies, despite the known feelings and wishes of the people there, violated English principles. The Queen then made an attempt to drive in the wedge further between the King and his Minister President; she revealed that Bismarck had sent to Paris an account of the King's private conversation with Lord Augustus Loftus at the reception. He was abusing his master's confidence in order to defeat the pacific views of the King.[17] When the Queen's letter arrived safely in Berlin at the end of March, the Crown Prince sent its contents by personal message to the King. There was no reply. Meanwhile, the Crown Princess forgot her delicate position enough to answer her mother's inquiries on the extent of Prussian mobilization. Five of the Prussian frontier forts had been armed, and four army divisions had been put on alert, ready to fight.[18] This military information reached Queen Victoria before she heard it from the Foreign Office.

It was now the turn of Queen Victoria's brother-in-law, Duke Ernest of Coburg, to intervene. He secured a letter from the Austrian Foreign Minister declaring the Emperor's wish for peace. He traveled to Berlin personally to see that it reached the King of Prussia, for it might be intercepted by Bismarck's agents on the way. No one wished for war the Duke reported from Berlin, not the King or the princess or any mortal. The fault was singly and solely with Bismarck.

This comment was ingenuous. The General Staff wanted war, as did many of the *Junkers* and reactionaries at court. It suited the war party and the King to put all the responsibility for Prussia's policy on Bismarck, who wanted only to unite Germany in the way Italy had been united. It suited the Coburgs and the peace party around the Queen of Prussia and the Crown Prince to cast Bismarck as sole and total villain, who was misleading the righteous King. The Tsar now intervened, sending his uncle the King of Prussia a peace proposal through Baron von Schleinitz, a former aide-de-camp of the Crown Prince. But the proposal was ignored. The Duke of Coburg and the rulers of the other small German states were now worrying about a circular from Bismarck demanding to know who would fight for and who against Prussia. In the Duke's opinion, only a serious warning from England and France together would deter Bismarck from his disastrous course.[19]

While English diplomacy was trying and failing to secure French support against Bismarck's war, the King moved on his own. He proposed to send General Münster on a special secret mission to Vienna to see whether disarmament was still possible. Bismarck dissuaded him by offering his resignation if his policy were not followed. The King yielded, breathing peace and war alternately to different people. As he vacillated, he was incited against Austria all the time. Bismarck was intent on war, Lord Augustus Loftus reported, and war he would have if he remained in office. In short, the King had to decide: Bismarck or peace?[20]

The strain of stimulating the King to fight and frustrating

the Coburg intrigue was telling on Bismarck. He was fed up
with foreign monarchies trying to stick a finger into the national omelet. He hardly left the residence of the Minister
President. There the Austrian Ambassador found him, lying
on his red sofa, like a wounded boar—in agony, but a threat
to any hunter who came into his lair. He was said to be ill
or dying; actually he was suffering from indigestion, neuralgia
and varicose veins. In the mornings, he was usually bilious
and hung-over. Rumors of his resignation were widespread
in early April. He had boldly proposed that the German Confederation at Frankfurt should be ruled by deputies elected
by universal male suffrage, a proposal meant to steal the Coburg clique's thunder and attract liberal and national support
for Prussian policy. But the idea of one man, one vote offended
the King. He told Bismarck: "What you are proposing to me
is revolution!"[21]

The contradictions and swerves in Bismarck's policies baf-
fled his supporters as well as his enemies. At this low point
of his unpopularity, Queen Victoria struck her hardest blow.
She sent a personal letter to the King of Prussia through Lord
Augustus Loftus, who handed it to the King in the royal railway carriage. The British Ambassador told the King that the
letter was the private act of Her Majesty and did not involve
her government. Then and there, the King read the letter with
interest and attention, while Loftus watched him. The letter
ran:

BELOVED BROTHER,
    At this fearful moment I cannot be silent, without rais-
ing my voice earnestly, and in the name of all that is most
holy and sacred against the threatened probability of war.
It is in your power to avert the calamities of a war, the
results of which are too fearful to be even thought of,
and in which thousands of innocent lives will be lost, and
brother will be arrayed against brother.
    War is ever fearful, but when it is begun for mere

objects of ambition, for imaginary affronts and wrongs, it is still more fearful. You are deceived, you are made to believe that you are to be attacked, and I, your true friend and sister, hear your honoured name attacked and abused for the faults and recklessness of others—or, rather more, of ONE man! . . .

Ever your affectionate and unhappy Sister and Friend
Victoria R.[22]

After reading the letter, the King told Loftus that the latest Austrian dispatch had made it difficult for him to hold back from war. Loftus answered that, as the Emperor of Austria desired peace as much as the King said he desired it, there must be a way to find it. But the King replied, "I do not see how it could be effected."[23] The fact was that the King had not read the latest Austrian dispatch. It had been misrepresented to him by Bismarck. This gave the Coburg intriguers their opportunity to drive home the wedge between the King and his Minister President. The King had forbidden Queen Augusta to approach him directly on political matters because of her intrigues against Bismarck, but she sent a copy of the Austrian dispatch to the Duke of Coburg, who had it printed in the state *Gazette.* Once printed, the Queen could lay the full text in front of the King. His anger at having been tricked by Bismarck into thinking it offensive was very great. Queen Victoria's allegations in her letter were proved true.

The Duke of Coburg had asked his influential contacts in Vienna to verify whether Austria wanted war or not. The answer was that Austria wanted peace and was hardly arming. Full details of all Austrian military movements were sent to the Duke of Coburg, who had them passed on to the King by the trusted Schleinitz.[24] Again, Bismarck's assertions about Austrian mobilization were exaggerations. The Crown Prince called them "frivolous frauds." At this time, the fall of Bismarck was a real possibility. Austria prepared to withdraw its reinforcements from Bohemia and Silesia. If this were done, the King declared that Prussia would begin disarming the day after Austria did. Bismarck seemed too ill to protest. "My illness and death might prevent the war," he said. "If I had been in health, I would have insisted on it."[25]

Now the secret pact with Italy saved him and restored the King's faith in him. He had persuaded his ally to move most of its army towards Lombardy. The Austrians could not leave Venetia undefended against such a threat. On April 21, the Austrian Emperor felt obliged to declare a partial mobilization for his southern army. He appeared to be deceiving the King of Prussia about disarming and wanting peace. Bismarck had asserted just that. War with Austria was necessary.

It was the end of the Coburg intrigue. The King again trusted Bismarck's tactics and sources of intelligence. Far from dismissing his Minister President, the King feared that Bismarck might resign if his recommendations were not followed. Bismarck knew that Austria would also have to defend itself in the north. It could hardly risk committing its armies to an Italian campaign and inviting a stab in the back from Prussia, and its slow process of mobilization at half Prussia's speed meant that it had to prepare for war first. So six days after the partial mobilization in the south, the Austrian Emperor reluctantly ordered the mobilization of the northern army in Bohemia. Even if this would provoke a full Prussian response, there seemed nothing else to do.

Bismarck had got what he wanted, an apparent Austrian threat against Prussia. His health suddenly and wonderfully improved. To the Crown Princess, he seemed dangerously well. His audacity was rising with his spirits. Lord Augustus Loftus confirmed her view. When peace was apparently agreed, Bismarck was down and depressed, but now he had revived with his war policy. Sooner or later, war was inevitable because of him. As he joked to the British Ambassador, he would prefer to go down to posterity in the character of Attila.[26] There would have to be a conflict to remove so dangerous a man—or an assassination.

❧

On the fine spring day of May 7, the Minister President left his red sofa to confer with the King in the royal palace. He returned on foot and unguarded along the Unter den Linden. A student from Tübingen, Ferdinand Cohen-Blind, stepped from under the trees and fired five shots at Bismarck at point-blank range. The Minister gripped his assailant and held him until he could hand him over to a couple of passing guards. In the struggle, the revolver was pressed to Bismarck's thick coat, which was pierced by two bullets. One of the bullets bruised his ribs without breaking the skin. Bismarck told the King that he was wearing a breastplate of silk and wadding, which had saved his life. He told his political secretary that the shots had little effect because the gun was against his coat and the bullets had little velocity.

The assassination attempt was strangely timely. It provoked the first demonstration for Bismarck. A crowd assembled in the Wilhelmstrasse and cheered Bismarck until he appeared on his balcony. The would-be assassin was the Jewish stepson of a socialist revolutionary from southern Germany, Karl Blind, then in exile in London. Bismarck's spies immediately linked the assassination attempt to a secret society of republicans in Württemberg with plans to murder the King of Prussia and leading members of his government. The King was confirmed in his fears of revolutionaries and in his dependence on Bismarck's agents, while the British were linked to the conspiracy. Cohen-Blind had intended to flee to London after the attempt and had sent on his bags in advance. The Prussian police had the luggage receipt. A police officer left for London to recover the bags in case there were papers in them which would incriminate the members of the secret society, and British police cooperation was demanded.[27]

The timing of the attempt on Bismarck's life was perfect for him. It rallied popular support for his policy against the enemy within as much as the enemy outside. The fact that he was wearing a thick coat or padded breastplate on that day was very fortunate. The identity of his assassin was a godsend, a Jew and a radical connected with two opponents of Bismarck's diplomacy, Württemberg and England. The quality of the revolver used in the attempt was incredibly poor. Bismarck's explanation of the bullet holes was improbable; shots fired at point-blank range have more power, not less, and murderers prefer to put the muzzle against their victim to make sure of his death. The sequel was also odd. Cohen-Blind was able to cut his own throat in his cell that night. His attempted assassination seemed even more spurious. He was either murdered by police agents or given a razor and encouraged to commit suicide. It was beyond belief that such an important witness should not have been kept alive, unless there were good reasons to shut his mouth. As it was, he could not give evidence at his trial. He could not say who had set him up in Bismarck's path armed with a revolver so defective that it worked little better than a popgun.

In Berlin, even Bismarck's critics thought that the attempt on his life was genuine. They could not believe that a gullible youth might have been found to act out a fatal part in a political charade. The Crown Princess called the dead man a poor, well-meaning, mistaken, shortsighted wretch. It was better that Bismarck should live to see the consequences of his reckless madness than die a martyr.[28] Her mother in England was more vengeful and skeptical. She could not quite agree that it was better that Bismarck had not been shot. "Here people think it was all got up on purpose and don't believe that the man really tried to shoot Bismarck—else why did he not succeed?"[29]

The temptation to shoot Bismarck was great, for Prussian aggression threatened to swallow up all the small independent German states such as Württemberg. On May 2, Bismarck's Cabinet sent a unanimous resolution to the King, asking for full mobilization against Austria. The next day, the Crown

Prince was summoned to a secret meeting of the Crown Council. It was decided to put the four army corps on alert onto a full war footing. The news that Hanover, with its connections to the British Crown, would not support Prussia and was arming against it made Bismarck savage. The whole Prussian army and the reserves were called up. Bismarck intended to cut the Gordian knot of Germany with the sword.[30]

That May, as Austria and Prussia and Italy prepared to fight, the feeling of helplessness among the Anglo-Coburg group grew into despair. Everybody was arming against somebody, Queen Victoria recorded, and everybody declared they wanted to attack nobody.[31] At least she was on the sidelines of the war, involved only through her children and cousins. The Crown Princess was threatened with worse than the end of the Coburg dream. Her own husband might have to try and kill her sister's husband in Hesse and her close relatives in Hanover and Coburg. It was all absurdity and horror. She dissected daily her family's ruined future, contrasting it with the castles in the air she had been building for eight years. She felt wretchedly low and depressed. Her husband had been given command of a major Prussian army. The King had never been in better spirits. He might not wish for a war any more than the Crown Prince did, but his passion for soldiering put other considerations in the shade. "I fear," the Crown Princess told her mother, "it is a characteristic trait of the whole family, you know."[32]

She was writing in reply to one of Queen Victoria's more absurd suggestions. Her mother wished the Crown Prince to be firm and say he refused to take part in such an iniquitous war. This would raise him in the eyes of all the world.[33] That might well have been true, but it would also have put him inside a military prison on a charge of treason. Queen Victoria would not admit what her daughter knew very well, that the Crown Prince thought himself primarily a soldier and a Prussian commander. He would not be such a fool as to appear a traitor when the tide of Prussian nationalism had begun to run so strongly. Better to accept the gift of an army than to serve time as a public enemy.

The Crown Princess's blood relations forced her to divide her loyalties. Nearly all the people close to her in Germany belonged to princely families in the south. They would necessarily side with Austria. Her sister Alice's husband Louis and his youngest brother William would have to fight with the Grand Duke of Hesse-Darmstadt against Prussia. Yet the second brother, Henry, was in command of the Second Prussian Lancers and would have to fight with the Crown Prince, perhaps against Hesse. The members of family might be killing one another. The Crown Princess assured Alice that whatever happened she would always love and help her sister. She passed the same message of personal support to her cousin the King of Hanover.

The defection of Hanover particularly enraged Bismarck. The state was in northern Germany and should have been within the Prussian sphere of influence. Bismarck saw its opposition as the dying kick of the Anglo-Coburg conspiracy against him. The blind King George showed courage and put his small forces in the field against a Prussian invasion. He might have expected support from England because of his dynastic connections with the throne, but Lord Clarendon put a stop to that. He advised Queen Victoria that the fact of the King of Hanover's being a member of the English royal family did not mean that she should take any special measures in the event of Hanover's being invaded by Prussia.[34] The Queen of England could not risk the storm of unpopularity if she tried to involve her country in a war abroad to protect her German cousins or her own daughters.

The greatest instinct for survival was shown by the leading Coburg intriguer, Duke Ernest himself. Certain that the Prussian military machine would win the war, he applied for a command in its army. Although he thought Prussia was in the wrong, he joined Bismarck's side to preserve his duchy. His lack of courage displeased Queen Victoria. He could have agreed to be neutral—that might have been necessary—but to change colors she could not think right.[35]

Austria now made the mistake of repudiating the agreement to split the Danish border duchies with Prussia. In reply, the King sent Prussian troops into Holstein. The Austrian forces would not fight, but withdrew over the border into Hanover. Not a shot had been fired; peace was still just possible. But on June 14, Austria called for the mobilization of all the smaller German states against Prussia. Most of them wanted to be neutral, but they were caught between the hammer and the anvil. They agreed to mobilize, but only to defend their individual frontiers. Their weak decision meant that Prussia could gobble them up piecemeal. Bismarck immediately sent an ultimatum to Hanover and Saxony. They must allow Prussian troops to march through their territory or be destroyed. The two states rejected the ultimatum and prepared to fight the war forced upon them.

The war was coming at the worst possible time for the Crown Princess. In April, she had borne her second daughter, also called Victoria. Princess Alice, too, was having another child in Darmstadt. Both the sisters needed their husbands' support in the recovery from their pregnancies, yet the two men were called to arms on opposite sides. The Crown Prince was ordered to take command of the Second Army of 120,000 men in Silesia, while Prince Louis was sent to command a Hessian brigade of Cavalry. The Crown Princess was left to cope with her fears and her nightmares alone. "Last night I dreamed of a battlefield where nothing but heads and arms and legs lay about," she wrote to her husband in the field. "I was so glad when I woke up and thought: Thank God, it was only a dream. But how soon may it become a reality."[36]

All too soon, death in the family became a reality. Her adored Sigismund, not quite two years old, fell ill with meningitis. He was her adored child, her special love. He died suddenly, with his father away on campaign. Four weeks after the brilliant Potsdam christening of the infant Princess Victoria, a funeral procession followed the little coffin. Too old to go to war, Field Marshal Wrangel bared his head to the dead child who would never serve as a Prussian prince must do. The Crown Princess was overcome with grief. She had nobody to comfort her. "What I suffer none can know," she wrote to her mother. "Few know how I loved! It was my own happy secret—the long cry of agony which rises from the inmost depth of my soul reaches Heaven alone."[37] She was so pierced to the heart that she devoted herself more and more to the nursery. Her eldest boy, William, noted the change in her. After Sigismund's death, her younger children now had the full benefit of her love, which had been mostly given to her husband.[38] But then, William was always jealous to have more of his mother's love.

彩

Sigismund died as Prussian troops were marching, virtually unopposed, into Saxony and Hanover. The brave, blind King George ordered the Hanoverians to fight at Lagenalza, but they were swept away. By the end of June, most of northern Germany was in Prussian hands. An army was striking south to punish Frankfurt for having decided to mobilize the smaller German states. The First Army under Prince Frederick Karl of Prussia was moving to join another Prussian army on the Elbe and engage the Austrians. The Second Army under the Crown Prince was advancing through Silesia. Moltke had planned that a three-pronged force should converge and force battle on the enemy. The Austrian General Benedek wanted to defeat the Prussian armies separately. All depended upon the Crown Prince's breaking through some scattered Austrian Corps and joining the other two armies in time for the vital battle.

Now that he had what he wanted, Bismarck became superfluous. He could do nothing to influence the conduct of the war; he could only observe the military forces, which he had raised and equipped. He was given his uniform for sweating it out in the summer sun, the long gray cloak and pointed helmet of a cavalry major in the *Landwehr*. He lingered with the King in Berlin until the news came that the decisive battle was imminent. Then he joined the royal retinue in the six special trains commandeered to take the great and the curious to the front line. Not for them the rigors and rehearsals of war. Only the grand finale.

The Crown Prince had a hard time of it, advancing through Bohemia toward his rendezvous with the First Army. He won three engagements on three successive days at Nachod, Skalicz and Schweinschädel. Benedek's outlying Corps desperately tried to hold him off. The Austrian commander wanted to provoke the First Army into attacking him on its own. His defensive position was near the village of Sadowa, only seven miles away from Frederick the Great's old headquarters at Königgrätz, where a fortress now dominated the junction of the Adler and the Elbe Rivers.

The Crown Princess could not hide her pride at her husband's bravery, energy and modesty. His troops cheered him whenever they saw him and were said to adore him. He was often thirteen hours in the saddle at a stretch, but he never complained. Sensitive man that he was, he found the fatigue as nothing to the mental excitement and exertion of directing so dangerous an undertaking. Above all, he felt himself pulled apart by the violent emotions of the fight and the awful sight of the horrors of the battlefield. "To one so kind," the Crown Princess said, "I know what the shock to his nerves must be."[39] She herself felt the most conflicting emotions. She wrote to Queen Victoria imploring her to understand her feelings, which had to be on the side of her country and her husband. Of course, she was in despair at being forced to think of other Germans as her enemies and wish for their destruction. Yet she had death in her heart, the death of her darling Sigismund. "I can only regret that I did not die before all this," she wrote to her mother, "or was born after it comes to an end. And what the end of it will be—Heaven knows! I cannot describe what a cruel contradiction of feelings one had to pass through—but over all sounds my darling's last cry—and the tears that I shed for all the poor fallen and wounded and their afflicted families flow over his little grave."[40]

As her husband moved his army toward his accounting at Königgrätz, she had to put aside her grief and think of the injured soldiers. She worked hard to scrape together necessaries for the field hospitals, now full of Prussians and Austrians and Saxons, all pell-mell. She begged her mother to send her sponges and old linen, just as Princess Alice was asking her mother for the same things to staunch the wounds of the retreating Hessians serving in the Federal Army.

With the Crown Prince rode a British military attaché, Colonel Walker. The position of the military attachés was curious at the time: if ambassadors were sent to lie abroad, attachés were sent to spy abroad. But they were official spies, licensed to inform. The Crown Prince wanted a British colonel, whose reports on his behavior and successes would go directly back to Queen Victoria. He had waited so long to do something of consequence which might win her admiration. Even at the price of revealing certain military secrets of the Prussian war machine, he knew the value of Walker's reports in terms of deterrence and propaganda. If the Colonel could give detailed accounts of the effect of the Prussian needle gun and rifled Krupps cannon, he could also point out how formidable the Prussian armies were. The King and Moltke would want that.

Walker was with the Crown Prince when the news came that Prince Frederick Karl and the First Army, which now incorporated the smaller Army of the Elbe, were to engage the main Austrian and Saxon forces on July 3 near Königgrätz. The Crown Prince was in the position of Blücher at Waterloo: if he could not reach the battlefield in time, Prince Frederick Karl, playing Wellington, might be defeated by Benedek. The

Crown Prince's army was encamped many miles away. At midnight, on the eve of the battle, he was ordered by an officer of the general staff to make for the flank and rear of the Austrian position. Rousing his weary troops, he set off in the night toward his destination. His energy and example were extraordinary. He kept his men moving through the dark and the morning for the next twenty-four hours.

Nearly half a million men were engaged in the battle of Königgrätz. It was the herald of the triumph of the railway carriage over the horse-drawn wagon. It was a greater concentration of men than even in the time of Napoleon. The battle would decide whether Germany was to be united at last by a greater Prussia, or whether the Austrian Emperor and the King of Saxony and the gaggle of minor German princes leading the Federal Army in the Southwest would keep Germany as divided and impotent as Italy had been before the Austrian defeat there. It would decide the future of Germany, which had been so long confused with the Holy Roman Empire and its usual Emperors, the Hapsburgs, who had unfortunately looked more toward the Danube and the Mediterranean than to the Rhine and the Elbe.

Bismarck watched the battle from the hills behind the Prussian lines. He was riding a large red horse and became saddle sore and blistered during the eight hours of the struggle. He stayed close to the King and his military advisers. Austrian shells whizzed past unpleasantly close, and he scolded the King for taking unnecessary risks. The staff officers thought he was really afraid of risking his own precious person, but the King listened to him and took up a less exposed position to view the battle below.

It did not go too well. The Saxons fought valiantly under the two sons of their King. Benedek's men checked the advance of Prince Frederick Karl's troops and put them on the defensive. The Austrian cavalry was massing for a charge which might end in a Prussian rout. Then, toward one o'clock, Bismarck saw a line of gray trees five miles away advancing from the east. It was the Crown Prince's army making for the Austrian flank and rear, exactly where it should be. Heavily bombarded by the Austrian artillery, the Crown Prince's advance guard stormed the village of Chlum and menaced Benedek's line of retreat to the south through Königgrätz. The Austrian commander sent in his reserves to retake Chlum, but the Crown Prince held on, pushing up more and more of his men. Benedek had to fall back or risk the loss of his whole army. Through the courage of his rear guard and the Saxons, he managed to escape with 180,000 men, leaving 40,000 dead or wounded or taken prisoner. The Prussian cavalry, which had not been used in the action, failed to charge in hot pursuit and break up the defeated Austrians. Benedek still stood with a large army between the Prussians and Vienna.

Bismarck was depressed, not elated, by the carnage. He was thinking that his son Herbert, in the services, might be among the piles of dead. He rode into a nearby village in the dark, broke into a cottage to spend the night there, and fell into a manure pit. It was a watershed of European history. If that pit had been twenty feet deep and full, Bismarck reminisced later, they would have had a long search next morning for their Minister President.[41] The great Bismarck would have suffocated in horsedung.

In Colonel Walker's opinion, the First Army had been very hard pressed before the arrival of the Crown Prince, whose judgment and decision, firmness of execution and calmness could not be surpassed.[42] Of course, Moltke's strategical planning had aimed to bring the Prussian armies together at Sadowa, yet he depended on the vigor and skill of the field commanders, particularly of the Crown Prince. The princes also had to rely on the fighting qualities of their men, armed with the needle gun against stubborn opponents more used to the bayonet than the rifle. At the first sight of the Crown Prince's men, Moltke's reliance on strategy prompted him to declare: "The campaign is decided. Success is total. Vienna lies at Your Majesty's feet." The King was very angry at such a preposterous statement. His commanders must still lead his men to victory. War was more than communications; it was will and timing, iron and blood.

For once the Crown Prince had done the right thing in the right place at the right moment. He had done it in front of his father at the most decisive battle in Europe since Waterloo. When the papal secretary heard of the Austrian catastrophe, he said: "The world topples."[43] The King of Prussia was overwhelmed by the Crown Prince's superb display on the field. He put the coveted Order *Pour le Mérite* around his son's neck and embraced him among the dead and the dying. The result of Königgrätz turned a disgraced and isolated Crown Prince into a national war hero. Ironically, it also made the dangerous policy of his chief enemy Bismarck seem the superhuman statesmanship of a genius. Victory changed all and hallowed all. The past was shriven. The Crown Prince and Bismarck were now the joint saviors and makers of the new nation.

As if to show this, they formed a misalliance of convenience against the King. The extent of the Prussian victory had gone to His Majesty's head. He wanted to march into Vienna as a conqueror, then annex great sections of independent Germany and Austrian Silesia. William I of Prussia, Loftus wrote gloomily, would prove as ambitious and audacious as Napoleon I and put all Europe in a blaze.[44] The King's aggressiveness did not suit Bismarck, who clearly saw new dangers for Prussia. The victory had been too quick and too great, yet not great enough. Benedek still had a large army in the field, that might not be able to defend Vienna, but could still retire to the east. The allied Federal Army in southern Germany was still intact. The French and the Russians were waiting to intervene. Only a swift and moderate peace would stop the other great powers from interfering. Bismarck also knew the danger of a war of revenge. If the peace terms were too harsh, Austria would be bound to ally itself with France, so that it could reconquer its lost territories. Better to make a future friend out of a foe, than a certain enemy through greed.

The drama between the King and Bismarck was played out at Deitrichstein Castle at Nikolsburg. Finding the King unmovable, Bismarck threatened to resign and sent for the Crown Prince to aid him. Surprised at this appeal, the Crown Prince wrote to his wife that he might now be able to act on her ideas. As usual, he agreed with her views down to the last detail. "If God is as good to us as He has been so far," he declared, "Germany's renaissance may really be achieved in spite of Bismarck."[45]

Moltke was waiting for the Crown Prince as he walked up the hill to the castle. Things were in a terrible state. The King and Bismarck would not even see each other. The French Emperor was threatening to come into the war, if his peace proposals were not accepted. They were very much what Bismarck wanted: Austria was to cede no territory, but was to be excluded from Germany; Prussia was to get Schleswig and Holstein and a large indemnity; France would receive Venetia and hand it over immediately to Italy. Nothing was to be agreed about northern Germany, where Bismarck and the King were to have a free hand. Prussia could swallow up the small states in due time. The way to do it was not to gulp, but slowly, bite by bite.

The Crown Prince agreed with Bismarck. The Coburg plan had always wanted the unification of Germany by Prussia. It was sad that it was being done by the drawn sword, not by the liberal word. Germany was going to be merged into Prussia, as Bismarck wished. Prussia was not going to be merged into Germany, as the Crown Prince and his wife wished. Yet Bismarck seemed to want to conciliate his old opponents. His proposed North German Confederation would have a *Reichstag,* an elected parliament, as a fig leaf over naked

Prussian control. The Crown Prince hoped against hope in Bismarck's show of moderation, but he was watchful of his unlikely ally. As he wrote in his diary, he would not allow himself to be led astray.[46]

He alone tried to induce the King to accept the reasonable terms of peace. For three days, he was the contact between his father and Bismarck. When he finally persuaded them to meet, he shocked his father by supporting the Minister President. "It is a topsy-turvy world," he had to admit. "For the last three days Papa has said such things to Bismarck that he actually cried last evening and was really afraid to go in again. I had to calm down both of them."[47]

Bismarck was so depressed by the resistance of the King and the generals that he even thought of throwing himself out of the open window of his room on the fourth floor. As he stood in front of it, he heard the door open behind him, then felt a hand on his shoulder. "You know that I was against this war," the Crown Prince was saying to him. "You considered it necessary, and the responsibility for it lies on you." But, the Crown Prince continued, if Bismarck thought it was the time for peace, then there would be peace. He would go to his father once more, and he did so. He returned to Bismarck's room within half an hour. "It has been a very difficult business," he told Bismarck, "but my father has consented."

So the Crown Prince saved Bismarck and his policy twice over, once by his determined march to Königgrätz, and again by his persuasion of the stubborn King. Bismarck could not have convinced the King. In time of war, he was a despised civilian, but the Crown Prince was the hero of Prussia's great victory. This finally made the King give way and stop his army fighting in the middle of another battle. He hated to do it. He could see himself entering Vienna at the head of his troops. Now he was deprived of that triumph. He wrote a bitter note in the margin of Bismarck's last memorandum to him. He accused his minister of leaving him in the lurch in the face of the enemy by threatening to resign. He could not replace Bismarck at that moment, and his son supported Bismarck's opinions, so he found himself reluctantly compelled, after such brilliant victories on the part of the army, to bite this sour apple and accept so disgraceful a peace.[48]

✻

The fighting was not yet finished. By making a separate peace with Prussia, Austria left its German allies in the lurch. All the Prussian armies could now turn and crush the small states. Princess Alice, in despair in Hesse-Darmstadt, wrote to her mother in England that all the bloodshed was useless— that made it harder to bear. The small countries would have been wiser to submit sooner, as their enemy was too mighty.[49] Robert Morier was commanded by Queen Victoria to make his way through the fighting and see how Princess Alice was coping. She broke down completely in front of him. She did not know what was happening to her husband Prince Louis with his cavalry brigade in the Federal Army. It had already suffered severe losses at the hands of the Prussians, and the Federal soldiers were living on raw potatoes and green apples, while Prince Louis himself had survived for two days on one piece of black bread.[50]

The Federal forces were not wiped out because the states began to defect from the common cause and submit to Prussia. Bavaria was the first to make a separate peace, followed by Baden. The other minor German states soon gave up the fight and trembled at what might happen to them. All of Queen Victoria's German relatives appealed to her to intercede with the victors. Hesse-Darmstadt was occupied by Prussians and menaced with the loss of the largest and oldest part of the state. "If we lose it," Princess Alice complained, "we shall not only be very poor, but may as well give up the name of *Hessian*." It was a thankless task, but if her mother could write to the victorious Crown Prince of Prussia to use his influence for them, she would be deeply and truly grateful.[51]

There were other pleas to Queen Victoria, particularly a noble and moving one from the King of Saxony, who had felt that he had to defend the independence of his country. His troops had been loyal and courageous, and he could say with the clearest conscience that he could not, he ought not, to have acted in any other way than he did.[52] Queen Victoria could only reply to him that her heart bled for his country, a land to which she was tied by ancestry and affection, yet she could do nothing for him. The policy of her government was to keep out of any situation that might involve England in the war.[53]

The case of Hanover was the closest to home. Queen Victoria's soldier cousin, the Duke of Cambridge, was next in line of succession to the throne after the blind King and his son. He wrote in great distress to the Queen. To see all their old German associates knocked on the head and their friends and relatives scattered to the winds made the stoutest heart shudder at the bare thought. His feelings chiefly went with the poor Hanoverians. What would the Queen do?[54] Little, she answered, beyond expressing her deep interest in Hanover's integrity and welfare. She had heard, anyway, that there was no intention of annexing it.

She had heard wrong. Bismarck wanted Hanover to strengthen Prussia's new position on the North Sea and to act as a buffer in case of a French invasion. He also wanted to lay his hands on the Hanoverian King's treasury, that would give him a secret fund to use on influencing the press and his intelligence system. Stieber had formed a counterespionage group to protect Prussian headquarters and to inform his master Bismarck what the military were thinking. He would be as useful after the war as in it.

Queen Victoria tried to plead for her German relatives through her son-in-law, the Crown Prince. She expected he could do little and admitted to writing only to ease her conscience. She knew that such a total victory by Prussia had given it the power to annex by right of conquest. All kingdoms

had been assembled by her method, royal marriage, or by
Bismarck's method, war. Her feelings about Prussia's victory
were ambivalent. She did believe that Prussia should unify
Germany. And she was influenced by her eldest daughter's
pride in the Crown Prince's success and example on the battlefield.

Her son-in-law seemed such a splendid contrast to her
eldest son, who appeared to live only for pleasure. She had
Colonel Walker's reports praising the Crown Prince sent to
the Prince of Wales. They were meant to inspire him and
"germanize" him. They enraged him. Prussia's outright annexation of Schleswig and Holstein, a serious blow for Denmark
and his wife's family, had made him angry. Unlike his mother
and his elder sister, the Prince of Wales did not believe in
the Protestant alliance between England and Prussia; he believed that England needed an alliance with France—and even
with the old enemy Russia.

Because Queen Victoria's government did not protest
about the annexations, the old feeling of respect for England
was revived in Berlin. It made life easier for the Crown Princess. Her elastic nature led her to rejoice in her absent husband's triumphs and forget the loss of her child some of the
time. The war had confirmed her in her newfound Prussian
patriotism. "I am NOW every bit as proud of being a Prussian
as I am of being an Englishwoman and that is saying a *very
great deal*," she wrote to her mother, who knew what a John
Bull she was and how enthusiastic she was about her home.
Yet now she praised the Prussians for their intelligence and
humanity. Their army had behaved excellently. Their only
fault lay in Bismarck's conduct. She could never believe that
the war was justified, although good for Germany might come
out of it.[55]

If she could not justify the war, she could justify Bismarck's
harsh policies toward the conquered German states. Her memory of her husband's danger, her pride in him, her anguish
at the loss of her child, her pain at seeing the wounded in

the hospitals, these had given her a new maturity and clarity. At this sad time, she told her mother, she must quite separate her feelings for her relations from her judgment of political necessities.

Bismarck's voice might have been speaking from her. The success of his diplomacy had turned the Crown Prince to support him against the King. Now it was turning the Crown Princess, his opponent. She was talking of political necessity, not of moral judgment and family feeling. Of course, she assured her mother that she and her husband were not giving up their liberal principles. But as Queen Victoria knew, political events had their own imperative. Those rulers who were now threatened with annexation might have foreseen what danger they were running into. They were told beforehand what they would have to expect and they chose to go with Austria, so they had broken their own necks.[56]

Such political realism finally convinced Queen Victoria to make the best of a bad job. Prussia had won. Willy-nilly, Germany would be united. This was the main thing and a good thing. If it was not being done the Coburg way, it was being done. The Crown Prince would inherit what he had won with the sword Bismarck had put in his hand. If the present was brutal and in Bismarck's grasp, the future was bright and in the hands of her son-in-law and her daughter. So the Queen compromised with the dead Prince Consort's gospel about Germany. She praised her daughter for her strength of mind. She could see in every one of her Vicky's letters how her great mind and large heart were developing. "How proud adored Papa would have been of you," she wrote to the Crown Princess. "But Oh! If only Papa's great maxim of Prussia becoming Germany and a great German empire could be realized."[57]

It was already being realized in Bismarck's way. All were following where he was leading the King of Prussia. His critics suspended their judgment for the time being. They called it the logic of events, not the power of the one man. Even his enemy Robert Morier had to admit that Bismarck was a man of genius, although he remained the unprincipled scoundrel after the battle of Königgrätz that he was before.[58]

On August 10, the Crown Prince came home from the war. His wife took the children in a carriage and drove out to meet him in a wood. He looked well, but thinner and bearded and serious. He was depressed not only by the death of small Sigismund, but also by the scenes of war, and the loss of tens of thousands of lives hung heavy on his soul. All the struggle and the suffering, what were they for? Nothing had really changed for him in his own country. Do what he would, as long as Bismarck and the King remained as they were the good of Germany and Prussia never could be secure.[59]

7

Waiting on Ceremony

HE VICTORY PARADE was led by the King on horse-back. At his back rode the Crown Prince looking like a Teutonic hero, bearded and erect. Bismarck had been promoted to the rank of a *Landwehr* cavalry general. He rode along the Unter den Linden, large and pale under his helmet, a garland of flowers round the neck of his tunic. The strain of the past months made him have a nervous collapse immediately after the parade. He called it a softening of the brain.

It certainly led to a softening of his hard line at home and abroad. When he had recovered, he made his peace with the right wing of the liberals. His years of governing unconstitutionally were forgiven by an Indemnity Bill, which passed by a vote of three to one. The King was opposed to asking for absolution from the Chamber, but again the Crown Prince gave Bismarck his support. Even among the liberals, Prussia's victory had tossed a halo over the spike of Bismarck's helmet. The angel of darkness—Liebknecht wrote—had become the angel of light. Before him, the people lay in the dust and adored.[1]

There was another softening in Bismarck's policy toward the conquered small German states. Helped by the Crown Prince's former adviser Max Duncker, he created a North German Confederation above the River Main. It had a *Reichstag,* an elected parliament with few powers, in which the new National Liberal Party continued the compact with Bismarck, who became Chancellor. The National Liberals supported their old oppressor because they thought that a strong and united Germany should come first. Personal liberties could wait. There was no hurry to assimilate the whole of Germany; it would take years for Prussia to digest the petty northern states without swallowing the different and difficult Catholic states of the south.

The seventy-year-old King agreed with Bismarck's softer policy. He went out of his way to assure the British Ambassador that he did not expect to see the unity of Germany in his lifetime. It would not be carried out by force, but should be left to time and public opinion.[2] Neither he nor the new Chancellor trusted the support of south Germany. If there was to be a war with France, Bismarck would rather have the southern states as enemies. "It would be necessary," he said, "to place a Pomeranian behind every Bavarian."[3]

By waiting too long, Napoleon III got nothing from the German civil war, and he began to push for the frontier fortress of Mainz or Luxembourg, both garrisoned by the Prussians. There was no question of Mainz being yielded, but Luxembourg was another matter. Bismarck favored giving a sop to the French Emperor while Prussia consolidated its gains. He helped to persuade the indebted King of Holland, the nominal sovereign of Luxembourg, to sell the buffer duchy to France. It seemed a good deal for all sides.

Yet Bismarck had sown the dragon's teeth. The Prussian generals and the King would not allow the French army a base so close to the heartland of Germany. War threatened.

Both countries armed furiously. Even the Crown Princess held on to her new allegiance. She told her mother that Bismarck was not in the wrong, the aggression came from France; it was there they wished for war. For her part, she thought it better the war should be now rather than later—horrible as it was. The great united empire of Germany would never consolidate itself in peace until the power of France had been reduced.[4]

Queen Victoria was shocked at her daughter's belligerence. Bismarck seemed to be leading her on as well. Queen Augusta of Prussia was quite right in wishing for no war; that is what every woman should do. Bismarck was wrong because he had encouraged the French Emperor to believe he could get Luxembourg. As for reducing the proud old state of France to a second-rate power when Prussia itself had become a great power only recently, that was a sorry thing to say. "I am afraid the time may come," the Queen wrote prophetically, "when Europe will wish France to be strong to keep the ambition of Germany in check."[5]

She had already put the blame of trying to start a new war onto Prussia alone. Writing directly to the King, she had taken the side of Napoleon III, who was only asking now for the disarmament of Luxembourg. An imperious refusal to make this small concession would put Prussia in the wrong. The French Emperor, Queen Victoria asserted, was very anxious that peace should be maintained. The British government would arbitrate. It rested entirely with the Prussians whether there was war or not.[6] This surprising letter from Queen Victoria did much to stop the outbreak of hostilities in 1867. Prussia could not risk England supporting France against it, so Bismarck accepted from the British government a meaningless collective guarantee of Luxembourg's neutrality. The Prussian garrison was withdrawn, the fortifications were razed, and the duchy was left with the King of Holland. Napoleon III had opened one of the gateways into Germany without having to capture it.

Queen Victoria was praised by both the King of Prussia and the French Emperor for keeping the peace between them. It was not flattery. In the world of royal diplomacy, she had acted as an honest broker between the rival rulers. She had made her reluctant government negotiate a piece of paper that saved face and allowed Prussia to back down with honor. The Crown Princess also had played her part in keeping the peace. She had even dared to speak to Bismarck on politics. With her usual candor, she told the Chancellor that she was no blind admirer of his, yet he would increase her admiration if he could preserve peace. He said that the French were rearming so fast that Prussia must rearm against them. She then proposed mutual disarmament, but he would not give her an answer. She could not fathom what he intended to do. She had heard that he was not inclined to go to war, but she never could know what he really meant.[7]

She was so afraid that her candid letters might fall into the hands of Bismarck's spies that she asked her mother to burn them. She knew they revealed state secrets. These might reach the ears of the German Embassy in London through the indiscretions of British ministers briefed by her mother. But Queen Victoria thought the letters of such importance that she kept them to use in her own diplomacy. The royal group of the Coburg sympathizers still survived, although it was reduced to Duke Ernest, Queen Augusta of Prussia, the Crown Prince and Princess, King Leopold II of the Belgians and the Grand Duke of Baden. All of them had worked hard to keep the peace.

The understanding in Europe allowed the Prussian royal family to go with the Russian and Austrian imperial families to the World Exhibition in Paris. It was a lavish and exhausting occasion, marred only by an attempt on the lives of the Tsar and the Tsarina. A refugee Pole shot at them, but only wounded an attaché's horse. Their consternation was obvious to the Crown Princess: the Tsarina cried all the evening and would not be comforted, while the Tsar was as white as a sheet. Both of them said they regretted the French Emperor had not been touched.[8]

To royalty, assassination seemed a form of sacrilege. Regicide was worse than a murder in the family; it was unholy. Although the Crown Princess rather admired Cromwell, Queen Victoria would never forgive him for having had Charles I's head cut off. When, shortly after the Paris Exhibition, the Mexican revolutionaries executed the Emperor Maximilian, the Queen of England was shocked and outraged. It was too awful. "How dreadful that we can do nothing to avenge this horrible murder," she lamented to her eldest daughter, "and that the days of chivalry have passed away."[9] Their Coburg cousin Charlotte, who had married Maximilian, went mad with worry and grief.

The temporary understanding between the great powers helped to heal the wounds within Queen Victoria's own family. The healing began during the Prince of Wales's visit with his wife to Berlin. They were returning from the wedding of his sister-in-law Princess Dagmar to the Tsarevitch. Queen Victoria had not wanted her eldest son to go to St. Petersburg. She objected to his remaining so little at home and always running about.[10] But he went all the same, for his mother would give him nothing important to do in England. Diplomatically it was an important marriage. The new royal alliance between the Danes and the Russians was a further guarantee against Prussian expansion. "A young life is thus being sold and sacrificed," the Crown Princess wrote about Dagmar, "to the doctrines of the great conventions."[11] She could have said the same about her own marriage, even though it was a love match.

The Crown Prince was sent to the wedding celebrations as Prussia's ceremonial representative. He took the opportunity to try and persuade the Danish Princesses and their husbands, the heirs to the English and Russian thrones, to accept Prussia's friendship. The Prince of Wales was too good-natured and diplomatic to give pain to his brother-in-law. He

was friendly to the Crown Prince in St. Petersburg, and on
his return journey to England he found himself welcomed
by the Prussian court. Like the Crown Prince, he looked ill
from the long nights spent in railway carriages, followed by
interminable receptions and banquets in overheated palace
rooms. For both of them, representing their countries abroad
was bad for their health and a quicker way to the grave.

It seemed a policy of Bismarck's to weaken the Crown
Prince slowly with ceremony, travel, political isolation and
kindness. The long court season in the Berlin winters was a
trial by heat and cold, etiquette and rigor. The Crown Princess
found it more and more intolerable for her and her husband.
It nearly killed them, yet it renewed the vigor of the couple
they were waiting to replace—the King and Queen of Prussia.
"I am quite knocked up by all the Balls," the Crown Princess
complained to her mother in March 1867. "I have been out
every night since Sunday and rarely home before two. I cannot
stand it. My digestion, my hands, my eyes—all suffer. But
the King and Queen so delight in it that they seem to go
out oftener and stay longer every year."

The Queen of Prussia had a passion for the season. She
dressed at the height of fashion like a young girl of twenty,
and wore a new gown each night. The Crown Princess did
not understand how a woman in her late sixties should care
so much for the *grande monde.* Fritz looked pale and ill, and
complained of feeling always tired from the constant social
occasions.[12] Every now and then, the Queen would decide
to leave a ball before the late supper. Then she would make
her daughter-in-law take the place of honor and receive everybody in her place. "I wish she had a heap of daughters and
daughters-in-law," the Crown Princess wrote in desperation.
"Then she would not always want me for everything." The
Crown Princess was sure that people were sick of seeing her
so perpetually. She almost felt inclined to beg their pardon
for boring them so often.[13]

The winter seasons were now more glittering and prolonged because Berlin was becoming an international capital,
rather than the chief city of a major German state. There
were the affairs of the North German Confederation to be
settled. There was the foreign business necessary for a new
great power. The ceremonies of the court were also diplomatic
occasions where negotiations were carried on discreetly, as
the King showed favor to one country or another by choosing
to speak to a particular ambassador. Royalty in Berlin communicated as well as condescended. The King saw that every
important person knew his shifting place. The interminable
balls were not so much a dance of wasted time as a game
of musical chairs.

The five winter seasons after the defeat of Austria saw
the Crown Prince and Princess forced to keep their stance
just behind the throne. This ceremonious lingering was against
their natures and cost them a lot. By May of 1870, the Crown
Princess was extremely worried about her husband's health.
"*Soirées* follow one another daily," she reported to her mother.
"You would be sorry to see Fritz so pale and yellow. I really
feel quite anxious about him. The Queen has no mercy. This
week she has not been in bed *once* before two o'clock, and
on the move all day long. I wonder it does not kill the King
outright. As for Fritz, it is injuring his health, and I have no
means of stopping it."[14]

Dancing attendance at court wore down the Crown Prince
less than did his long foreign missions. Apparently Bismarck
wanted to prolong the King's life by keeping him at home.
The Crown Prince would be exposed to risk and possible scandal by sending him abroad—something which also kept him
away from the influence of his English wife. In 1868, he was
sent off to represent the Prussian royal family in Turin at
the wedding of Prince Humbert to Princess Margherita of
Genoa. The following year, he was delegated to attend the
opening of the Suez Canal.

On both occasions, the Crown Prince gave some ammuni-
tion to Bismarck's propaganda machine. In Turin, he was on

good terms with Prince Napoleon and seemed to be appeasing France. In Egypt, he was photographed with the Emperor and Empress of Austria—a peaceful picture that suited Bismarck well. The Chancellor wanted Austria as a friendly power in the forthcoming war against France to complete the unification of Germany. The outbreak of the conflict had only been postponed. When it came, Bismarck wanted all the other powers as allies or neutrals.

The Crown Princess found her husband's long absences difficult to bear. He had come to dominate much of her life. Command in war had given him confidence in his judgment, and his wife now looked to him for advice as she once had to the Prince Consort. "It is extraordinary how Fritz has grown mature of late years," she told Queen Victoria. "I often tell him he is not only Husband but Father and Mother to me now."[15] To write that was heresy, but the Crown Princess did. She was determined to be a good Prussian now. She knew her mother did not like Prussia at the moment because of Bismarck's treatment of the Augustenburgs and the King of Hanover, but she could do nothing about that. Her heart was thoroughly with the interests of her new nation. Her work was for its future.[16] For three years, the Crown Princess did not go to England to visit her mother, which proved her new commitment to Prussia. On the anniversary of her mother's wedding, she bore another son, Waldemar. He seemed sent to her to assuage the ache in her heart left by the loss of Sigismund—heaven forbid that he too might be taken from her. Her large family as well as her political sensibility kept her at home. Finally, at the end of 1868, she and her husband paid a two-month visit to Queen Victoria, who made them feel England was a second home. They stayed over Christmas and were rebuked by the King of Prussia for missing the opening of the Berlin season. Going to England always caused bad blood between father and son.

Ever since the victory at Königgrätz, the King had been kind to them as long as they did not talk to him about politics.

There seemed to be none of the anger and suspicion of the years before the war. The King knew his son was waiting for his place on the throne. The unspoken compromise between them was that while the father lived, the son would not speak out. Even so, the Crown Prince and his wife were required to remain near the court most of the time. The moment they went away or were sent away from the King, the Crown Princess knew that ill-natured people would find some way to make him dissatisfied with what they did.[17]

She was spied upon in her own household. The ladies-in-waiting and the Prince's aides were often Bismarck's creatures in liberal disguise. Lady Ponsonby was horrified at the espionage and intrigues that surrounded the Crown Princess, who had grown indifferent. She expected nothing better in Prussia. She said fatalistically to Morier that Bismarck was so clever she expected to be preaching his gospel one day without even knowing it. She still had the trustworthy Countess Blücher to help her with the household, and had engaged Count Seckendorff, a thrifty and honest man, to be court chamberlain. Bismarck had accepted this appointment, expecting to turn Seckendorff too. But he never did; the chamberlain remained loyal to the Crown Princess to the end, reserved, fastidious, devoted to a platonic love of her.

Bismarck went on isolating the heir to the throne from his advisers. Those who were not suborned were removed. The trusted Professor Geffcken was exiled to England, where the Crown Princess recommended him to her mother. He was the object of the special spite of Bismarck, who persecuted him until he was obliged to leave.[18] Young Stockmar spent over two years trying to recover from the nervous collapse induced in him by Bismarck's pressure. He clung to solitude as the best way to avoid persecution.

Her loss of advisers made the Crown Princess commit a political indiscretion. She knew that Morier was the one person especially feared by Bismarck, for Morier was as capable at intrigue as the Chancellor and had formed a network of his own spies and informants in Germany. The Crown Princess asked her mother to have Morier transferred back to Berlin as Secretary of the Embassy there. He would be the right man at the right place.[19] He would also provide the Crown Princess with the secret intelligence which Bismarck had taken away from her. Queen Victoria was grateful for the services Morier had given to the Coburg group and to her family, and she used to receive him privately in Windsor Castle when he brought the latest intelligence and confidential messages from the Crown Prince and Princess. So the Queen pressed the appointment in Berlin on her new Foreign Secretary, Sir Henry Stanley. He seemed ready to accept Morier's transfer, until he learned of Bismarck's absolute opposition. The fact that Morier felt so warmly and strongly about German politics made him think himself a German politician. His ideas were directly opposed to Bismarck's. If he meddled in political matters in Berlin, then England would lose all its influence there.[20]

Queen Victoria did not press the matter. Wherever Morier was, he would still serve her and her daughters. The Crown Prince and Princess continued to use him as an adviser and an agent. Their movements inside Germany itself were now restricted by the King and Bismarck, but they could not be stopped from visiting the spas in the spring and summer. All the court and the financiers went to them, to take the cure and exchange confidential information. At Karlsbad and at Gastein in 1869, the Crown Prince and Morier drank the waters together and went to the Crown Princess's rooms at night to discuss politics. Between them, they tried to work out what Bismarck was contemplating. A war with France was the assumption.

Another weapon in Bismarck's arsenal against the influence of the English royal family was the use of scandal. The most obvious target was the Prince of Wales. "There is not a horror in Germany that is not told of Bertie," the Crown Princess informed her mother in 1866, before her brother's visit to Berlin. He and his wife were represented "as a wretched couple and you as a most unhappy mother."[21] When four years later the Prince of Wales was wrongly accused of adultery by the hysterical Lady Mordaunt, he was condemned in his own country even though the lady was declared insane. In Berlin, he was utterly vilified. Queen Victoria believed in his innocence, but recognized that he ought never to have been mixed up with such people or his name dragged in the dirt.[22]

The Crown Princess was not spared from scandal. For the next thirty years, she was falsely accused of taking her chamberlain Count Seckendorff as her lover. When the Crown Prince was away at Suez and she traveled to Cannes with her enormous caravan of baggage and children, she put propriety above inconvenience and expense. "It would not be proper for me to be in a hotel in a foreign country with only one gentleman," she wrote to her mother, "—besides Count Seckendorff is much too young for that."[23] She knew that in the Prussian court, like Caesar's wife, she had to appear above suspicion.

Unfortunately, one of her favorite ladies-in-waiting, Valerie Countess Hohenthal, fell in love with the dashing Count Üxküll. A duel was fought over her, and she then eloped from Cannes to become the Count's mistress. She completely broke with her family and friends, only saying to the Crown Princess that she wanted to retire from court life. A dreadful scandal was certain to be made of it. The Crown Princess dreaded going back to Berlin more than she could say. She was pregnant again, and felt unfit to face up to her mother-in-law's anger at letting down Prussian standards. Queen Augusta was furious. She ordered her daughter-in-law to take on a *Grande Maîtresse* to run her ladies and their morals. The Crown Princess was obviously incapable of keeping up a decent household for her husband. The Crown Princess could not accept this. Another spy planted on her by the Prussian court would have been intolerable. She would rather her husband had brought back one of the overseers from the harem in Constantinople.[24]

The Crown Princess wanted a domestic life with as little ceremony as possible. Her family was large and growing. Another daughter, Sophie, would soon be born to join her five living brothers and sisters. Even Queen Victoria with her nine children thought it all too much. She had never devoted herself to infants as her eldest daughter did. "Very few worship babies as you do," she reminded the Crown Princess. Children were far more of a terrible anxiety than a pleasure.[25] She did not see that having children was a compensation for her daughter. During the four years of her greatest political activity, the Crown Princess had borne only one child, the dead Sigismund. She had come from a large and happy family, and reproducing that situation was an escape from feeling impotent in public affairs. She felt the need to create a small world of her own.

She was strict about the education of her two elder boys, who she believed should be taught the Spartan values of self-discipline. At whatever cost to her tender heart, she preferred to ignore her William's handicapped arm. He must learn to live with it and to ignore it himself. Sympathy would only encourage self-pity in him. She and her husband showed no signs of noticing the pain suffered by their eldest child during his fearful riding lessons. His riding master put the boy on his pony without stirrups and made him take the reins in his right hand. When the pony trotted off, the boy fell off. The master picked him up and put him again on the pony's back. The boy fell off. The master mercilessly ignored the child's prayers and tears and set him back on the pony after every tumble, until William could stay there and learn a sense of balance. By the age of ten, he had survived normal Prussian cavalry practice and could ride in a victory parade.

In the schoolroom, however, he showed the same defect as the Prince of Wales: he could not concentrate. All the severity of Hinzpeter could not turn the child into a scholar. William had an elusive and disobedient nature, full of pride and self-will, and he was not developing into the son his mother wanted. As she wrote to Queen Victoria, she was looking for her children to grow up "like my Fritz, like Papa, like you and as unlike the rest of the Prussian royal family as possible." Then they could be good patriots and useful to their country—call it Prussia or call it Germany. Their education was not an easy task by any means.[26]

William felt more and more that his mother was cold toward him and his father distant. His harsh schooling seemed to prove their indifference. He was to remember a joyless childhood in which renunciation was the law. It was dry bread for breakfast and no praise. Duty was the reason for all.[27] Although his father taught him German history and took him on long visits to castles and parks, he did not rescue him from Hinzpeter's severity. He wanted a soldier and a ruler to be made out of his son in spite of his handicap. Finding little tenderness or encouragement in his life, William began to react against his mother. He felt inadequate because of his arm, then blamed his feeling of inadequacy on her. It was her fault that he was a cripple, not his own; she had made him so. She was also a foreigner who was always praising the stoic virtues of an English gentleman, not a Prussian officer—which he would soon become, as his father had.

He did not feel the same when he visited his grandparents, the King and Queen of Prussia. They sympathized with him and encouraged his love of soldiers and uniforms. The King saw in the boy a way of transmitting his own royal traditions to the future, untainted by the heresies of his son and daughter-in-law. He encouraged William's childish self-assertion and resistance to his mother's ideas.

The Crown Princess hated the fact that her eldest son already had a military tutor, Schrötter, and was being trained as a recruit in the Grenadiers. A Sergeant Klee also taught him how to bang a march from a drum. It was in preparation for his tenth birthday, when he would be made a lieutenant in the First Regiment of Footguards. He was deeply impressed that the King would present him with the Order of the Black Eagle. It would be like receiving a knighthood. When his mother saw him wearing his little uniform, she thought he looked like some unfortunate little monkey dressed up and standing on top of an organ.[28] The Crown Princess, who knew the ceremony marked the turning of her eldest son away from her, confessed to her mother:

> It will go hard with me to make an amiable face when I see William seized upon—and all sorts of nonsense talked to him—which I have carefully kept from him till now. It cannot *fail* to make the child *quite* confused. He will receive his commission from the King, put on his uniform, and report himself to all sorts of military superiors. The King and the whole family are delighted. They fancy the child will be quite one of *them* from that day forward.[29]

William was becoming one of them together with his younger brother Henry. Both loved military and naval games. In his first letter to his grandmother Queen Victoria, William told her of having a large mast set up in the garden at Potsdam. He climbed to the foretop with a real captain to look down on the whole deck plan of a ship, laid out on the ground below. "We play in it, and about it and enjoy ourselves famously."[30]

Most impressive of all was a visit to the largest ironclad in the world, the *König Wilhelm.* The boy looked upward at the rows of huge guns with their heavily polished muzzles. Sailors manned the rigging and piped his father and himself aboard. They were given rich and forbidden cake in the admiral's cabin, fitted out in the solid English style. The boy thought what a joy it would be to command such a fine ship. The memory of it left him no rest.[31] It recurred again and again to him as a way to challenge his mother's authority and superiority. She was always telling him that the British navy was the best of them all. She would see.

France and Prussia continued to arm against one another. They would go to war soon if they did not disarm. Depending of which was the victor, Germany would be united or dismembered. Mutual disarmament was the best way out, but it could not be done, for the King of Prussia was devoted to his army. Queen Victoria's new Foreign Secretary, Lord Clarendon, agreed to try and ask the King to disarm, but he knew he would fail. The King did not desire war, Clarendon observed to Queen Victoria, but his army was his idol. He would not listen to any proposal to reduce it. He would not make any change in the Prussian system which compelled every man to serve.[32] And as for Bismarck, his maxim had always been that when he was traveling in dangerous company, the only thing to do was to have a revolver in his pocket.[33]

All the same, Bismarck put the British proposals for disarmament in front of the King, who was annoyed by them. They seemed dictated by the French, or else the policy of the King's enemies in Germany. In Bismarck's opinion, they were merely the act of a cool friend. "Put yourselves into our skin," he said. "You would then think—you would then act—differently. What would you say, if we were to observe to you that your Navy was too large? That you did not require so many ironclads?"[34]

There was no answer to that.

8

Empire

"WE COULD NOW FIGHT France and beat her too," Bismarck told his chief propagandist Moritz Busch in February 1870. "But that war would give rise to five or six others."[1] He was waiting for his opportunity to make France seem the aggressor. Time and Spain delivered the chance into his hands. The throne was vacant there, and as usual a German prince was the traditional choice to fill it. The Spanish parliament and its leader General Prim asked for a Hohenzollern prince to accept their crown. To France, this overture could seem to be a Prussian plot. In the event of war, Napoleon III would have to divide his armies to guard against a stab in the back from across the Pyrenees, yet how could he protest against the offer? How could a civilized modern country still go to war for dynastic reasons? "Please see that this theme, a new war of succession *in the nineteenth century*," Bismarck scoffed to Busch, "is thoroughly threshed out in the press."[2]

When the Spanish offer came to Prince Frederick of Hohenzollern-Sigmaringen, Bismarck encouraged him to accept it.

As head of the royal family, the King of Prussia would have to give his consent, and Bismarck sent him a strong memorandum in support of a Prussian prince on the Spanish throne. Prussia would benefit, France would feel threatened and humiliated. The King did not agree. Ignoring all advisers except the Crown Prince, he refused to give his permission. There might be too much trouble for too little gain. No Hohenzollern would take the Spanish throne, even if Bismarck wanted it.

The Crown Princess sent this information to her mother, as her husband had asked her to do in his name. In fact, it was no business of hers. It had to be kept most profoundly secret, because nobody wanted the French to know. The Crown Prince and the King would only trust Queen Victoria to tell the news confidentially to Lord Clarendon. Would the Queen give her own and her government's opinion on the Hohenzollern candidature as soon as possible? "Perhaps you would write it in German to Fritz," the Crown Princess concluded, "as it is particularly disagreeable to me to be a medium of communication in things so important and serious."[3]

It was more than disagreeable. The King was using her in this secret negotiation with England in order to counter his own Chancellor. The diplomacy came to nothing, because Lord Clarendon would not permit Queen Victoria to give any advice on the matter, and because Bismarck would not take no for an answer. Although Prince Frederick was persuaded by his father to refuse the offer, Bismarck sent a trusted agent and a military representative to Madrid to urge General Prim not to give up the idea of a Hohenzollern candidate, but accept the Prince's elder brother Leopold. He could change royal minds as he had often done before. By the end of May, Prince Leopold had decided that he would be a candidate for the throne, if the offer were made to him. Bismarck sent the news by cipher to Madrid early in June. He had carefully calculated that, because of the summer recess, nobody would interfere with his planning. The King was taking the cure at Bad Ems and Moltke was in Silesia, while he himself had retired to his country estate at Varzin. It would be difficult to convene a Crown Council to stop anything happening in Spain. In any event, Bismarck asserted that the matter had nothing to do with him, only with the King in his private capacity as head of the family. The King had no right either to grant permission or to refuse it, Bismarck said to the British Ambassador. The Hohenzollern Prince was in the same position as any other Prussian subject who wished to emigrate.[4]

This was a specious argument. Bismarck certainly protested enough when one of Queen Victoria's children or relatives made a marriage or took a throne that seemed to threaten Prussia's interests. He knew that there would be a furor in France when the secret was out. A plebiscite had confirmed Napoleon III's tenure by a huge majority, and he had chosen a new Foreign Minister, the Duke de Gramont, who wrongly believed he could count on Austrian support in a war against Prussia. When, at the end of June, the French discovered that General Prim had asked the Spanish parliament to "elect" Prince Leopold as king, all hell broke loose in Paris. And when the Hohenzollern Prince accepted the crown and the King of Prussia gave whatever consent he could, de Gramont's fury was even greater than the national anger. He made an inflammatory speech in the French parliament on July 6, threatening war if the Hohenzollern candidate did not refuse the Spanish throne.

French belligerence began to change the Crown Princess's mind just as it changed the King's. On the day of de Gramont's speech, she thought Prince Leopold's acceptance was a sad mistake. But two days later, she reflected court opinion by saying that she did not see why the French were complaining. Prince Leopold had made an independent decision. It was really nothing to do with the government or the King.

Her ingenuousness was due to Bismarck's cleverness in staying away at Varzin; nobody knew of his two agents' work in persuading General Prim to offer the crown again to a branch of the Hohenzollerns. But his astute leave of absence was nearly Bismarck's undoing. The French Ambassador to Berlin, Count Benedetti, was sent to speak directly to the King at Bad Ems, and there was no Chancellor to protect His Majesty and interpret the signals from France. Although Bismarck later blamed the King for dealing directly with the French in his absence, he had decided to stay away and allow French belligerence to lead to the necessary war. Absent from Bad Ems, he could not speak for his master. As it was, the King saw the French Ambassador on four successive days at Bad Ems. He was surprised at the violence of the French reaction to the Hohenzollern candidate, which Bismarck had always undervalued to him. He made grave diplomatic errors, which Bismarck would not have done. He admitted he had authorized Prince Leopold to accept the Spanish throne, but had done so only as head of the family, not as sovereign of his country—a meaningless distinction to the French. And he properly reported that Bismarck was aware of the giving of royal consent, which proved to the French that the whole affair was a Prussian plot. They demanded that the King withdraw his consent to Prince Leopold's candidature, which the King would not do.

Again British and French diplomacy used the system of royal communications to try to save the peace. The French Emperor wrote to King Leopold II of the Belgians to put direct pressure on his friend and namesake Prince Leopold. Queen Victoria was asked by her new Foreign Secretary, Lord Granville, to exert her influence by writing to Prince Leopold's brother-in-law Philippe, Count of Flanders. She asked him to tell his relative that the Queen of England begged him to withdraw and maintain the peace of Europe. For whatever reason, Prince Leopold did renounce the throne as a personal decision. The King of the Belgians claimed all the credit. He needed to boast to win friends for his country, which might be engulfed in a war between its two powerful neighbors.

The apparent success of direct royal diplomacy once more seemed to postpone the outbreak of war. Prince Leopold's renunciation was represented as a private decision influenced by pressure from friendly European sovereigns. It was not the result of an order from the King of Prussia, although he had listened to the entreaties of his wife and had sent a military aide from Bad Ems to advise Prince Leopold to withdraw. De Gramont remained bitter. Even if the cause of the quarrel was removed, the original insult of Prussia's secret backing of the Hohenzollern candidate was not.[5] The French Foreign Minister wanted more than a diplomatic victory; he wanted the public humiliation of a rival power which had sought to humiliate France by means of a dynastic device.

So Benedetti was sent to demand more from the King of Prussia, who now commanded Bismarck to leave his retreat and accept responsibility for Prussian policy. The Chancellor also had to try to unravel the royal peacemaking, which he had allowed by his studied absence. As usual, his first thought was to offer his resignation rather than accept a diplomatic defeat at the hands of France. But the War Minister, Roon, and Moltke and his secret agents all advised him that this was a good time for Prussia to fight. France's new weapons, the chassepot rifle and the mitrailleuse machine gun, were not yet operational. So Bismarck sent a message to the King, urging him to recall the Prussian Ambassador, Baron Werther, from Paris and to demand an explanation for de Gramont's belligerence. This would greatly increase the chances of an ultimatum from the French who, Bismarck thought, were running amok like a Malay who had got into a rage and rushed through the streets dagger in hand, foaming at the mouth, stabbing everyone who happened to cross his path.[6]

Meanwhile de Gramont was pushing his diplomatic luck too far. On July 12, he instructed Benedetti to ask the King of Prussia to state his approval of Prince Leopold's withdrawal. The King must also agree to refuse to authorize the Hohenzollern Prince to accept the Spanish crown if it were offered to him again.[7] The King hid his anger at being pestered once more on the promenade at Bad Ems. He turned down the new French demands, but said he would still consider the matter. His touchy sense of honor was provoked. All the same, the draft of his written reply to Benedetti did not break off negotiations with France. Using firm and moderate language, the King refused to bind himself for the future. He denied Prussian complicity in Prince Leopold's decisions. He also declared he would not deal directly any more with the French envoy; in future, Benedetti might only approach one of His Majesty's aides. Now that Bismarck was again in Berlin, the King sent him the draft letter by cipher telegram with authority to release the text at his discretion.

Strategically and politically, Bismarck had decided that this was the time to unite the German nation. Bavaria and the southern states were bound by a military alliance to support Prussia, now threatened by a foreign ultimatum and invasion. So Bismarck edited the King's text, cutting it until it became a curt refusal to negotiate in the face of French aggression and insolence. When he read the changed text to his dinner guests, Roon and Moltke, they became cheerful.

"It sounded before like a parley," von Moltke said. "Now it is like a flourish in answer to a challenge."

"Our God of old lives still," Roon added, "and will not let us perish in disgrace."

Bismarck may not have directly provoked the war by editing the King's draft reply, but he was reponsible for releasing the new brusque text to the press and the foreign ambassadors. Because the French demands were excessive and the King's refusal reasonable, Bismarck could brand the French as the aggressors. As he told his two dinner guests: To stop other great powers from intervening, it was important that Prussia should be the party attacked.[8] The edited Ems telegram made it appear so.

De Gramont made a further error by proposing that the King of Prussia should write a letter of apology to the French Emperor. Baron Werther, the Prussian Ambassador in Paris, was stupid enough to send this proposal back to Berlin. When the King heard of it, he was so angry that he agreed to recall his Ambassador. It appeared that he was breaking off diplomatic relations with France. Bismarck, of course, was still posing as the injured party. He told the credulous Lord Augustus Loftus that the Ambassador's recall was a personal matter, not a rupture with France. Prussia still desired peace, he said.[9] Werther's recall finally convinced the French that the Prussians would rather fight than admit their plot to install the Hohenzollern candidate on the Spanish throne. Both nations began to mobilize, and the French also called up their reserves. Remembering the victories of the first Napoleon, most people other than Bismarck and the General Staff thought that the French had a superiority in numbers and weapons. The Crown Princess made herself hysterical at the vision of possible defeat. On July 13, she had a violent headache and a choked throat, because she thought that the French were well prepared and the Prussians not at all. The tension she felt was taking its toll, and three days later her mind was rambling and incoherent because her nerves were so shaken. She was convinced Prussia faced devastation, ruin and perhaps annihilation, yet she was totally persuaded by Bismarck's insistence that the French had shamefully forced the Prussians into war. It was a crying injustice. There was a universal cry "To arms" to resist an enemy who had so wantonly insulted them.[10]

Fortunately, while his wife was falling apart, the Crown Prince kept his head. He had seen Bismarck on the crucial day of July 13 and had been hoodwinked by him. The Chancellor had told him that since Prince Leopold had renounced the throne peace was assured. "He gave me the impression," the Crown Prince wrote in his war diary, "of being taken completely unawares by the sudden and threatening turn of affairs in France." Two days later, when war was almost certain, Bismarck, Roon and Moltke revealed to the Crown Prince the truth which they knew, that the French army was less strong and prepared than the Prussian one. They went to Brandenburg together to meet the King returning from Bad Ems.

He was surprised to see them, but was soon convinced of the need to mobilize the army. The Crown Prince urged him also to mobilize the *Landwehr* and the fleet. The King again consented and embraced his son with emotion. They would fight together again. That was the true bond between a Prussian King and his heir.

They had never been more popular with the Prussian people. So dense was the crowd in front of the Royal Palace, the Crown Prince recorded, that he and his father had great difficulty in pushing their way through to the terrace, which was packed with officers. The cheering never stopped. Again and again the King had to show himself. The whole multitude sang with one voice, *"Die Wacht am Rhein."* At that moment, all realized the solemn meaning of the song.[11]

Queen Victoria was convinced that Prussia was wholly in the right and France absolutely in the wrong. Three of her closest German male relatives were in the army, her Coburg brother-in-law and her two sons-in-law, the Crown Prince of Prussia and Prince Louis of Hesse. She pressed her Liberal Government to intervene, but her Prime Minister Gladstone would not listen. England must continue its policy of strict neutrality, whatever the Queen might feel about her kith and kin in Germany. In a summing up for the Queen, the Foreign Secretary, Lord Granville, assigned the blame for the war with elegance and prescience, knowing very little of Bismarck's hand in provoking it.

> The last week seems like a feverish dream. The result today is dreadful. Every one seems to have been in the wrong. The King of Prussia probably did not give his consent to the candidature of Prince Leopold without the knowledge of M. Bismarck. The latter must have known how distasteful it would be, rightly or wrongly, to the French. The secrecy of the negotiation, and the suddenness of the announcement was discourteous. The violent language used by the French Ministry was undiplomatic and unstatesmanlike. France is morally unpardonable, but perhaps

militarily right, in making such haste. But it is inconceiv-
able that, in the present state of civilization, hundreds
of thousands of Frenchmen should be hurled against
like numbers of Germans, on a point limited to a matter
of etiquette.

In Lord Granville's opinion, Her Majesty the Queen had
done all that she could have done to make Prince Leopold
withdraw. Her Majesty's ministers had done all they could
do to keep the peace, so they could do nothing more but
rest on their oars.[12] Bismarck was right. Britain was a happy
island which could afford to coast along and keep out.

Britain's refusal to come into the war was taken badly
in Prussia. In the previous continental war against Napoleon
I, the British and the Prussians had fought together until the
French Emperor met his Waterloo. Even now, most informed
opinion did not think Prussia could fight alone. Although the
combined German forces numbered 1,500,000 men and
400,000 could be mobilized and sent to the front within four
weeks, the illusion of French superiority was still paramount.
The odds were fearfully against Prussia in the awful struggle,
the Crown Princess informed Queen Victoria. "There is not
a family that is not torn asunder, not a woman's heart that
is not near to breaking and for what?! Oh that England could
help us."[13]

England could, but England would not. Queen Victoria
sent on her eldest daughter's impassioned plea to her ministers,
but they would not budge. England would stay put and its
Queen would have to hide her partiality. "Can there be a
more cruel position than the unhappy Queen's?" she complained to Lord Granville. "She knows what her duty is and
will do what must be done, but she will suffer dreadfully,
and were Germany, dear Germany, the land of her Husband
and her Mother—of her only Sister and Brother—to be
crushed, she hardly knows how she could ever get over it!"[14]

She confided to the Crown Princess that her whole heart and her fervent prayers were with beloved Germany, and that she would suffer cruelly for all of them. Her dead husband would have gone to fight for Germany if he could.[15]

While revealing her private feelings, the Queen did not forget to ask about the Prussian plans of defense and attack, but the Crown Princess knew little of her country's strategy. Her husband was ordered to lead the Third Army in the south. Known for his tact as well as for his military skill, he was always given the most difficult post. His Second Army at Königgrätz had been full of dissident Poles; his new one would be full of south Germans, who had fought against the Prussians four years before. Two Prussian divisions would stiffen the forces of Bavaria, Württemberg and Baden, and they were expected to hold off a French invasion from across the Rhine until the main Prussian armies could assemble. The Crown Prince did not think much of their chances, but he would do his duty.

The sad christening ceremony of his infant daughter Sophie seemed more like a farewell party than a festival. Afterward, he left for the front without telling his wife. The thought was kind, and yet she felt as if her heart would break. He was gone without a kiss or a word of farewell and she did not know whether she would ever see him again.[16] He did not know whether his south German troops would fight alongside the Prussians. It might be a just war, but the Crown Prince had not yet tested national feeling in the states near the Rhine.

Bismarck wanted to play the injured party in public and use propaganda to win allies abroad. He gave a long interview to William Russell, the famous war correspondent of *The Times*, even though its editor Delane was no friend of Prussia and bet on "Casquette against Pumpernickel." The Chancellor was so reckless and indiscreet in the interview that Russell felt his hair curling tighter and tighter with alarm. The war correspondent's position was privileged. He was attached to the

Crown Prince's headquarters along with the British military observer Walker (now a general) and most of the commander's old Anglo-Coburg group: Duke Ernest himself, the historian Freytag, the Baden minister Baron Roggenbach, and briefly Morier, who came to glean what information he could. Morier was on his way to Darmstadt to check on Princess Alice's well-being and to watch the Hessian troops march off to become part of the Prussian advance guard—a military detail which Morier cabled in cipher to Lord Granville.[17]

Although the English were favored in the Crown Prince's army of the south, they were hated elsewhere. Before he joined his armies, the King of Prussia told both the Crown Princess and her mother that he was deeply grieved by a secret intelligence report from London that England was supplying France with shipping coal for its fleet, with horses for its artillery, and with millions of cartridges. Was this neutrality?[18] Morier confirmed the national feeling against England. Many sons of Germany might now be killed by English bullets. He knew his own country believed in free trade and could not control its exports, yet how could such an explanation convince in time of war, when England's neutrality seemed biased and little less than desertion?[19]

Bismarck was orchestrating the anti-English campaign, which was easy to do. As the Crown Princess told her mother, the King and Queen of Prussia believed the innuendos against England because with a pistol to one's breast no one was inclined to investigate much.[20] A supposed gaffe by the Prince of Wales—that he hoped Austria would join France and Prussia would fare ill—was publicized everywhere. Bismarck also alleged there were treasonable foreign intrigues going on in Hanover, whose treasury, ironically, was now the "Reptile Fund" used by him to bribe the press. He saw no harm in inflaming the German newspapers against England while encouraging the English press to support Prussia in the war.

He had a fresh weapon of communication to hand. In 1869, he secretly gave government funds to Bernhard Wolff to keep his news agency, the Continental Telegraph Company, from being taken over by its rivals, Reuter of London and Havas of Paris. Wolff was given a virtual monopoly in Germany as long as all telegrams of a political nature were immediately reported to government agents. Bismarck also had the right to censor or to originate news stories, which were sent by telegraph to all local German newspapers. It was a fundamental way to influence the press through the only rapid method of transmitting news. Bismarck always saw the press as a dangerous and despicable opponent, to be bullied or bought or cowed. Although he despised journalists, he was conscious of their power, and his sensitivity to criticism in print and his ruthlessness in dealing with it were extraordinary. "Every press attack must be smashed," he once declared, "every insult must be avenged."[21] In war and peace, he used Busch and Stieber to run a central clearing house for government propaganda and for counterattacks on hostile sources of information.

It was the development of a modern system of media manipulation in the interests of the new nation-state. Against it, the old royal system of suggesting or planting an occasional article was inefficient and out of date. In the greater Prussia he was creating, Bismarck's methods overwhelmed the few newspaper pieces which the Anglo-Coburg group could arrange to be printed. Most of its scribes were now with the Third Army and the Crown Prince, and even he believed Bismarck's accusations against Lord Granville and the British government. He told General Walker that the English governing class was blindly hostile to Prussia, and that all hope of a good understanding between the two countries had broken down.[22] Temporarily, the Crown Prince felt isolated and betrayed by his long support of his wife's homeland.

He had also become Bismarck's ally in the great emerging vision of a united German Empire. The extraordinary welcome he had received in Bavaria and Württemberg had persuaded him that even the people of the southern states felt German above all. "The Union of Germany is effected," he confided to Morier, "and it is the *people* of Germany by whom it has been effected." It was a national feeling, not mere hatred for the French. He had pledged himself to lead the combined German forces to victory in order to create a united Germany with his father as Emperor. "If you hear after some great battle of my suddenly quitting my army," he told Morier, "do not think I have run away. I shall have gone straight to Headquarters to urge and plead this cause with the King. *I shall have Bismarck on my side.*" This assertion startled Morier, who knew of the enmity between the Chancellor and the Crown Prince. The English diplomat knew the significance of their strange alliance: In war their aims were the same, a moderate peace which would end by uniting Germay; in peace they were opposed, because the Crown Prince wanted a free Germany. But the heir to the throne could hope to inherit the title which he and the Chancellor desired the traditional King to take—German Emperor instead of monarch of Prussia.

Yet first, victories had to be won against France. The Crown Prince thought the Germans would win in the end, but Morier was one of the few to think that they would win in the beginning. He sent back an opinion which the Foreign Office found ridiculous: the Germans would be before Paris in three weeks.[23]

✻

Speed of mobilization was all. Three German armies were ready to advance across the Rhine while the French were still straggling toward the front. In the south, the Crown Prince could hardly believe it. There was no invasion of Germany. He could push forward into Alsace. "For all the French sabre rattling," he wrote in his diary, "and all their age-long preparation against a sudden onslaught, *we* must be the aggressors. Who could ever have thought it?"[24]

The walled town of Weissenburg barred the way into France. As the Crown Prince advanced with the Third Army, the French pushed troops into the fortifications. With his usual speed of maneuver, the Crown Prince launched two simultaneous attacks by the Bavarians and the Prussians. To his surprise, the Bavarians fought well. The French finally had to flee to avoid being surrounded. Their vaunted mitrailleuses seemed cumbersome and ineffective, and their intermittent rain of bullets did not stop the bayonet charges of the German troops.

It was the first German victory against the French in fifty-five years, and even better was to follow. Two days later, on August 6, the Crown Prince totally defeated Marshal Mac-Mahon at Wörth. The French commander took up a strong defensive position on the steep slopes of the valley of the Sauerbach, protected by the stream and water meadows. Improving on the strategy and success of Königgrätz, the Crown Prince set out his Army Corps with the center laid back and the two wings projecting in long horns. He would rather outflank than attack frontally. He would try to cut off, not to batter down. He might have encircled the whole of Mac-Mahon's army if the Bavarians had shown more stomach for the fight. Throughout the long day of the struggle, the French held the heights above the town with tenacity and courage. The mitrailleuses and the chassepots began to thin the Prussian ranks, and Zouaves bounded in great leaps to counterattack down the slope. Toward the late afternoon, the Württembergers broke through and threatened MacMahon's line of retreat, and in spite of a Balaclava-style cavalry attack on the German artillery, the French army had to withdraw. Soon the retreat became a rout. The roads for miles around were littered with discarded French weapons.

It was hard-won victory. The Germans lost more than 10,000 men, the French double that number. The annihilation of the cavalry brigade of Cuirassiers was particularly horrible: their charge at the guns had become entangled in vineyards and orchards, where they had been shot down or taken prisoner almost to a man. General Walker saw the woods and fields covered with breastplates and helmets, swords and lances, dead horses heaped in piles and broken riders lying beside them. Though the French had fought well and had been commanded well, the Prussians were too quick for them, both strategically and tactically. For once in history, the élan of the French troops had been surpassed.[25]

The Crown Prince had won the first major victory against the French, shattering the myth of their superiority. With his speed of attack and ability to inspire his troops, he had proved himself the best of the Prussian field commanders. If the Bavarians had shown more fury, he might have surrounded MacMahon and won a total victory. As it was, he was the hero of the hour. His success encouraged the First and Second Armies above him, striking down through Lorraine toward Metz and Marshal Bazaine's forces.

The Crown Prince loved and hated being a warrior. He looked the role, mounted on his bay horse, his yellow beard and whiskers in an aureole under his cavalry cap, but the sight of the dead after the battle affected him deeply. The fallen had stiffened into the last spasm of their death agony, their arms and legs stuck out at odd angles under their faces, contorted in frozen pain. Set above a mass grave, a simple wooden cross was held up by the piled and broken muskets of the dead. "When once we get back home," the Crown Prince recorded, "the Fatherland will be drowned in tears."[26]

The wounded were the special problem of the Crown Princess. She supervised the building of a temporary hospital of wooden huts in the Kreutzberg at Berlin, meant to accommodate 1,600 injured soldiers. She begged her mother for more old linen. Sending it would hardly be a breach of British neutrality; a wounded man had ceased to be an enemy, she told Queen Victoria, he was only a suffering human creature entitled to everyone's help.

She was being accused of supplying her mother with secret information, which the Foreign Office was passing on to the French, so she took care to define her delicate position. The information she relayed was a personal act, not an affair of state. "I hope I am only doing what you wish," she confided to Queen Victoria, "in writing openly what I hear, see and *think*. I only write as a private individual to you as my dear Mama, at the same time thinking it may be agreeable and useful to you to hear what is thought and said on this side of the water from an *unofficial* source. Of course *I* am looked on with suspicious eyes—as England is supposed to be on the other side."[27]

She was increasingly under suspicion. In time of war, all foreign-born people tend to be accused of being unpatriotic or of sending vital information abroad. Queen Augusta became jealous of her daughter-in-law's success at organizing the temporary hospital in Berlin and wanted to stop her from founding another one at Homburg, but the King permitted it at the Crown Prince's request. He could refuse little to his victorious son, although he too was becoming jealous of the hero worship of the Crown Prince within the ranks of the German army. The soldiers seemed to know that the Crown Prince cared for their lives and would win his victories at the minimum cost. But the King and his wife wanted no child to steal their glory in battle or at the bedside of the wounded.

The King's advance on Metz with the other Prussian armies was bloodier. At Gravelotte, the French caught the Prussians in a defile and punished them with chassepots and mitrailleuses. The King himself was in great danger from shot and shell, and he won only a Pyrrhic victory at the cost of some 20,000 Prussian dead and wounded while the French retired with lighter losses. An attempt by Marshal Bazaine to break out of the fortress of Metz was shattered at another bloody battle at Mars la Tour, a field where poor tactics allowed much more death than glory.

There, the leaden rain of the chassepots was literally like a hailstorm.[28] The Prussian dragoon guards were destroyed in a useless charge, repeating the French mistake at Wörth. The whole ground was littered white and blue with the bodies. Bismarck's elder son Herbert was hit by three bullets and reported dead. His father, in the yellow undress uniform of the *Landwehr* heavy cavalry, rode to look for him and found him wounded and cheerful in a field ambulance station. The American General Sheridan was visiting the Chancellor and condemned the unnecessary slaughter. "Your infantry is the best in the world," he said, "but it was wrong of your generals to advance their cavalry as they did."[29]

The Crown Prince never wasted the lives of his men; he maneuvered his army into victory. He was ordered to join the King's main army and advance on Paris with 300,000 men. But intelligence came that MacMahon's army was striking along the Belgian border to relieve Metz, still besieged by the dogged Prince Frederick Karl with seven army corps. "The time is now ripe to set the mousetrap for the enemy," the Crown Prince wrote in his diary. With his father the King, he swung northward, and pushed MacMahon out of a strong defensive position on the rocky crag of Senuc toward the border fortress of Sedan. The guaranteed neutrality of Belgium should prevent the French army from escaping across the Meuse and the frontier. To stop any such retreat, the Crown Prince once again executed one of his brilliant strategical marches. He sent his two Prussian army corps on a flanking movement across the Meuse. The early morning mists hid the maneuver, so MacMahon's forces thought they were only facing a Prussian and Saxon army to the front and flank. Instead, the Crown Prince's army corps took up their positions in the French rear and blocked the last loophole of escape. Desperately, the French charged with Chausseurs and Cuirassiers, Turkos and Zouaves, but the Prussian needle guns cut them down. The demoralized French infantry fell back on Sedan in a panic. "Our plan was being carried to completion with mathematical precision," the Crown Prince recorded. "Marshal MacMahon was surrounded!"[30]

Although it had been Moltke's plan, its success was once again due to the Crown Prince's execution of his part of it. Once the battle was won, he rode from his observation post to report to the King, who had ordered a short bombardment of Sedan. The burning town of Bazeilles sent up a dense gray-yellow pillar of smoke into the clear air. The setting sun gilded the bodies of the fallen and the crests of the hills about doomed Sedan, where the French Emperor himself was now thought to be trapped. When the Crown Prince reached his father's side, he heard the news that Napoleon III wished to capitulate with all his army. "That is a grand success!" the King exclaimed, offering his hand to be kissed by his son. "I thank thee for thy share in it."[31]

Once more the Crown Prince had marched his men to the right place at the right time. He had prevented the escape of the French Emperor, whose surrender might well end the struggle. "The War had reached its culminating point," the Crown Prince wrote, "the instigator of the crying wrong was in our power. Peace could not now be long delayed."[32] Soon a plenipotentiary appeared with Napoleon's written offer to surrender his sword to the King of Prussia and the King accepted the surrender, using his son's writing paper and sealing his answer with the eagle signet from his son's holster. Then father and son threw themselves into each other's arms, deeply moved by a victory greater than Königgrätz.

The illusion did not last. Peace was not won. The King and the Crown Prince were not reconciled. When the Crown Prince begged the King not to humiliate the French Emperor by making him hand over his sword on the hilltop among the Prussian generals, he was thought to be showing too much sympathy with the enemy. At the peace parley in the villa where the French Emperor had fled, Napoleon III accepted defeat and exile in Germany, but he stressed that he could only speak for himself, not for his government which might choose to carry on the war. His short and podgy figure made the King of Prussia's tall and commanding form look wonderfully imposing. But when Napoleon III wept and said he had never even wanted to go to war, the Crown Prince did not know what to say.

Soon after the capitulation, the Crown Prince was visited

by his strange ally Bismarck and together they planned how they might put pressure on the King to establish a German Empire. Bismarck now insisted on taking Alsace and Metz from France, even if it meant prolonging the war. The capture of the Emperor with an army of 80,000 men had changed the conditions of peace.

At the time of the battle of Sedan, Bismarck confided to his creature Busch his views of the Crown Prince and his wife. He claimed that he was now quite good friends with the Prince. "Why should he not be pleased?" Bismarck asked. He was the heir apparent to one of the most powerful kingdoms in the world: he would turn out to be reasonable and would allow his ministers to govern for him, he would learn not to thrust himself too much forward. In general he would get rid of many bad habits that made old gentlemen of his trade rather troublesome.

As for the Crown Princess, Bismarck did not consider that she had too much influence over her husband. He found her a clever woman, but far too candid. Because she could not disguise her feelings, she was very vulnerable. "I have cost her many tears," Bismarck said. She could not conceal how angry she was with him at the time of the annexations of Schleswig and Hanover. She could hardly bear the sight of him. She had once asked him to bring her a glass of water, and as he handed it to her she had said to a lady-in-waiting, "He has cost me as many tears as there is water in this glass." But, Bismarck said, that was all over now.[33]

It was all over—but only for the duration of the war, which was not all over. Bazaine's army in Metz was still making ever more bloody and futile attempts to break out. A Third Republic was declared under General Trochu and Jules Favre to forestall a red revolution in Paris, feared by the Rothschilds and the financiers. With the north lost and the road to Paris open, a *levée en masse* was decreed to create new French armies in the south, but it seemed too little too late.

The rapidity and extent of the German successes had been

incredible. The Crown Prince found them almost terrifying. He took Rheims only four weeks after his first victory at Weissenburg. To his wife, the surrender of the French Emperor at Sedan had a moral. Such a downfall was a melancholy thing, she wrote to Queen Victoria, but it was meant to teach deep lessons. "May we all learn what frivolity, conceit and immorality lead to! The French people have trusted in their own excellence, have completely deceived themselves. Where is their army, where are their statesmen?"[34]

The inexorable German advance on the French capital caused panic there. Many refugees fled west. By September 20, the blockade was completed with the Crown Prince making his headquarters at Versailles. There was general depression within the besieged city. It was felt, the British ambassador reported, that while respectable citizens were on the ramparts, the reds might pillage the town. Foreign diplomats, however, would stay on in Paris unless it were bombarded.[35]

That was the question. In military terms, there had to be a bombardment to force a surrender, particularly as the French had heavy artillery in their fortifications around the city. Yet in terms of international propaganda, any destruction of such a center of civilization would be a fatal mistake. Abroad, anger at the French provocation of the war was already turning into sympathy after their continual defeats.

Many stories of brutalities in the conquered countryside began to circulate. The strategy of living off the land by forced requisitions from Stieber's lists of resources involved coercion and violence. Guerrilla resistance invited the reprisals Napoleon I had used in Spain. Bismarck had no pity on men caught with weapons and without uniform; he had them shot at once, saying that human life was of little value. "If we lived four hundred years, it would be another matter."[36] Even the Crown Prince accepted the necessity of reprisals. If a shot was fired from a house at a Prussian patrol it was burned down, or else its owner was flogged and stripped of food and money.

It was horrible, the Crown Prince admitted, but consistent with the proclamation of martial law.[37]

Luckily for the field generals, the responsibility for the atrocities landed on the generals of the occupying forces or on the military police led by Stieber. He understood the use of terror in order to control the local population. Any peasant who watched Prussian troop movements was liable to be tortured or hanged as a spy, and so was any balloonist who came down while trying to escape from Paris. When the King followed the Crown Prince and set up his headquarters at Versailles for the siege of the French capital, Stieber was always at His Majesty's side, feeding the royal paranoia with stories of hundreds of French spies and assassins. In reprisal for a trivial anti-Prussian demonstration, Stieber threatened to hang ten town councillors. When an innocent young man on his honeymoon was sentenced to the gallows for keeping a diary, Stieber answered army pleas for clemency with the words: "That only makes my task the more painful"—and had the young bridegroom hanged all the same.

Security measures and the rigors of martial law had to be applied more and more against a French population now recovering from the shock of total defeat and adopting guerrilla war tactics against the invaders. The Italians took the opportunity to seize Rome from the French, but Garibaldi came to teach the French republican government how to fight with irregulars. A scratch army was put together on the Loire and managed to retake Orleans, while another instant army advanced toward Alsace. Even though Bazaine eventually capitulated at Metz with 175,000 men, Paris still held out, firing from its fortifications at the forward positions of the Germans. The besiegers began to feel more and more besieged, a huge force of 300,000 men surrounding an enemy city, but surrounded by a hostile nation. The bombardment of the enemy capital seemed the quick solution.

Bismarck certainly wanted that. Opposed to him was the

Crown Prince, now general in command of the siege, and Moltke. From the military point of view, an immediate bombardment would be stupid. The Germans had not brought up the long-range artillery nor the munitions to keep up a continuous shelling of Paris. With the guns they had, they could only hit the rich faubourgs instead of the industrial and workers' *quartiers* where a red reign of terror was already said to be starting. The Crown Prince refused to sacrifice his men's lives by storming the fortresses outside Paris or to waste his few shells on a symbolic bombardment. "Fritz regrets every shot that is fired," his wife wrote to her mother, "and every death."[38] For four months, he refused all demands to shell Paris, until he was overruled by the King. The new year of 1871 would see the bombardment. Hunger had not forced the city to surrender.

The Crown Prince's stand against the folly of bombarding the French capital led to a vicious smear campaign against him and his wife. "In Berlin it is now the order of the day to vilify my wife," he wrote in his diary, "as being mainly responsible for the postponement of the bombardment of Paris and to accuse her of acting under the direction of the Queen of England. All this exasperates me beyond measure."[39] Bismarck himself orchestrated the campaign through his wife at home, and recorded the accusation in his memoirs. He found it absurd that Paris should not be treated like any other fortress. Making it into a special case was a notion imported from London by the roundabout route of Berlin—the cant of English public opinion.[40] To Bismarck, heavy artillery and assault must end the siege quickly. Each month Paris still held out, intervention was more likely from England or Austria, Italy or Russia.

Bismarck had begun by courting international opinion, but now he did not mind alienating it. He and the King and the Prussian generals became domineering with their victories, demanding a French capitulation. Only the Crown Prince seemed conscious of the shifting tides of opinion. The English

and American correspondents at Versailles were now condem-
ning the Germans as a greedy and brutal people—no longer
innocent victims but arrogant victors. "What good to us is
all power," the Crown Prince asked himself, "all martial glory
and renown, if hatred and mistrust meet us at every turn?
If every step we advance in our development is a subject
for suspicion and grudging? Bismarck has made us great and
powerful, but he has robbed us of our friends, the sympathies
of the world, and—our conscience."[41]

So the commanding general of the siege agonized and was
accused of pro-French sympathies under English direction.
In point of fact, his mother-in-law Queen Victoria was being
herself accused of foreign sympathies because she continued
to back the German cause when public opinion was swinging
to support the gallant resistance of the French. She hated the
war because of the intolerable strain put on her. She was
on the side of Germany but remained Queen of England. These
divided interests in royal families were quite unbearable; human nature was not made for such fearful trials—especially
not mothers' and wives' hearts.[42]

In the long struggle to change the King into a German
Emperor, the Crown Prince was the instigator and conciliator,
calming both the King and the Chancellor when they would
not speak to each other on the subject. He had been taught
to be an imperialist by Prince Albert, whose dream always
was a free liberal German Empire as the leader of civilization.
The Crown Prince wanted a revival of the ancient imperial
crown, more than a thousand years old. He was not disinter-
ested. He hoped soon to inherit the imperial title from his
aged father. "The Crown Prince is as stupid and vain as any
man," Bismarck complained. "He has been made crazy again
by all that Kaiser madness."[43]

Bismarck also wanted a united Germany, and the title of
Emperor was a convenient umbrella for it. He hammered out
separate treaties with the south German states and used his
Reptile Fund to pay off King Ludwig II of Bavaria, who sent

a letter drafted by Bismarck requesting the King of Prussia to assume the imperial crown. Although the King protested that it would only be a cross for him to bear, Bismarck and the Crown Prince clasped hands outside his room. This formal request by the leading minor German sovereign would lead to a change of mind. The only thing preventing the actual ceremony was the King of Prussia's wish not to take the imperial title until he had taken the French capital.

The siege of Paris, however, dragged on into the new year. Even the bombardment was ineffective, as the Crown Prince had predicted. His wife was more ferocious about it than he was, telling her mother that it might annoy the English that *their* beautiful and charming Paris should be battered to pieces, but these were the unavoidable consequences of fortifying the city and prolonging the war.[44] To the Crown Prince, Gambetta seemed a mere butcher by raising scratch armies with no hope of beating the professional Prussian corps. The Government of National Defense seemed to Princess Alice of Hesse to be a form of terrorism; the Republic with which the English were so enchanted was a far worse despotism than that of the Empire.[45]

Under the pressure of his son and his Chancellor, the King of Prussia assumed the title of German Emperor in the Hall of Mirrors at Versailles. Paris still would not fall, but the German princes could not hang around headquarters forever waiting for the ceremony. On January 18, 1871, all the dignitaries assembled in their military dress uniforms and insignia. The King put on the Russian Order of St. George, while the Crown Prince wore the Garter at his knee to show his love of England. The palace of Versailles was packed with Prussian and German officers and picked soldiers carrying their regimental colors, torn by shot and shell. Under a central window of the huge Hall of Mirrors before a field altar, the King stood with the royal princes. After the Crown Prince had ordered "Off helmets for prayer!" a Potsdam chaplain read a short liturgy. Massed military bands then struck up the hymn *"Sei*

Lob und Ehr" under the painted ceiling which glorified the triumphs of *Le Roi Soleil.* The Te Deum was sung before the King proceeded to the *Salon de la Guerre,* where he read a short address to the German sovereigns, followed by a grim Bismarck, who read another address to the German people as if he were reciting an agenda. Then the Grand Duke of Baden cried in a loud voice, "Long live His Imperial Majesty the Emperor William!" Flags waved, huzzahs shook the tapestries, the Crown Prince knelt and kissed his father's hand. He was raised and warmly embraced. He was His Imperial Highness now—which he declared he did not want to be called.

The new Emperor also said he did not want his title. He fought not to be called Emperor of Germany. He had wept and had threatened to abdicate if he could not get his way, but as this title implied a territorial claim Bismarck had insisted that the King of Prussia should be called the German Emperor. "Delivering the imperial baby was a difficult case," Bismarck wrote to his wife. "At such a time, kings—like women—have strange longings." As midwife at so protracted a labor, Bismarck had felt ready to explode like a shell and blow up the whole palace.[46]

The acquisition of the imperial title was the last great service that the Crown Prince would perform for his father. He had been the major agent in winning three great battles. If the fortune of war had gone the other way, there would have been no Prussian solution to the German problem. By his military skill, the Crown Prince had helped achieve the Coburg dream of a united German Empire. In spite of his forced cooperation with Bismarck, he secretly wanted to pension off the Chancellor.[47] Bismarck was not eternal, as the Crown Princess pointed out to her mother. She thought he would soon be as quickly forgotten as the Louis Napoleon who had once so frightened Europe.[48] Only the heartbeat of one old man fluttered between the Chancellor and dismissal. Bismarck might try to speak and act like the new German Emperor, but he could fall as quickly as he had risen. In any event, his power was limited as long as the war continued. When he tried to interfere with military strategy, Moltke quarreled with him, and again the Crown Prince had to try to heal the breach. Moltke wanted a war of extermination against the French, while Bismarck wanted peace and a resumption of his total control.

The Chancellor kept the new Emperor's ear and won his peace. Unlike at Sedan, he was appointed to negotiate the terms for the capitulation of Paris and the ending of the war with France. He made the Crown Prince and the other generals bitter by excluding them from the peace preliminaries. The French negotiators, Favre and Thiers, stood in awe of Bismarck and knew that further resistance was useless. Paris was starving, and the recruits in the *levées en masse* were hardly more than boys. By the end of February, the French capital had formally surrendered. By the end of the first week of March, the deputies of the newly elected National Assembly at Bordeaux had ratified the peace terms. The war was over.

France had to pay a great price. It lost Alsace and the northern part of Lorraine, including Metz. It also had to suffer a German army of occupation living off the land "like caterpillars on a tree" until a war indemnity of five billion francs ($400 million) had been paid.[49] Throughout the negotiations, Bismarck behaved like a bully, conducting himself with monstrous and intentional rudeness. At the last moment, he spared Thiers the indignity of submitting the French capital to a German triumph through its streets; instead, the new German Emperor twice reviewed 30,000 of his troops on the race course at Longchamps. Bismarck had again snatched from him the chance of a victory parade through a conquered capital.

In March, the Crown Prince returned, an embittered victor, to his wife in Berlin. His cousin Frederick Karl had been made a Field Marshal for his dull and costly victories. His gracious words as he accepted his baton were: "At last!" The Crown Prince could not even say that. His exploits were being consigned to oblivion. He must take no glory from the Chancellor or the Emperor, and must wait until the victory parade in June to be given his marshal's baton covered with sky-blue satin and studded with crowns and eagles.

The award had come too late and was hardly noticed in the triumph. The Crown Prince's son William, riding behind him on his dappled pony, was more fascinated by his grandfather the Emperor, who halted under the Brandenburg Gate to receive the keys of Berlin from a group of maidens in white. The Emperor saw his grandson's devotion and put a hand on the boy's shoulder among the ranks of the Guards and the cheering crowds and the massed booming bands.

"This is a day you will not forget," the Emperor said.

The boy never did.

9

How Long, O Lord, How Long?

ISMARCK WAS CREATED a prince and given an enormous estate. In himself, he seemed able to concentrate the whole German Empire. He controlled the Reichstag through the National Liberals and national communications through his agents and the Reptile Fund. The new Emperor was little more than the ceremonial head of state, while Bismarck ran all the business of the country. After a long visit to England to recover from the hardships of the war, the Crown Prince found himself again excluded from the Council of State and the War Cabinet. The only formidable opposition to Bismarck came from the General Staff, always jealous of its military powers and privileges, from the Junker reactionaries he was deserting, and the Catholic aristocrats clustering around the implacable Empress Augusta. As for the German princes, most had been reduced to figureheads on pensions. "They no longer want to govern," Bismarck told Busch, "and are glad when someone relieves them of the trouble."[1]

Even the liberals and the middle classes, who had once

looked to the ideals of the Crown Prince and his wife, now made Bismarck their idol because he was enriching them. France managed to pay off its war indemnity of five billion francs within three years. The flow of money into Berlin provoked a speculative boom there, which spread over the whole Empire. Money was so abundant, the British representative reported from Leipzig in 1871, that people did not know what to do with it.[2] In Berlin itself, the excessive liquidity led to enormous stock and property speculation as great as in the South Sea Bubble of London or the Panama scheme of Paris. "The market had bullish orgies," a contemporary wrote. "Millions, coined right out of the ground, were won. National prosperity rose to apparently unimagined heights. A shower of gold rained down on the drunken city."[3] Much of the risk capital went into the railway schemes of Baron Strousberg, who was set on creating a railway empire in eastern Europe as large as those of a Vanderbilt or a Gould—and by the same methods of watering stocks until they were drowned under the inevitable deluge. Industry flourished with the orders for rolling stock and track, building materials and luxuries. A new word was coined, the *Gründerjahre,* to describe the postwar boom years of ostentation and speculation, greed and display.

Bismarck had performed a miracle of balance and compromise between the new and the old. The liberals were placated with a Reichstag and prosperity and free trade within the German Empire. For these benefits, they gave up their demands for a bill of rights and control over the Cabinet and the Chancellor. Although the Junkers lost their feudal privileges, many were pleased by confirmation of their power and position in Prussia and at court. The social system remained a caste system, where appointments were reserved for aristocrats and their sons. Even the generals were tolerably pleased when Bismarck arranged a deal between them and the Reichstag, by which military budgets would only have to be agreed upon every seven years instead of three. Through victory and German unity, Bismarck seemed to have found a synthesis for the irreconcilable conflicts of Prussian society. Giving every group something, he had reconciled the nation in the pride of unity. Only the masses stood outside the settlement—powerless, but patriotic and fairly prosperous. Their time was not yet, so Bismarck did not need to deal with them.

The forces that opposed Bismarck's plans for a united Germany seemed to him threefold: the Church, the unadaptable Junkers, and the crown, which still had the power to dismiss him. The Church was attacked through a mistaken policy of extending state control over parochial schools, both Catholic and Protestant. This policy pleased the liberals and the anti-clericals, while alienating the southern German Catholic states. Hundreds of bishops and priests were imprisoned or expelled; within five years, one-third of Prussian parishes had no pastors. This *Kulturkampf* was destroying the hardwon unity of Germany in the name of reason and State power.

The new British Ambassador, Odo Russell, managed the impossible; he was on good terms with the Chancellor as well as with the Crown Prince. He analyzed Bismarck's policy at home. The *Kulturkampf* would make the state supreme over all foreign influences, particularly papal, perhaps divine. The recent defining of the doctrine of papal infallibility was anathema to Bismarck: "thinking himself more infallible than the Pope he cannot tolerate two infallibles in Europe." The abolition of feudal rights and the increase of court ceremonial weakened the aristocracy by putting it in costume. Cleverest of all, Bismarck had persuaded the old German Emperor to distrust his family and the minor princes. The Chancellor alone appeared to hold the ring between liberals and aristocrats, the Emperor and the court, making himself indispensable to the German system he had created. The future sovereign, the British Ambassador concluded glumly, would be obliged to secure Bismarck's services.[4] He made all work.

❧

The future sovereign was being reduced with the former German sovereigns to exercises in etiquette. The ceremonies of the Empire were even more exhausting than those of the Kingdom of Prussia. "Party succeeds party—dinner after dinner," the Crown Princess complained to her mother. "It is really too much for one's nerves. Fritz says this last week has tried him more than the whole campaign."[5]

The German Emperor seemed to have taken over the tricks of Versailles, where *Le Roi Soleil* had used ceremony as a form of rule. Endless protocol and public displays of obedience made all the rival princes impotent and subservient. The Emperor and Empress kept their son and daughter-in-law firmly in their place, which was waiting meekly behind the throne. In fact, the Emperor's haughtiness to his heir made the Crown Prince pass on the same ill treatment to lesser princes in order to salvage some pride.

In an interesting aside to her Foreign Secretary, Queen Victoria criticized her son-in-law for his behavior on ceremony. "The Crown Prince *hates* intrigue," she declared, "and is *very* straightforward and honest and kindhearted but rather weak and to a certain extent obstinate, not *conceited,* but absurdly proud, as all his family are, thinking *no* family higher or greater than the Hohenzollerns; not proud to those below him, that is to the people, but proud and overbearing to other *Princes.*"[6]

Attendance at all great ceremonies was absolutely required; absence was an insult, if not a little treasonous. When the former British Ambassador stayed away on holiday from the Victory Parade in June 1871, it was taken as a political affront that contributed to his replacement by Odo Russell—very much persona grata at the court. At other special state occasions, such as the funeral of the Queen Dowager in 1873, Queen Victoria insisted that a distinguished British representative be sent from England to be in attendance. These royal princes or noble lords were invariably struck by the number of orders and decorations worn by the imperial guests, even at a funeral. Although in mourning, most of the men glittered with the jeweled stars and embroidered sashes of their particular rank and distinction. That was why an English aristocrat had to be there; to show respect was all. The court sought "with the greatest avidity any small marks of favour from the Court of England."[7]

Especially important was the confirmation service of Prince William, the Emperor's grandson. Queen Victoria sent to her "Dearest Willie" a portrait of the Prince Consort, a large inscribed English Bible, and a small ivory bust of herself. She did not want him to forget his English and Coburg connections, and she exhorted him to stick to his Protestant faith during an age of religious strife. Disbelief was now trying to raise its poisonous head and under the form of science and intellect, progress and liberty, to shake the simple belief in the Heavenly Father and His blessed Son.[8] She also sent the Prince of Wales to the ceremony, feeling it important that her successor should be present at such a solemn step for an heir to the German crown.

The confirmation service was a demonstration of how the Hohenzollerns still saw themselves as the sword in the hand of God. Prince William himself wore the uniform of the First Foot Guards and the riband and star of the Black Eagle. His father, who led him to the altar to make his responses, also wore his Guards uniform. Even the Prince of Wales was dressed in the finery of a British general topped by the Black Eagle. The Emperor, too, was splendid in military dress and decorations, as were the invited princes of the blood and field marshals. Against this glorious array, only the ministers and the royal women looked drab, the Crown Princess in a black dress with a white bonnet, the Empress in a cream-colored gown. Like peacocks or Mayan warriors, the imperial family on ceremony displayed finer feathers on the males.

The Emperor's love of tradition and form made him quarrel over the education of his grandchildren. The Crown Princess and her husband wanted to send Prince William and his brother Henry to the Gymnasium at Kassel so that they could meet German boys from ordinary families and experience the

national system of education. The Emperor wanted to limit
his eldest grandson to more military training and keep him
ready to appear in the world on all occasions. That, the Crown
Princess told her mother, would be an end of all study at
once, and an end too of all hopes of his becoming a steady
and serious man.[9] So the parents fought the Emperor on the
subject through many unpleasant and violent scenes—and
won their point. William and his brother were sent to Kassel
for more than two years, but did not seem to profit much
from the experiment. Their tutor Hinzpeter went with them
and supervised them privately, ensuring that they made no
friends with their classmates. Hinzpeter thought the effect
of the school on Prince William was only skin-deep, while
the Prince complained to his imperial grandfather that he was
humiliated by scoring fewer marks than mere commoners.

The autocracy of the Emperor toward his son was galling.
The war hero of Wörth found himself treated like a child,
given little to do, but forbidden to go away. He was not allowed to leave Potsdam or Berlin without his father's permission, which was often refused. "Just think of Fritz at forty
being treated like a boy of six," the Crown Princess wrote
in indignation. "It is a tyranny which I consider quite insupportable. A General is put above our children against our will
with orders from the Emperor and our Home turned topsy-
turvy—I own I feel in a perfect rage." It was enough to make
a saint swear.[10]

Yet the Crown Princess held her tongue, except when the
continual attacks on England reached her ears. Then she could
become spiteful and savage in defending her homeland, finding it ridiculous that it should be thought a sin to be a stranger
in the Prussian court. Her sin became greater when she made
friends with the Hanoverian Ludwig Windthorst, the cultivated leader of the Catholic opposition party in the Reichstag.
Like the Emperor, Bismarck thought that princes were tainted
by the company they kept. If the Crown Prince's household
were entertaining the chief opponent of the *Kulturkampf*, he

might be considering Windhorst as Bismarck's replacement when the old Emperor died.

Bismarck was indispensable to his own system. His fear of a plot against him was chiefly directed at the Crown Prince's mother, for as the Emperor aged, the Empress gained more influence over him. In Bismarck's view, she had abandoned her support of the Liberals because he had swung over so many of them to his side. Now she was with Bismarck's old supporters, the reactionary Protestants and the devout Catholics opposed to the *Kulturkampf*. It was a way of undermining the Chancellor's power. "If she is not already a Catholic," Bismarck stated to Busch, "she will be so very soon."

Above all, Bismarck hated the Empress for indulging in direct royal diplomacy. "She also interferes in foreign policy," he confided to Busch, "having taken it into her head that it is her vocation to plead everywhere in favour of peace—to be an Angel of Peace. She therefore writes letters to foreign Sovereigns, to the Queen of England for instance, which she afterwards mentions to her consort, who, however, says nothing about them to me."[11] This brake on Bismarck's provocative diplomacy was especially disconcerting during the war scare with France in 1875, when royal intervention did much to scotch Bismarck's plans.

To protect himself, Bismarck had to pay daily calls on the Emperor in Berlin and Potsdam. But when they were separated during the long summer recess, the Chancellor could not prevent the Empress from playing on her husband's fear that a revolution might result from the radical changes of the *Kulturkampf*. Then Bismarck had to go out and rebuild the morale of the old Emperor. Once during the religious crisis he had to travel as far as Jueterbogk to join his royal master in his carriage. The Emperor was depressed, thinking of the scaffold once more and ready to abdicate. Acting as he had when he first became the chief minister of Prussia, Bismarck caught at the Emperor's sword knot and appealed to his sense of duty as an army officer. By the evening, the King was cheerful and refused to accept Bismarck's threat to resign, his counterstroke if he did not get his own way.

The Emperor still had the final say, but the Chancellor dominated him as long as he lived. Interest in the state of the Emperor's health was almost ghoulish, and provoked many secret messages in cipher. By the end of the war in 1871, he appeared feeble and wandering in his wits, then he seemed to recover, but, in June 1873, he began to suffer from sick headaches, giddiness and fainting fits. The symptoms were the same as at the beginning of his brother's madness. Bismarck took the matter seriously, and Odo Russell reported back to London that the Crown Prince might soon have to assume power.

That was Bismarck's nightmare, and his reason for hating the Crown Princess second only to the Empress. The Chancellor felt that he might be able to work around the Crown Prince despite his liberal convictions, if only his strong-minded wife were not his conscience and guide in peacetime. Bismarck told the British Ambassador's wife that he thought he could agree with the Crown Prince, but he feared never with the Crown Princess. As a result, he would be bound to persecute her through his control of the press, making her position with the public a very difficult one, in order to have his own way about the administration of Germany.[12] He knew where she was vulnerable. First, as a foreigner who could always be accused of being an English agent. Second, as the malign influence behind the Crown Prince. Third, as a dangerous reformer, with her new hospital systems and girls' schools so tainted with English innovations. Fourth, as a woman who disliked Prussian ceremonial and tradition, while favoring the artistic and the unconventional. Fifth, as a supporter of toleration for Catholics and even Jews. To all these exploitable weaknesses, the Crown Princess added candor and sensitivity. She was almost too easy a mark.

A reconciliation between the Chancellor and the Crown Prince, still lingering on the threshold of the throne, seemed probable, for the one must inherit what the other had created to be run by himself. There were attempts by mutual friends to make this possible, but all ended in nothing. War might make for a strange alliance, but peace would not. While Bismarck could control the old Emperor, he did not want the bother of dealing with the heir apparent and his difficult wife. He would rather ignore the problem until it was real, reducing the Crown Prince's political role to insignificance because he still had his head stuffed full with English notions about parliamentary government. "The Crown Prince wants me to obey the majority," Bismarck once exploded. "That demands a suppleness of character and conviction that I do not possess."[13]

Anyway, the English alliance desired by the Crown Prince and the Empress did not suit the Chancellor's book. The armies of Russia and France were the real threat to German security, while a naval power could be treated with suspicion and contempt. It was a favorite saying of Bismarck's, his *bête noire* Morier reported, that he lost five years of his political life through the foolish belief that England was still a great power.[14] Morier had been the first to accuse Bismarck of fomenting the war against France by arranging the second Spanish offer to the Hohenzollern candidate. Now Morier's confidential meetings with diplomats at spas, and his dining with the German Emperor and Empress at Baden, persuaded Bismarck that English intrigues against him never stopped. Morier was his sworn enemy, sent from southern Germany to spy on him and to concoct his fall. England might not be able to fight, but it could still plot against him through its agents abroad and in the imperial family itself.

Although Bismarck did not actually threaten England, once Moltke did at one of the Chancellor's dinner parties. He was seated next to the British Ambassador and told him that an invasion of England was strategically easy, that the people had no discipline and were unprepared to resist. As for a war of revenge with France, that had to happen; it was the main reason Germany kept such a large standing army. War, anyway, would last as long as humanity. God Himself favored it, as the Bible proved.[15] When the Crown Prince visited Queen Victoria in 1871, he told her that they were living on a volcano. Some day, he said, Bismarck might try to make war on England.[16]

※

The Crown Princess knew that she offended Prussian society by her intelligence and independence, yet she had been trained to be what she was. She insisted on trying to provide an equal opportunity for suppressed Prussian girls, and she worked actively to found three schools which would give them a higher education. Two of them were called after her, the *Victoria Schule* and the *Victoria Lyceum* which even had an English headmistress. If the court was shocked by the alien Princess's efforts to improve young women's minds, it was horrified by her insistence on sports and physical training for their bodies which seemed unfeminine and improper as well as foreign and pernicious.

Her efforts to reform German hospitals and nurses' training provoked a similar reaction, but she had not met Florence Nightingale in vain. At the time of the war against France, Prussian care for the wounded was on a level with British neglect before the Crimean War. The hospital the Crown Princess had fought to set up at Homburg was run on the new English model, scrubbed and hygienic, with open windows to let in the air and let out the carbolic. The wounded soldiers recovered faster there. They were grateful and learned to value the Crown Princess almost as highly as they did her military husband, but the German doctors thought her reforms dangerous and foreign. It was reported back in Berlin that her methods were killing off the wounded rather than curing them. Her attempts in the years of peace to carry on her hospital work were blocked by her mother-in-law, suspicious of her innovations, jealous of her success. Only in the training of nurses were some of her reforms adopted.

The price the Crown Princess paid for insisting on better education for women was to appear interfering and radical. She seemed to be acting like a Victorian missionary in a backward and savage country. She offended not only the court, but also most of the teaching and medical professions. She particularly offended the fundamentalist Protestant clergy, who were becoming increasingly powerful at court, to whom church and home and children should be the only concerns of Prussian women. What the Crown Princess called reform, they called subversion.

Her three elder children were learning to rebel against her teaching. They did not like the quiet life at Bornstadt, where their mother fled from the stifling rooms and long ceremonies of Potsdam. William did not enjoy being made to groom horses and look after dogs. He preferred the mess and the parade ground, the court and the glitter of life in the capital, where his grandparents encouraged him to resist his mother's foreign ways. In point of fact, his mother's insistence on a Spartan English education had benefited her crippled child. He was becoming self-reliant and learning to suppress his self-pity. He worked all the time at developing his good right arm until he had a mighty grip, strong enough to make one hand do the job of two. His left arm was six inches shorter than the other and unable to lift a thing, but he learned to balance it unobtrusively on a belt or a sword hilt. He did use it to hold the reins of his horse, but he could only direct his mount with his knees and his right hand.

His mastery over his infirmity gave him increasing self-confidence. He became the ringleader of his brother Henry and sister Charlotte in rebellion against their parents' authority. Charlotte was the first to defy her mother openly. A capricious and frivolous princess, she wanted to get away from home as soon as she could. Since marriage was the only way out, she chose the shy, retiring and studious Prince Bernhard of Saxe-Meiningen, who tried to teach her about Greek archaeology instead of listening to her chatter. As the Prince was a suitable husband, and as her daughter was making trouble in the house, the Crown Princess agreed to Charlotte's marriage when she reached the age of seventeen. This caused a strong reaction from Queen Victoria, who accused her daughter of making a victim out of Charlotte because the young girl was unhappy at home. The Crown Princess found such an accusation unfair. Her mother had never visited her home in Germany and had never seen how they lived, so how could she judge whether Charlotte was happy or not? The family circle was usually all simplicity and harmony when the Emperor and Empress left them alone, and when she and the Crown Prince were not forced to go about and entertain too much.[17]

The Crown Princess was living in a state of self-delusion about her three elder children, who were forming a little cabal against their parents. They doted on the Emperor and Empress, loving the splendor and importance of the old Prussian traditions. Always careful to show great honor to those who cared so much, Queen Victoria sent in 1878 two of her sons, the Prince of Wales and the Duke of Connaught, to the double wedding ceremony of Princess Charlotte and another Prussian princess. The Crown Princess went through the tears and the sense of loss that her mother had suffered twenty years before on losing her own daughter—and Queen Victoria did not mince her words about it, declaring: "I think a daughter's marriage dreadful, repulsive."[18]

The long and elaborate wedding ceremonies caused comments in *The Times.* Its editorial wrongly stated that royal marriages no longer had any important effect on the conduct of nations—a senseless thing to say after recent royal efforts at keeping the peace and a war caused by a Hohenzollern candidate for the Spanish throne. But *The Times* did praise the resolution of those who went through the observances, including an interminable torchlight procession of the Prussian ministers. The thoroughness of the national character was seen in its etiquette, *The Times* noted. The aged Emperor might have the satisfaction of thinking, as he watched the twenty-two repetitions of the same ceremony, that the spirit of discipline and the instinct of obedience presided over the court as well as the camp.[19]

One of the Prince of Wales's aides wrote back to Queen Victoria about the strange marriage customs; she was always avid for such details. Apparently the *Grande Maîtresse* of Princess Charlotte's household distributed *Strumpfbänder* for the princes to wear in their buttonholes. These were pieces of embroidered ribbon which looked like bookmarkers, remnants of an old custom in which the youngest Hohenzollern prince had helped to disrobe the bride and had cut up her garters to give to the male guests. The aide also noticed what other Englishmen had noticed before him; the military splendor of the court with its many magnificent uniforms bespattered with orders and medals was equaled only by the exceeding plainness of the women.[20]

The Crown Princess was not one of them. Although her figure had thickened with the bearing of her eighth and last child, Margaret or "Mossy," her face was young and alive with the intelligence she could not hide. She remained in love with her husband, who treated her with trust as well as devotion. As the long years passed and the throne seemed no nearer, he learned to admire his wife's commitment to her ideals and constancy in withstanding the pressures and pinpricks inflicted on them.

Bismarck was enraged again by Queen Victoria's marriage game, when her son Prince Alfred was engaged to the Tsar's only daughter, the Grand Duchess Marie. Her children seemed to be trying to surround Germany with their blood alliances. Even the Crown Prince accused the Prince of Wales of working to populate northern Europe with anti-German marriages.[21] Ever since the defeat of the French and the founding of the German Empire, Bismarck had been aiming to preserve the peace of Europe and consolidate the new nation. His greatest fear was a conflict on two or three fronts. France might combine with Austria or Russia in a war of revenge. In five years, the Third Republic had paid off its reparations, achieved national prosperity and equipped new armies. The German general staff feared French rearmament and wanted a quick preventative strike against the revived enemy across the Rhine.

This was not Bismarck's desire. Just as royal alliances prejudiced his diplomatic efforts to keep rival powers isolated or friendly with Germany, so the dominance of the general staff in time of war threatened the delicate balance of forces within Germany which he manipulated in order to give the new nation time to develop and grow together. A powerful army was essential for national security, but Bismarck never forgot his own loss of control during the wars against Austria and France. The war scare of 1875 had shown just how dangerous the high military command could be. Although Bismarck had allowed a press campaign to be run, alleging that France would soon attack Germany at the head of a combination of Catholic powers, he had meant to intimidate the Third Republic, not to open hostilities. His problem was that, once Moltke and the general staff scented the possibility of war, they would not be put off. They impressed on the Emperor the need to attack France in order to prevent an invasion of Germany. And the Emperor had listened to them rather than to his Chancellor.[22]

The French government, however, had not repeated the mistakes of 1870. It did not wish to fight and mounted a diplomatic campaign in order to threaten Germany with Bismarck's nightmare, the condition of all the European powers against the new Empire. The Austrian Emperor warned his German cousin not to fight France again, and the Tsar traveled to Prussia to repeat the same message. Queen Victoria sent a special messenger to Berlin carrying a letter to the Tsar, in which she reminded him of the recent joining of their two families and begged him to use his influence with his uncle the German Emperor. As all the monarchs of Europe said they wanted peace, why should Germany have to fight?[23]

Faced with a possible war on three fronts, Bismarck had regained control over the general staff without admitting that he had lost it. Humiliated and on the edge of a nervous collapse, he declared that he would have to resign or retire to the country. If he went on overworking, his doctor had told him, he would be dead in a few months.[24] He denied responsibility for the war scare, telling the British Ambassador that it had been caused by the irresponsible press and various stockjobbers. Military men had the right to desire a preventative war, but not to make one. In fact, Bismarck did not subscribe to the "up and at 'em" principle; his was "Let them come on!"[25]

The Emperor would not accept Bismarck's resignation, but sent him away on sick leave to the country for five months. Before the Chancellor left, he took care to see the Crown Prince and assert his innocence in the matter of the scare, saying he regretted England's unfriendly attitude. Queen Victoria herself had come out against Germany—something which she did not deny. "It was I ALONE," she informed the Crown Princess, "who on hearing from ALL sides from our Ministers abroad of the danger of war, told My Ministers that *every thing* MUST be done to *prevent* it, that it was too intolerable that a *war* should be got up." No one wished more than she did that England and Germany might go well together, but Bismarck was so overbearing, violent, grasping and unprincipled that no one could stand it. All agreed that he was becoming like Napoleon I who caused Europe to join together in putting him down.[26]

Queen Victoria had not known that Bismarck had briefly lost control to the military machine and had taken the blame for a war scare that he had initiated, but regretted. In fact, the combination of great powers against Germany had proved to the general staff and the Emperor that Bismarck was essential. His diplomacy had never allowed such a coalition to form against Germany. He had only permitted wars to break out when Austria or France stood alone. He was indispensable in preserving the new German Empire. Even the Crown Princess had to admit that. Although she thought him a very doubtful blessing, "the idea that Bismarck has made us *great*—has made us *feared,* and therefore is *perfectly* INFALLIBLE—is the presiding one!"[27] The Emperor himself found it useful to put all responsibility onto Bismarck by implication. When he wrote personally to Queen Victoria, he declared that the war scare of 1875 had been entirely a fabrication by the newspapers, especially *The Times.* He and Moltke had never even considered a preventative war.[28]

On reading the letter, Queen Victoria's Prime Minister had commented drily that the Emperor was not allowed to know what was said and done in his name.[29] The truth was that it suited the Emperor to make Bismarck seem responsible for all policy—and it suited Bismarck to appear so. The Emperor could do no wrong. The Chancellor was all-powerful. He stood between the throne and the German people. His domestic policies during the first seven years of the Empire were based on a series of checks and balances between various social groups and classes, that allowed for national prosperity and a bourgeois economic revolution. Bismarck saw himself as the architect of the new Germany, and any attack on his authority appeared an attack on national security. In a real sense, he was the state he was making.

To protect his power and to make his countervailing policies work at home and abroad, Bismarck had to fragment his opposition. His persecution of any potential rival could approach paranoia. The ambitious Count Harry von Arnim was thought to be forming a Catholic opposition group with himself as the prospective Chancellor. As a consequence, Bismarck had him prosecuted as a traitor who had betrayed government secrets. The Count was eventually sentenced to five years' penal servitude.

Bismarck was also determined to destroy the influence of the Empress Augusta, who attracted those elements who could not be reconciled to Bismarck's immense authority. The Crown

Princess remained his lesser target in the attack on the integrity of the Empress, whom Bismarck's agents suggested should be banished or imprisoned. The Emperor did not come to his wife's defense, and the more she was abused and accused, the more civil, subservient and devoted did everyone at Berlin become to the Chancellor.[30] No one seemed to have the courage to counterattack against his press and spy network. "It is an abominable system of his," the Crown Princess protested, "trying to pull down the royal family in the eyes of the public to appear a *martyr*! It is wicked, disloyal and ungenerous especially to women who cannot defend themselves; and the German public are *so blind* in their adoration of Bismarck that they would believe *anything bad* of us, if it came from him or was sanctioned by him."[31]

She would not see the rationale behind Bismarck's assaults on any possible leader of an opposition. Bismarck believed that his policies were the best for the new Germany, and most were proving successful. The Crown Prince and Princess thought that other liberal policies would be more successful, but they had no power and resented their exclusion from it.

They particularly misunderstood Bismarck's constant supervision of them and efforts to keep them isolated. They felt themselves at the center of a conspiracy by the Chancellor to make them impotent. In fact, they were only a small element in his grand designs, only two of several potential leaders of an opposition. Even Queen Victoria thought that her daughter had reacted too strongly against the Chancellor's surveillance when she had asked her mother's permission to burn all her letters. "Every scrap that you have written—I have hoarded up, but the idea is dreadful to me that anyone should read them or meddle with them in the event of my death. Will you not burn all mine? I should feel so much relieved. . . . I am sure that keeping them is a bad plan."[32]

Queen Victoria had told her daughter to keep the correspondence. So survived perhaps the most valuable evidence of the power of royal kinship and diplomacy in the nineteenth century, which was dedicated to keeping the peace between England and Germany and in all of Europe. The apparent opponent of this policy, Bismarck, was now working for much the same end. After the nightmare of the coalition against Germany in 1875, he had realized that his country must not appear too powerful. He wished to preserve the status quo between England, Austria and Russia, while keeping France too isolated to attack Germany. The most likely conflict was between the British Empire and the Russian one, particularly on the Black Sea, where England used Turkey as a bastion to keep the Russians from the Mediterranean. Germany's interests were not to take the side of either Russia or England, but to act as the honest broker between them and keep them as friendly nations.[32]

Unfortunately for Bismarck's policy of holding the balance of power in Europe, the Tsar in 1877 was going to war against Turkey on behalf of the persecuted Serbs. The German Emperor wanted to support Russia, although Bismarck insisted on remaining neutral. This displeased the Emperor, who retaliated by making Bismarck keep General Albrecht von Stosch as head of the admiralty. He was close to the Crown Prince and seemed to Bismarck another rival as Chancellor. Bismarck threatened to resign if Stosch were not dismissed, but the Emperor insisted on retaining him and sent Bismarck away on a long leave of absence. But Bismarck still knew only too well how to get his way even with his opponents. He succeeded in priming the Crown Princess to write to her mother in defense of his emerging plans: England was to take Egypt from Turkey and leave Russia and Austria to pick up other choice pieces from the carcass of the Sick Man of Europe. Queen Victoria was outraged. She and Lord Beaconsfield were both fanatics about supporting Turkey and keeping the Russians from Constantinople. When she showed her Prime Minister the Crown Princess's letter, he declared that it must have been dictated by Bismarck.

So the Crown Princess's worst fear had been realized: Bismarck had been so clever that she was saying his words without knowing it. When her mother told her that England would do what it intended *without* Bismarck's permission, she knew she had been duped. When British warships were sent to the Bosporus, her old patriotism was rekindled. "*How* I do long for *one* good roar of the British Lion from the housetops," she wrote, "and for the *thunder* of a British broadside!"[34]

The thunder was not heard or needed. A combined threat from Austria and England was enough to halt the Russian armies just short of Constantinople. The peace imposed by the Treaty of San Stefano was made subject to a Congress of the great powers in Berlin, of which Bismarck was to be the arbiter. His policy and his country's armies had made Germany the center of European diplomacy. Now he could let other nations fight and call the end game.

❧

The long wait of the Crown Prince seemed to be over. On May 11, 1878 a plumber named Max Hödel came out from between two carts and fired two shots at the Emperor's open victoria carriage as it was passing down the Unter den Linden. The Emperor was with his daughter Louise, the Grand Duchess of Baden, who saw the would-be assassin; his complexion was sallow and gray, his expression was one of calm despair.[35] He had fired too high. The Emperor's *Jäger* jumped down from the box to pursue the man, while the carriage drove on. Hödel was captured and nobody was hurt—except for the socialists. He claimed to be one of them, and Bismarck introduced a bill to muzzle them and their newspapers. The National Liberals in the Reichstag feared that the new law might be used against them and opposed it, to Bismarck's fury.

There was less opposition to repression after June 2, the day Dr. Karl Nobiling, a socialist and journalist, fired a double-barreled shotgun at the Emperor's open carriage from the upper window of a Berlin house. Twenty-seven pellets lodged in the Emperor's arms, five in his neck, and six in his left cheek and brow. Two lead slugs also penetrated his jaw and wrist. An artery was nicked, and torrents of blood flowed over the upholstery of the carriage, which was driven at snail's pace back to the palace. There the old man insisted on walking inside unaided before fainting from loss of blood.

The Crown Prince and Princess were on a visit to England. There had been a disaster in the Channel on the day before, when the German flagship *König Wilhelm* had rammed and sunk the ironclad *Grosser Kurfürst* with the loss of the lives of 250 German sailors. The British navy had been ordered to give all assistance, and the Crown Prince had hurried to Dover to see what could be done. But the news of his father's wounding in Berlin sent the Crown Prince and his wife dashing back to Germany. Both thought that the old man of eighty-two would not recover from such serious injuries. Special trains brought them to Berlin in less than two days, and they hurried to the Emperor's palace which was crowded with generals and ministers and servants and attendants of all sorts. "Most uncomfortable," the Crown Princess thought. Everyone showed the utmost concern and horror and alarm. The Emperor himself seemed calm and far more reasonable than all the others, who appeared to have lost their heads.

He did seem to be on the point of death. He was without his usual false teeth, which changed him, the Crown Princess noted. His head was bandaged, his arms were bandaged, and he was unable to move at all. His face was swollen and he was lying on a horrible old bed with only relatives to nurse him. The Crown Princess soon changed that, bringing in a good English bed and arranging for proper medical care. "Poor dear—my heart felt I cannot say what—" she wrote "to see him a *venerable* man of 82 struck down by the hand of lawless violence if not murder, lying so patient and helpless in his bed—a most pitiable object!"

Politically, of course, all was in a great mess. The question was whether the Crown Prince would become the formal Regent during the Emperor's illness. Strong repressive measures would have to be taken and, since they were bound to be unpopular, the Crown Princess thought they should not be her husband's responsibility. Bismarck's mistakes had led to social strife; it was the Chancellor's duty to put things straight.[36]

A Regency Bill was brought to the Emperor to sign. Bismarck was by the bedside, also the Crown Prince and Princess. His son was only to represent him, the Emperor said; the government was to be as before. Bismarck was to have unchecked power to halt subversion and to run the imminent Congress of Berlin. The Crown Prince was to remain a ceremonial figurehead, until the day when the old Emperor might pass away.

At the first State Council, the Crown Prince had to watch, while Bismarck decided whether to dissolve the Reichstag, with its Liberal majority against repressive measures, or to proclaim martial law.[37] Anti-radical feeling was running high. New elections were likely to bring in a majority in the center and on the right, and if this happened, Bismarck could secure the passage of an "Exceptional Measure" giving the state the power to proceed against any subversives or troublemakers in society. It put a big stick in the hand of the Chancellor, with his elaborate system of spying and denunciation. He could threaten his enemies legally whenever they dared to show their heads.

The Crown Prince could do nothing about Bismarck's swing back to the right. He had only the responsibility and agony of deciding on the execution of Hödel, who probably was mentally defective. For weeks he would not sign the death warrant, but finally did so because of the need to deter future assassins. The Emperor thanked his son for sparing him the ordeal of taking another man's life. The Crown Prince had done right and God was pleased with him. Hödel himself refused all religious help and shouted "Bravo for the Commune!" before his head was struck off.[38]

Like Cohen-Blind before him, Dr. Nobiling died of self-inflicted wounds before he could stand trial. He was reported as having said that his reasons for trying to kill the Emperor were political and that he had had accomplices. This alleged evidence was enough to secure public support for the Exceptional Measure. Nobiling's bloody work was also a piece of good luck, as Bismarck told Busch. If the pro-Russian Emperor had not been removed from the scene, Bismarck would not have had his way at the Congress of Berlin.[39]

As it was, Bismarck and Lord Beaconsfield got on splendidly. They seemed to recognize in each other a cunning and a candor as well as a certain reckless, romantic imagination. Beaconsfield thought Bismarck behaved like a sweet-voiced ogre, while Bismarck loudly praised Beaconsfield for being so straightforward, and for never stopping at small things but going for the important things at once.[40] He rammed through the business in his normal hectoring way. The Russians were outsmarted and outgunned, but the German Emperor always blamed the Crown Prince for the Russian losses at the Congress. As Regent, his son should have stood up for them against Bismarck, who had declared that the eastern question was not worth the bones of a single Pomeranian grenadier. When the Crown Prince pointed out to his father that the Chancellor had not consulted him, the Emperor replied, "I was ill and not expected to recover."

Perhaps Bismarck had tried to please the next Emperor by favoring England's position at the Congress. He certainly told his intimates that he found it easier to deal with the Crown Prince and Princess than with the Emperor and Empress, who were becoming opinionated in their old age. While the Emperor liked the appearance of authority, the Crown Prince was modest and unassuming. He did not say, "I have won the battle, I have conducted the campaign." He said that his Chief of Staff had done it and deserved the rewards. The Crown Princess was also preferable to the Empress, because she was unaffected and sincere. Family considerations had once made her troublesome, but these were now less important.[41]

So Bismarck trimmed his sails while the aged Emperor was ill, trying to make his peace with his next master. But when the Emperor was driven back in triumph through the Brandenburg Gate at the end of the year, to take back the appearance of ruling from his son, it was the same performance as before. Incredibly, the peppering by lead slugs and pellets seemed to have improved the Emperor's health. His rheumatism and nervous attacks had gone, in acupuncture by attempted assassination. He looked as if he would live for ever. Dr. Nobiling, he often used to say, was the best physician he had ever had.

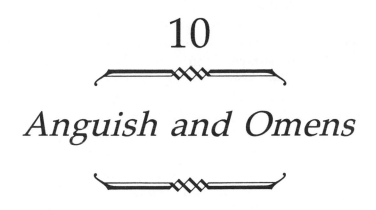

10

Anguish and Omens

DIPHTHERIA STALKED Germany. It struck in the garret and the palace, the back room and the nursery. In Hesse, Princess Alice watched three of her children and her husband, the new Grand Duke, stricken. Her daughter "May" died. When she told her sick son he burst into tears and, trying to comfort him, she kissed him. It was the kiss of death. She caught diphtheria herself and died on December 14, 1878, the anniversary of the death of her father the Prince Consort. The Crown Princess had been particularly close to Alice. "Our darling!" she wrote to Queen Victoria. "I can hardly bear to write her dear name: she was my particular sister, the nearest in age, the only one living in the same country with me! We had so many interests in common and all our children were so near of an age! . . . Her last letter to me, a little pencil note, which, alas, I did not keep, was a cry of anguish for her sweet little flower, so rudely torn from its stem. I never heard from her again."[1]

Three months later, her own little flower was torn from her. The ten-year-old Prince Waldemar also caught diphtheria.

His tonsils swelled to the size of a walnut, and he could hardly swallow or shut his mouth. In spite of her sister's death, the Crown Princess insisted on nursing her son. She kept him isolated and was sprayed with carbolic before she would see her other children. After four days of choking with a rattle in his throat, the boy's heart stopped beating. Waldemar was dead. His mother thought him the dearest and most promising of her boys. It tortured her to go from his room, where he was lying so silent and so still, and see his pets in the next room, all his birds and the fishes in his aquarium, his three dogs and his small crocodiles. His mother could not bear the sight.[2] The Crown Princess never recovered from the death of her youngest son. For months, she was in a state of shock and depression, and year after year, she would dwell on the memory of him. The pain and grief were like a hidden spring that would rise up and bubble with a force that would not be controlled. For twenty years she had always had a boy to put to bed. Now all that was over. The two elder boys had left home, and the two beloved younger ones were gone forever. The thought was terribly bitter.[3]

At the funeral, the Crown Prince threw himself on the little coffin, lined with white satin and full of camelias and white roses. He had to take leave of his beloved son before he was laid to rest beside his dead brother Sigismund. It seemed a trial beyond endurance. The two elder sons had left home like their married sister, who was shortly expecting her first child. Only the three younger girls remained—and the ceremonial duties of acting as the Crown Prince.

In spite of the grief of the parents, the Emperor and the court did not wish to spare them from their official duties. After Alice's death, Queen Victoria had to intervene personally to make the Emperor allow her daughter to wear public mourning and miss most court occasions. "Everyone in colours!" the Crown Princess complained. "How could they think that I could go!!"[4] With Waldemar's death, the Crown Princess's withdrawal into black and isolation was greater than ever, a display of grief and solitude that antagonized the court. Although the Prussians had an official cult of the great dead, they found Queen Victoria and her daughter's private grief too excessive.

The Crown Prince took his son's burial so badly that he was ordered to take the cure at the baths in Kissingen. His wife was crippled with rheumatism and neuralgia, and only the birth of her first grandchild Feodore in May lightened her mood. With Charlotte's daughter the Crown Princess became a grandmother at the age of only thirty-nine. "I should have far preferred a Baby of my own to a grandchild," she confessed to her mother," but the happiness lasts too short a time. . . . A wee thing is really more to me than it is to many people."

The thought of her daughter giving birth made the Crown Princess reflect on how awful and terrifying the process was, which she had undergone so often. To her mother, she gave a revealing insight of the double vision which so many Victorian women used to view their physical functions. "This animal fabric of ours," she wrote, "has many aspects which are not so easy to get over—and which we should prefer to do without—still one must think as little as one *can* of this fact— and queer as nature is—look at that which is to be admired which ought to thrust the rest into the background!"[5]

Her dislike of Berlin society now became a revulsion, although she bore up courageously through the christening of her granddaughter and the Golden Wedding of the Emperor and the Empress, even wearing white for the occasions. But she found intolerable the spirit of espionage, malevolence, jealousy and malice that was rampant in the German capital. Home life as in her dear England was not known. It might be possible for her to have it if she were left independent, but habit and tradition ruled all at the retrogressive court where people were frigid and bitter, stiff and dull. Things and people grated harshly on her feelings. She felt herself in isolation.[6]

She must go away. She begged the Emperor to permit her and her husband and her three young daughters to spend the winter in Italy. It was a fight, but the imperial consent was reluctantly given. They went to Venice, then on to Pegli, an enchanting place with five old villas, magnolias, palms, cypresses, laurels, cedars, orange and lemon groves. The Crown Princess thought it a fairyland after the cold, dank north. She lingered there, missing the Berlin Season, letting her husband be called away on his official missions, but keeping to her daughters and her own warm ground.

The price she was paying was the surrender of her two elder sons to their professions and to other influences. Prince Henry had entered the navy at the age of ten, when a gunboat the *Blitz* had fired a salute of honor to mark the occasion. It was the famous gunboat which had fired a shot across the bows of a negligent British trawler in German waters, forcing her to dip her Red Ensign as the sign of respect. "Mark this gun well!" Hinzpeter had told his two pupils. "It is a historic gun, from which a historic shot was fired!"[7]

Prince William was not yet in a position to apply the historical lesson. He had always taken a great interest in the British navy, whenever he went to visit his grandmother in England: he had clambered all over Nelson's *Victory,* he had inspected ironclads at Plymouth, he had even gone undersea in a diving bell. At Osborne, he could stand by the old cannon in the model redoubt where his British uncles had played. He felt more loved by Queen Victoria than by his own mother and was treated as if he were her youngest boy, a relationship which he liked to feel never changed during his grandmother's life.[8]

The one particular favor he craved, the Queen wisely granted: the Order of the Garter. She had given the Order to his grandfather and father; now her grandson wanted the same mark of favor to prove he had come of age. The Crown Princess pointed out to her mother that the Emperors of Russia and Austria had sent him their highest decorations; could England do less? Queen Victoria consulted Lord Beaconsfield, who thought there was every reason for giving Prince William the Garter. The young Prince would never forget that he received from Her Majesty the most illustrious order in Christendom.[9]

The Crown Prince was almost as delighted as his son at the gift. It was not only that the Hohenzollerns cared so much for honors and orders; it would be a way of linking Prince William to England. The Emperor was also grateful, because it was the first time the Garter had been conferred on three generations of a royal house. And when Prince William paid his next summer visit to Osborne and declared on his return that he would like to live always "with Grandmamma of England," it seemed that Queen Victoria's personal diplomacy could do nothing better to help future relations.

Prince William also revered his grandfather the Emperor, who took special care to see him, often dining alone with his grandson on a small, shaky, green card table in the Unter den Linden palace. A bottle of champagne would be served and the Emperor would pour out one glass each, then cork it again for the morrow, marking the level on the label. He told stories of the glorious past, of the battles he had won, all the conquests and the marching. He impressed on Prince William's adolescent mind the grandeur and the power of the imperial position.

The Empress Augusta made her grandson literally her support, using his strong right arm as her crutch whenever she held her court. He learned to endure boredom and small talk during the interminable levées, standing stiffly, listening to her kind words to the endless queues of courtiers and diplomats.

Following his father's example, he had attended Bonn University for four terms, and had joined the same student corps, Borussia. But his studies were cut short, when his grandfather insisted that he return to serve with his regiment. War training was the first duty of a Prussian prince. He was happiest when with the Sixth Company of the First Regiment of

Footguards. His father had served in the Company and was proud of his son's quick grasp of military maneuvers.

At the time, the British military attaché in Berlin was the extraordinary Colonel Leopold Swaine, who had the great gift of inspiring trust in those he was sent to observe. All things to all soldiers, he was more specially the agent of certain English masters. Valued by both the German Emperor and Prince William because of his genuine admiration for their country's military machine, he reported specially and directly to Queen Victoria and to the Prince of Wales as well as to the War Office and to the Foreign Office. He particularly cultivated the difficult Prince William, who was becoming increasingly estranged from his parents. Swaine's private account to Lord Salisbury of the young man's character was most revealing, particularly on his love and hatred of England. It had been continually instilled into him from his early youth, Swaine reported, that everything English was better than everything else. This had an unfortunate effect not only upon the Prince himself, increasing his natural obstinacy on certain points, but also on his entourage, who became so embittered by this forcing of England upon them that their advice was not always the best or the wisest. Falling as it did on strong Prussian soil, it frequently made the Prince appear to be anti-English, which he was not.

The Prince was inherently German. He insisted on being considered a German prince before anything else, and looked upon the other countries only from the point of their usefulness to Germany. Brought up as he had been to regard the military strength of a country as the test by which everything else must be gauged, he saw England as comparatively weak and possessing a system of government which he could not understand.[10]

Swaine's character analysis was interesting because it accused the Crown Princess of forcing the example of her homeland down her eldest son's throat until he gagged on it. There was some truth in the charge, particularly after his marriage, when he became independent and could react more positively against his upbringing. Unexpectedly, he had fallen in love with an Augustenburg princess, the daughter of the ignored claimant to Schleswig and Holstein. Both of his parents approved of his choice of Augusta Victoria or "Dona," but they feared that the Emperor and Bismarck would never allow such a match. In point of fact, both William's grandfather and the Chancellor did not want to thwart the opinionated young man. They wanted to wean him from English influences and make him of their persuasion—something for which he was only too willing. "I shall with the greatest pleasure enter my beloved Regiment, *as the Emperor wishes it,"* he informed his mother as early as 1879, "because I long for the dear Potsdam and the life there is so pleasant and nice. And the stern and regular duty will do me good."[11]

Initially, the Crown Prince had to wait on Bismarck to make a personal plea for his eldest son's choice of a wife. "We all have to dance attendance whenever it pleases *him,"* the Crown Princess complained.[12] Bismarck was surprisingly willing to agree. He had humbled the Augustenburg family too much to see a threat in one of their princesses, especially as she seemed to have all the German female domestic virtues. The Berlin people might not consider her grand enough, the Crown Princess thought, but "they dislike everything *foreign* SO much, that I fancy they will be better pleased with a Princess bred and born and educated in Germany—and more spite, ill will, backbiting and criticism of the unkindest sort, she never can have to endure—than I have gone through for twenty-two years."[13]

In fact, Bismarck intended to use Prince William as a counterweight to his father. He and his wife even came to the engagement party, which surprised the Crown Princess. It was something that the Chancellor never did. She did not yet see Bismarck's policy of turning her son against his parents. It was easy enough, for William was opposing them more and more. "Willy is *chauvinistic* and *ultra* Prussian to a degree and with a violence which is often very painful to me. . . . Prussian Princes have a certain *genre* and it runs in the blood! With my children I often feel like a hen—that has hatched Ducklings."[14]

Prince William's marriage was treated with great importance by Queen Victoria. The Prince of Wales and his brother, the Duke of Edinburgh, were sent along with a supreme courtier, Lord Torrington, who admired the magnificence of the troops, so fine and healthy and strong in contrast to the reformed British army of boys. While the bride was driven like Cinderella in a glass coach pulled by eight white horses, Prince William commanded the Guard of Honor in front of the royal palace, lit with thousands of large wax candles. Nobody was allowed to sit down for five hours, and many of the ladies fainted, but all the same, Lord Torrington found it a fairy scene and a miracle of complicated splendor.[15] Not so the Crown Princess, who hated to stand on ceremony; to her, it was exhausting, suffocating and interminable as all the Berlin state weddings were. She had her diadem on for seven-and-a-half hours, and the standing was so bad that her legs felt as if they were going to come off.[16]

Prince William's marriage came at a time when the Crown Prince again seemed to be attracting an opposition party around him. Bismarck had given up his alliance in the Reichstag with the National Liberals, working with a loose coalition of the center and the right, sometimes supported by the few socialists. But in the elections of 1881, the Liberals won enough seats to threaten Bismarck's majority against them. The Crown Princess thought he did not care one bit. She wondered why he did not say straight out, "As long as I live—both the Constitution and the Crown are suspended."[17]

Bismarck's reaction to the Liberals' victory was to become more reactionary. His authority depended on pulling the teeth of an opposition. Early the following year, the Emperor issued an imperial rescript countersigned by Bismarck, that stressed his royal authority. The English press throughout the rescript resembled one of King Charles I's messages to the Long Parliament.[18] The Crown Prince had not been consulted and privately disapproved, but his public silence was considered a kind of acquiescence. His two sons thought that Bismarck's policies were sublime. People were saying that the Crown Prince would approve of anything the government did were it not for his English wife. She felt quite worn out. "If you hear I have the typhus or am off my head," she told her mother, "*pray* do *not* be astonished."[19]

Things were not as bad as the Crown Princess made out. The Liberals had been successful, and the extreme age of the Emperor made them look to the Crown Prince as the guarantor of the fall of Bismarck. Their leader, Eugen Richter, was invited by the Crown Prince to a secret consultation. The go-between was young Stockmar's successor, Karl von Normann, who was now the Prince's court marshal, a trusted and devoted aide who arranged the meeting in his rooms beside the Neue Palais. One of Bismarck's spies informed the Chancellor who told the Emperor that there was a conspiracy by the opposition, and Normann was summarily banished to the tiny duchy of Oldenburg. As he left, the Crown Prince embraced him and said: "When I am Emperor, you will be the first whom I will recall."

The new court marshal was one of Bismarck's creatures, the intriguing Count Radolinski. He was not suspected of treachery by the Crown Prince or his wife, although his orders were to report back on everything to Bismarck and to get rid of the faithful Count Seckendorff, who was still running the household. Radolinski failed to incriminate Seckendorff, but his brother was dismissed by the enraged Bismarck after twenty years' service in the Foreign Office. The Crown Princess's friend Lady Ponsonby told Queen Victoria that she would not be able to believe all the espionage and intrigue in Germany. Radolinski had been brought in because Bismarck wanted a man of his own near the Crown Princess in order to control the Crown Prince when he became Emperor. The new court marshal's mission was to betray her and to detach her family from her.[20]

≈

Until his son's marriage, the Crown Prince had been sent on ceremonial missions abroad: to Italy to attend the funeral of King Victor Emmanuel, to Russia for two imperial funerals. The Tsarina Marie had died in 1880, and the Crown Prince was sent to St. Petersburg to represent his father, the Tsar's uncle. A gale was blowing, the Neva rising, and the bridge over the rushing river so buffeted that it nearly collapsed as the funeral procession was passing over it. Almost immediately, and most indecently, the Tsar married his mistress, a Russian countess kept by him in the Winter Palace and the mother of four of his children. He did not live long to enjoy her. He was assassinated with a bomb the following March. Bismarck seemed to take pleasure in sending the Crown Prince again into the place of danger; the heir to the throne received threatening letters in Berlin before he left. In fact, police protection was so stringent in St. Petersburg that the funeral went off without incident. "I felt sure it would," the Crown Princess told her mother, "as there could be no object in attempting the life of so many Foreigners at once."[21]

Murder by unknown hands remained the terror of all royalty. Voltaire had called Russia a despotism tempered by assassination, which it was. The Crown Prince returned from St. Petersburg convinced that all sovereigns were to be killed by nihilists and socialists. The Crown Princess did not agree. She hoped that the days of Guy Fawkes and the Gunpowder Plot were things of the past, which they were not in Europe. She even read the whole of Karl Marx's *Das Kapital* and was so interested that she asked a Member of Parliament in London to send her a report on the author. Marx spoke of her and the Crown Prince with due respect and propriety. It would not be Marx, the report concluded, who would turn the world upside down.[22]

The Crown Princess distrusted communists and socialists, but because of her liberal faith she could not accept persecution of them. Another rift between her and the government was her refusal to accept a new wave of anti-Semitism and social discrimination. "In the royal family we stand quite alone with our opinion," she informed Queen Victoria, "and in what is called society."[23] The Crown Prince went out of his way to condemn any discrimination when speaking to Baron Magnus, the president of the Jewish community of Berlin. He knowingly made his opposition to the government clearer and his isolation greater.

Bismarck noted the heir apparent's flickers of rebellion and promoted the son in his place. Prince William was shown confidential Foreign Office dispatches and was given hours of briefing in diplomacy by the Chancellor himself. When the Crown Prince wrote to protest that it was unsafe to give an indiscreet young man secret information, Bismarck threw the letter on the fire and did not reply. By stressing his version of foreign policy to Prince William, Bismarck widened the split between the son and his pro-English parents. He even went so far as to accept a campaign over colonies in order to have beginning counters with England in his efforts to hold the balance of power in Europe. Prince William always wanted to emulate England more than he would admit. He desired a large German navy and possessions overseas. "The sole aim of German colonial policy," Bismarck told the new Tsar, "was to drive a wedge between the Crown Prince and England."[24] It would also drive a wedge between Prince William and his parents. Bismarck's sudden claims to Southwest Africa and the Cameroons, Togoland and Fiji and New Guinea were not a matter of the flag following trade; they were domestic sugar plums for Prince William and the German people. Diplomatically, the policy was of small value. As Bismarck said, his map of Africa lay in Europe. He needed to revive the League of the Three Emperors and protect Germany's eastern and southern fronts. The push overseas was only a matter

of forcing the colonial powers, England and France, to deal
with him. If he needed help in Europe, he could always give
either of them concessions abroad. Yet colonies implied con-
frontations. As the Crown Princess prophesied, "This colonial
sugar plum might easily turn into a bitter almond."[25]

After fulfilling delicate missions to Madrid and to Rome,
the Crown Prince found himself abruptly replaced as Prussia's
royal representative abroad. Bismarck knew that Prince William was a devoted supporter of the revived League of the
Three Emperors, but the Crown Prince was not in favor of
such a reactionary alliance. So, in 1884, Prince William was
ordered to St. Petersburg instead of his father to attend the
wedding of the Tsar's brother to Princess Elizabeth of Hesse.
The Crown Prince was completely dumbfounded at being replaced; he had never dreamed of such a thing.

In St. Petersburg, Prince William believed that he had
struck up a friendship with Tsar Alexander III. He made no
bones about his belief that a foreign conspiracy was being
carried on by his mother and his British relatives. "On no
account trust my English uncles," he wrote to the Tsar. "Do
not be alarmed by anything you may hear from my father.
You know him, he loves being contrary and is under my mother's thumb, and she, in turn, is guided by the Queen of England, and makes him see everything through English eyes. I
assure you, the Emperor, Prince Bismarck and I are of one
mind, and I shall not cease to regard it as my highest duty
to consolidate and support the Three Emperors' alliance."[26]

So Prince William betrayed his parents and accused them
of being foreign agents. It was an extraordinary situation:
grandfather, grandson and Chancellor were making pariahs
of the heir to the throne and his foreign-born wife. As if
performing a state duty, Prince William and his wife Dona
were producing son after son to secure the succession to the
throne. They quite ignored and forgot their parents' existence,
the Crown Princess complained; they always asked the Emperor and Empress about everything and took all their orders

directly from them. She was not even informed of what they meant to do. "Willy goes daily to his Grandpapa for all he wants and cuts his Papa—of course it is a great deal more convenient for them, but for *us* it is most painful and disagreeable."[27]

Inexorably, the rift between the Crown Princess and her eldest son was becoming an abyss of misunderstanding. They were so similar that they could not recognize themselves in each other. As a young diplomat James Rennell Rodd noted on his frequent summer visits to the Neue Palais, Prince William and his mother were temperamentally too alike ever to get on. Both were idealistic, indiscreet, impetuous and impatient of opposition, and both had the unconscious habit of royalty, the prerogative of always being right.[28]

From their own points of view, both were right over the next falling out. The Crown Princess's daughter Victoria, or "Moretta," fell in love with "Sandro," Prince Alexander of Battenberg, who had accepted the throne of Bulgaria and was seeking to make his new country independent from the Russians. This royal mismatch might become a time-bomb given the explosive situation in the Balkans and in the complex diplomacy among Germany, Russia and England. To make matters worse, Queen Victoria's youngest daughter, Beatrice, was becoming engaged to Sandro's younger brother "Liko," Prince Henry of Battenberg. The Queen of England and the Crown Princess seemed determined to cause international complications by marrying their daughters to minor German princelings who might be charming and good-looking but were unsuitable by rank and politics. Prince William was outraged, and even the Crown Prince annoyed. Nothing angered the Hohenzollerns more than Queen Victoria's preference for a love match to any arranged mingling of the correct blood royal.

Bismarck might discount the importance of royal marriages in his brand new world of great-power diplomacy, but he knew their relevance. The old Tsar had been pro-German because he was the nephew of the German Emperor. Alexander III was anti-German because of his Danish wife. Marriages implied alliances, and the Chancellor could not accept that there were no political considerations behind the two love matches with the Battenberg brothers. Sandro, Prince of Bulgaria, seemed to Bismarck an English tool against Russian expansion. His engagement to Queen Victoria's granddaughter, a princess of the German imperial family, was killing two birds with one precious stone. It gave the impression of Anglo-German support against the Tsar.

"The old Queen is fond of matchmaking, like all old women," Bismarck said to Busch, ". . . but obviously her main objects are political—a permanent estrangement between ourselves and Russia."[29] What he did not know was that the Crown Princess had already brought up diplomatic reasons to make her mother back Moretta's choice of a husband. Queen Victoria was set on the Russians never reaching Constantinople; what could be better than Anglo-German backing of a strong buffer state on the border zone of Turkey?[30]

Bismarck's political objections to the marriage were cogent. It might break up the League of the Three Emperors. The German Emperor recognized this and vetoed the match, which was very unpleasant for the Crown Princess,[31] but the veto and the unpleasantness would only last as long as the Emperor lasted. The Crown Prince might be against the marriage because he was touchy on the subject of inferior Battenberg breeding, but if he assumed the crown he would not withstand the pressure of his wife and her mother. In family matters, Bismarck knew that Queen Victoria was not accustomed to contradiction. She would bring with her, he joked, the parson in her traveling bag and the bridegroom in her trunk, and the marriage would come off at once.[32]

Bismarck used the Sandro affair to set Prince William even more against his English mother. William spoke so badly of his younger sister's suitor that his father found it difficult to keep his temper. His mother spent sleepless nights worrying over the rift in the family. Worse than angering his parents by his insolence, William had taken to staying away altogether.

"How can you justify your behavior toward us?" the Crown Prince asked his son.

"I thought I would not be welcome," William replied, "because you, dear father, have for a long time shown me quite openly that you cannot bear me."[33]

His father and mother might adopt a policy of perfect passive patience, but Queen Victoria would not be thwarted by a grandson or allow a child to insult his royal mother. She told her daughter that William was a very foolish, undutiful and unfeeling boy who needed a good "skelping" as the Scots would say and, seriously, a good setting down.[34] She offended him by refusing to see him when he wanted to come to England in 1885. Unable to understand the effect of his candor and rudeness on other people, he could not fathom the reason for his rejection by his favorite grandmother. "He never sees his own behavior in the right light," his mother wrote of him, "and fancies his opinion quite infallible—and that his conduct is always perfect—and cannot stand the smallest rebuke—though he criticizes and abuses his elders and his relations, as though he knew far better than they did."[35]

The Tsar had already been moving against the Prince of Bulgaria without prompting from Germany. Russian connivance led to an invasion by the Serbian army but, unexpectedly, Sandro led the Bulgarians to victory at Slivnitza, and only an Austrian threat to intervene stopped him from annihilating the Serbian army. A pro-Russian faction in Sofia, however, kidnapped him in a coup and sent him into exile up the Danube. He was forced to abdicate, returned briefly to take back power, then was finally made to abdicate once more. Eventually, another ruler was chosen for Bulgaria, the Coburg Prince Ferdinand, who now seemed an enemy of his own relations, putting a foreign throne before his own family.

Queen Victoria sent off dozens of letters to her Foreign Secretary demanding support for Sandro in Bulgaria, but the British had no warships in the Black Sea and no troops nearby. They could not repeat their bluff at the Congress of Berlin, which had originally made Sandro the prince of an independent Bulgaria. Morier, now Ambassador at St. Petersburg, was trying to maintain some British influence there and threw Sandro's cause to the wolves, incurring Queen Victoria's displeasure. On the Queen's instructions, he received a severe reprimand from the Foreign Office, but he was not replaced. The Crown Princess thought her mother very kind to their fat friend.[36]

Bismarck continued stalking the Prince of Bulgaria even in exile, telling the Emperor that the young Prince wanted to become leader of the opposition in Germany as a tool of English influence. He persecuted Sandro as he had persecuted Harry von Arnim, and made the Emperor refuse him a place at court or a commission in the German army. Hounded and broken and penniless, Sandro retired to Darmstadt. Despairing of marrying Moretta over the Emperor's veto, he began a liaison with a blonde Austrian singer called Johanna Loisinger.

Bismarck was so successful at plaguing those who crossed him that the Crown Princess became increasingly afraid of him. Although she would not give up the idea of her Moretta marrying Sandro, she had to stay silent because of the Emperor's implacable opposition to the match. Her unwavering support of Sandro and her constant use of royal messengers and private ciphers convinced Bismarck that she was still her mother's agent in Germany. Now she was betrayed by an old member of the Coburg group, who had wisely backed Prussia in its war against Austria. Duke Ernest wrote an anonymous pamphlet, *Co-Regents and Foreign Influence in Germany*, that might have been dictated by Bismarck himself.

The Duke knew of the liberal political ideas once shared among his dead brother, Queen Victoria, the Crown Princess, the Kings of the Belgians and the Stockmars. He used his inside knowledge to confirm Bismarck's suspicion of a working partnership between Queen Victoria and her eldest daughter. In England they did not tolerate any foreign influence, Bismarck declared. Lord Palmerston had opposed and persecuted the Prince Consort for his alleged or real influence over the Queen. Germans were expected to submit to that sort of thing and regard it as a matter of course. "We are an inferior race," Bismarck said ironically, "ordained to serve them."[37]

Bismarck's hatred of English assumptions of superiority exaggerated his suspicions, but these had an element of truth. The Crown Princess remained half-English in Germany, half-German in England; divided between the two nations, she could seem disloyal to both of them. It was the snare in a successful royal marriage that had now lasted until its silver wedding—the snare that *The Times* had foreseen on the first news of the engagement. The Crown Princess was an educated and inquiring woman, who wanted to know what was happening in Europe, which was also her right and duty because she would soon be the German Empress. The result was that Queen Victoria asked every visiting English dignitary to call on the Crown Princess, brief her thoroughly and act as a personal courier for confidential messages between Berlin and Windsor Castle.

These constant and clandestine communications with England seemed proof to Bismarck of his worst fears about the Crown Princess, yet in her firm conviction that England and Germany must get on, she could see herself only as an agent of mutual understanding. Her royal duty was to bridge the gap between the two countries. She believed in a linked group of royalty and aristocrats still ruling Europe and preventing wars by their personal contacts.

❧

The aged Emperor was failing at last. As he approached his ninetieth birthday, he had to take morphine for kidney and bladder trouble. When he walked, he shuffled his feet so that people felt that the least crease in the carpet would trip him up and he might tumble at any moment.[38] His birthday celebrations in March 1887 were curtailed so as to spare him too much fatigue. All the same, he was flattered by all of Europe coming to honor him—perhaps for the last time. Every royal house sent a major prince or grand duke. Queen Victoria sent the Prince of Wales, who took the opportunity to play the peacemaker with Prince William. He suggested that the military-minded young man come to England in the summer to attend the army review and that there be an exchange of officers between the British and German armies—an idea that found favor with the old Emperor.

As the first Emperor was sinking, the Crown Prince fell ill. Just before the birthday celebrations, his throat swelled up, and he found it difficult to swallow and to speak. Cancer was a possibility; his life might be in question. He had waited too long. He might never be Emperor after all.

ABOVE: *Emperor William I of Germany,*
Crown Prince Frederick William, Prince William and his son,
Prince William. June 1882.

Victoria, Crown Princess of Germany,
January 18, 1883.
(Reichard and Lindner)

The Crown Prince of Germany with his horse in the year 1887.
(Loescher and Petsch)

The Crown Princess. 1876. (Von Angeli)

*Crown Prince Frederick William in white
military uniform, June 9, 1887.
(Ottomar Anschütz)*

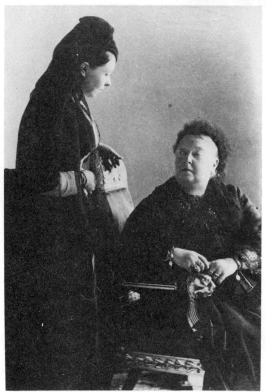

ABOVE: *Emperor Frederick III, 1888.*
(Byrne)

LEFT: *Empress Frederick of Germany*
with her mother, Queen Victoria,
February 1889. (Byrne)

The Empress Frederick and Bismarck, c. the 1890s.

Group assembled at Coburg for the wedding of Princess Victoria Melita of Saxe-Coburg-Gotha and the Grand Duke of Hesse. 1894. Queen Victoria is seated in center of front row, Victoria, Empress Frederick of Germany is to the right of her mother, Emperor William II of Germany is on the left.

Schloss Friedrichshof: the South Front, 1895.   (H. Rückwardt)

Queen Victoria. 1899.   (Von Angeli)

Empress Frederick of Germany, 1900.
(T. H. Voigt)

11

At the Throat

"HOARSENESS, GENTLEMEN," the Crown Prince joked to a deputation from the Reichstag, "prevents me from singing to you."[1] All that winter of 1887 his throat had been irritated, and in early March his doctor, Wegner, called in a specialist, Professor Gerhardt, who discovered a nodule at the bottom of the left vocal cord. Instead of leaving it alone, the professor decided to remove it. Every day he tortured the Crown Prince, first with a snare, then with a ring knife, and finally with a red-hot electric wire to burn out the growth. The voice would return completely,[2] the Crown Princess told her mother on Gerhardt's authority.

It did not. The Crown Prince was often unable to complete a sentence. Another specialist was called in, Professor Ernest von Bergmann, a surgeon and a liberal supporter of the Crown Prince. The swelling on the vocal cord had not healed, and Bergmann thought that it was deeply rooted and should be surgically removed by splitting the larynx from the outside. The appalling diagnosis reached the ears of the Crown Princess. "I was more dead than alive with horror and distress when I heard this," she wrote to Queen Victoria. "The idea of a knife touching his dear throat is terrible to me." The Crown Prince was very depressed. He now often thought his father would survive him.[3]

When the news of the proposed surgery came to Bismarck, he was distressed and annoyed. He had not been informed officially of a dangerous operation on the heir to the throne, and he intended to stop it. Through the Emperor, a further consultation was ordered, this time with three more specialists. After a careful examination of the growth, four of the six doctors decided that they had detected cancer and that the diseased area should be cut out at once. Gerhardt and another doctor disagreed. They reported to Bismarck that the throat operation would be at the risk of the Crown Prince's life. Although Bergmann assured the Crown Prince that the operation was suitable for old people and children, he told Prince William privately that the Crown Prince would lose his voice altogether and might die.[4] Certainly, when Bergmann performed the same operation years later to prove to medical students that he could have saved the Crown Prince, his patient died under the knife.[5]

At this point, Bismarck intervened again and forbade the operation without the consent of the Crown Prince and the Emperor. According to Rennell Rodd, he visited the British Embassy to determine the best available throat specialist for a further opinion. The choice lay among three authorities, one French, one Austrian and one English. Political considerations favored the London specialist, Morell Mackenzie, who spoke fluent German, was known in Germany from his textbook on throat diseases, and was socially prominent at home. To Bismarck and to the six German doctors, he seemed the best choice as an outside adviser, and they told the Crown Prince of their wish to bring in the London man.

Up to this point, the Crown Princess had played no part in selecting a doctor for her husband. She knew perfectly well of the risk in asking for an English consultant. If the Crown Prince were to become more ill or to die under treatment, the alien doctor would be held responsible and, she told her mother, many would blame her for suggesting a foreigner. If Queen Victoria would have the goodness to help them out of the difficulty and say that she was sending Mackenzie to report to her on the state of the patient's throat, then no one could take offense.[6]

Later, the Crown Princess was widely blamed for sending for Morell Mackenzie. The evidence is that she did not even know his name until he was recommended by the German specialists and the British Embassy, although her preference for a London doctor was undoubted. The German doctors' preference for a foreigner who would have to take all the blame if the Crown Prince were to die under the knife was equally clear. Bismarck's wish to have Mackenzie was not prompted by a desire to implicate the Crown Princess in yet another English conspiracy. He appears to have had second thoughts about the young Prince William succeeding his grandfather as Emperor, for the ill and weak Crown Prince would more surely depend on the Chancellor than would his ambitious and vainglorious heir.

The Crown Princess painstakingly prepared two rooms in the Neue Palais for the operation. A hard sofa was scrubbed down with carbolic acid for the patient, who was to be given chloroform. When Mackenzie arrived on the eve of the operation, his coolness and deftness reassured the Crown Princess. Diplomatically, he postponed making any decision, using forceps to remove a fragment of the growth for microscopic examination by a leading German expert, Dr. Virchow. Bismarck came himself to visit the Crown Princess and was surprisingly concerned. He said his wife advised her not to allow such an operation. The Crown Princess replied that she had nothing

to allow; she was forced to accept what the responsible authorities decided was best.[7]

Queen Victoria was not as confident about Morell Mackenzie as her daughter was. Her own doctor reported to her that
Mackenzie was very clever in dealing with throats, but that
he was greedy about money and was greatly disliked for that
reason.[8] Still, money was not the object when the Crown
Prince's life was in question. Virchow's analysis showed no
signs of cancerous tissue, but he wanted to examine a larger
fragment from the affected area. In removing that, Morell
Mackenzie apparently injured the Crown Prince's other vocal
cord, or so Gerhardt alleged. Mackenzie was even suspected
of deliberately cutting out tissue from the healthy vocal cord
for Virchow's microscope, which again showed no evidence
of cancer. The war between the rival doctors had begun.

The Crown Princess began to hope. She listened to Mackenzie, who promised that he would cure the Crown Prince
without an operation if the patient would come to England.
With her instinctive trust for the kind of doctors who had
treated her childhood ailments in her homeland, the Crown
Princess was only too ready to listen to somebody telling her
what she wanted to hear. The German doctors were still stressing the need for an immediate operation to remove the probably cancerous growth. "The Doctors will not allow that Dr.
Mackenzie's view is right and theirs is wrong," the Crown
Princess wrote to her mother. "But I am *convinced* of it! Fritz
ought to be under his care, and we must see *how*."[9]

Even the temporizing Dr. Gerhardt thought Mackenzie too
sanguine. The Crown Prince's friends saw in the London expert a shrewd self-advertiser who wanted the Crown Prince
as an exclusive patient. There was a struggle all along the
line about the treatment of the illness, with the Crown Princess
hoping against hope in Mackenzie's optimism, and the German
specialists priming Prince William's belief that the postponement of a throat operation was his father's death warrant.

Bismarck sat on the sidelines, wanting to preserve the Crown Prince's life for as long as possible.

A quarrel flared up as to who was to go to Queen Victoria's Jubilee. While his father was scheduled to have the operation, Prince William had assumed that he should represent the German imperial family for the occasion. He had bombarded Queen Victoria with telegrams, telling her that at the Emperor's command, he was coming in his father's place. But with the prospect of Mackenzie's treatment in England, the Crown Prince more than ever wanted to represent his country at his mother-in-law's great Jubilee. She had bidden him to come and ride in front of her coach as he had done before in the state ceremonies after the Prince Consort's death. "You both must not be absent on this day which will move me deeply," she wrote to her daughter. "You must take care of yourself, so as to be well for it. It would not be wise to speak much, but the procession to Westminster Abbey will not be too bad."[10]

The Crown Princess replied that her husband's one hope was to attend the Jubilee. The Emperor had given his consent, if the German doctors would approve. If he had been a few years younger, he would have come himself. As it was, the Crown Prince was terribly annoyed at William's coming forward so eagerly to take his place. Because of the Emperor's age people did not like the Crown Prince's leaving the country, yet he clearly ought to go to England to be cured by the only man who had offered him any hope.[11]

Bergmann himself approached the Emperor and tried to get the old monarch to stop his son from leaving for England in June, but the Emperor told him that the Crown Prince was not a child and should go for treatment where he thought best. When another analysis by Virchow found no cancerous tissue in two more fragments of the growth, the Emperor allowed the visit to England to proceed. Even the German specialists suspended their judgment. They were, the Crown

Princess thought, like the apostle Doubting Thomas and would at last believe that the growth was harmless.[12]

森

Although she appeared optimistic, the Crown Princess was terrified that her husband might die. With his death, she would have no protection. If she were widowed, his father or his eldest son might demand the right to go through his papers, most of them confidential and many showing his dealings with the liberal opposition in Germany and with Queen Victoria. Already, he and the Crown Princess had begun to destroy their papers, burning them with their own hands, and the trip to England was a heaven-sent opportunity to store the more compromising ones in a secure place. She turned to her mother for help. Under the present circumstances and for the moment, her daughter wanted to bring over all the private papers to England; could they be locked up in the iron room leading from the Prince Consort's library at Buckingham Palace? "We should feel much happier," the Crown Princess wrote. "I can explain more when we meet."[13]

Surveillance on the journey to England was being increased. Count Radolinski was one of many reporting back all the time to Bismarck, and to the supporters of Prince William who hoped that the Crown Prince might die before reaching the throne. At Balmoral, Radolinski arranged a quarrel with Count Seckendorff, the Crown Princess's most trusted servant, in a deliberate effort to get rid of him. But the Crown Princess countered Radolinski, defending her man, although she could not stop the insane endeavors to destroy Seckendorff. She was powerless to dismiss Radolinski, even though she knew he was a tool of Bismarck's intrigues.

Should the Crown Prince die, there was worse for her to fear. Her persistence in the Sandro affair had turned the Empress Augusta against her and her daughter Princess Victoria. The Empress despised the Battenberg family, and wanted the Emperor completely to disinherit the Crown Princess and her daughter if they disobeyed imperial orders and the Battenberg marriage took place. Bismarck had to plead with the Emperor not to give offense to his son by changing his will, but the threat remained. It was a question of whether the father or the son would die first, for the Crown Prince had little to leave to his wife if he did not inherit his father's private fortune.

The Crown Princess feared the worst, so she was forced to bring up a delicate matter. When her father the Prince Consort had died, she had begged Queen Victoria to exclude her from his legacy because so many of her sisters were still unmarried. Now she had to think of being left with an unmarried and disinherited daughter on her hands. "Perhaps you could find a small portion for *me*," she asked Queen Victoria, "which would go to that child." It was particularly important because her eldest son William was dead set against the Battenberg marriage. The Crown Prince feared that, if he died, his son would not deal kindly with his mother and Moretta.[14] Queen Victoria rallied to her daughter's support. There was a small amount of money which would go to the Crown Princess and Moretta if the Crown Prince died, or if they were cut out of the Emperor's will, or maltreated by Prince William for their disobedience. To the Crown Princess, the situation seemed intolerably like the Middle Ages, but she was still determined that the deposed Prince of Bulgaria would marry her daughter, even if a fortune were lost because of it.

The peace of Europe, however, meant more than a royal wedding. Bismarck took another step to block the marriage and render Sandro's return to the Bulgarian throne impossible. A Reinsurance Treaty was signed with Russia, in which Germany accepted that Bulgaria and its prince should be completely within the Tsar's sphere of influence. Moreover, Germany would not interfere if the Tsar wanted to take Constantinople. From Bismarck's point of view, he had neutralized Germany's eastern flank against attack leaving only the possibility of a French war of revenge in the west.

So, during the Crown Princess's absence, Bismarck had driven the final nail into the coffin of her prospective son-in-law's hopes of being recalled to his Balkan throne. The Chancellor was determined to defeat her and Queen Victoria in their championship of the Battenbergs. Even if the Crown Prince lived to be Emperor, Bismarck threatened to resign if the Battenberg marriage ever took place. A European war might threaten, if Germany seemed to be joining England in a Balkan conspiracy against Russia.

⚜

Riding a white charger in the Jubilee procession, the Crown Prince looked like a specter at this feast of empire. He wore the white uniform of the Pomeranian Cuirassiers, his helmet with its eagle crest and his silvered breastplate glittered in the sun, setting off the sash of the Order of the Garter and the sky-blue of his marshal's baton. Bearded and erect, silent and drawn, he was the white knight of his own glory, riding out in honor of the fifty years' reign of the Queen of England. Around him on their mounts were the princes of Europe and the world, the Hussars and the Horse Guards, all escorting the open gilt landau where Queen Victoria sat under her white bonnet spangled with diamonds, accompanied by the Princess of Wales and the Crown Princess. After the service of celebration in Westminster Abbey, the Queen kissed the Crown Prince on the cheek and then embraced him again on her way from the coronation chair, as if she knew this was the last time she might see him well.

He went nearly every day to visit Mackenzie in Harley Street. The swelling in the throat diminished and, at the end of June, Mackenzie succeeded in snipping off with his forceps the last of the growth on the vocal cord. Virchow's analysis of the tissue showed that it was a hard, compressed, warty growth, which showed no sign of spreading. Mackenzie seemed to have completed the cure that he had promised. The Crown Prince set off to Balmoral with the Crown Princess to recuperate. With them was a young doctor from the Throat Hospital, Mark Hovell, who was on a watching brief but only to oversee the Crown Prince's recovery. The Prince was able to speak in his natural voice again, to the delight of Queen Victoria who knighted Mackenzie for his skill and service.

Although there was strong pressure to return to Berlin, the Crown Princess insisted that her husband complete his cure in the pinewoods of the Tyrol. There, at Tolbach, he caught a severe cold and his larynx again became inflamed. Mackenzie was summoned to Tolbach and was dissatisfied at the state of his patient, particularly as he had assured the Crown Princess in August that everything was entirely favorable and that a complete cure was only a question of time.[15] He recommended Italy as the best place to recover, so the royal couple moved through Venice and the flowering gardens of Baveno on to the Villa Zirio at San Remo on the Italian Riviera. Although the powers in Berlin kept on demanding the return of the Crown Prince, his wife would not let him go.

She was right for his health, but wrong because of her standing in Germany. She was putting his life before her position. The fact was that if the Crown Prince were to die, the British Ambassador informed Queen Victoria and Lord Salisbury, it would hardly be possible for the Crown Princess to return to Germany, because she was keeping her husband abroad. The newspapers were demanding that German doctors be consulted, although Bismarck himself made no move as the ground was too delicate for him to tread.[16] The situation was made worse by the German Emperor catching a severe cold, which gave him abdominal pains and necessitated treatment by morphine. How could the heir to the throne remain absent when he might be Emperor the next day?

As the Crown Prince reached San Remo, his own condition deteriorated. Dr. Hovell examined his larynx and detected a new tumor below each vocal cord, and both tumors seemed to have a malignant appearance. Mackenzie was summoned by telegram and made another examination. At the end of it, the Crown Prince asked him whether it was cancer.

"I am sorry to say, sir," Mackenzie said, "it looks very much like it, but it is impossible to be certain."

The Crown Prince was silent for a moment, then managed a smile.

"I have lately been fearing something of this sort," he said before thanking Mackenzie for being so frank with him.[17]

Oddly enough, the relief of knowing the worst made the Crown Prince feel briefly cheerful and he was able to speak freely. It was the uncertainty that had made him melancholy. Recognizing the probability of cancer, Mackenzie immediately called in for consultation two specialists from Vienna and Berlin, Schrötter and Krause. Mackenzie saw the danger of being the only foreign doctor held responsible if the Crown Prince were to die, and he had to protect himself with other eminent opinions. Of course, had his treatment in England worked, he would have taken the sole credit.

Now that Mackenzie had confirmed the original diagnosis of the Berlin doctors, the storm broke on him and the Crown Princess. In Vienna, a professor told his audience that the Berlin doctors had always been right: an operation should have been carried out on the Crown Prince long ago; he should not have been sent traveling; cancer grew anywhere, whether in London, Berlin, Baveno or San Remo. Thirty newspaper reporters were dispatched by the European press to lie in wait for Mackenzie at the Hôtel Méditerranée. Daily reports on the state of the Crown Prince's throat publicized the doctors' disagreements.

Prince William now intervened. Acting on the old Emperor's orders, he arrived at San Remo with Dr. Moritz Schmidt, a bigoted laryngologist from Frankfurt. He called a medical conference in his hotel room and listened to the various opinions of the English and German doctors. Although there was general agreement that the throat was cancerous, no doctor wanted the total removal of the larynx unless the patient consented. Even if he survived such an operation, the Crown Prince would never speak again.

Prince William infuriated his mother, who was nursing her husband night and day, putting icebags on his throat and trying to keep him from despair. She was told to get the Crown Prince dressed, ready to return with him to Berlin for an operation. She refused, barring the way into the Crown Prince's bedroom and pitching into her son with considerable violence. He was present, however, when the doctors confirmed to the Crown Prince that he had cancer. Prince William wrote to his grandmother Queen Victoria:

> He received the news like a Hohenzollern and a soldier, upright, looking the doctors straight in the face. He knows that he is irretrievably lost and doomed! And yet he did not move an inch or a muscle. . . . It is quite horrible this confounded word "hopeless"! Poor Mama is doing wonders, she is perpetually on the verge of completely breaking down, and yet she keeps on that gigantic struggle against her feelings only not to distress Papa, and not to let the household see her grief. . . . I could not telegraph *en clair* as the French tap all telegrams going to England.[18]

Prince William did not mention his intervention to Queen Victoria, only his anxiety. His mother, however, complained bitterly about him to her mother, asserting that he had been misled. His advisers, including Dr. Schmidt, were telling him that the Crown Prince was so ill that he should not accept the succession if the Emperor died "but pass it on to William!!" That would be more than a death-blow to the Crown Princess. If her husband did not succeed to the throne, he would not be able to provide for her and her daughters, or be of any use to his country even for a limited time.[19]

Worse than Prince William's blundering was the behavior of Dr. Schmidt. Both he and Dr. Krause thought that the growth might be syphilitic in origin and advocated a course of potassium iodide. Schrötter considered this to be an old wives' tale.[20] Schmidt's nose for scandal was matched by his indiscretion. In a lecture at Frankfurt, he insinuated that the Crown Prince was suffering from something of contagious origins—an assertion which the French press immediately linked to false scandals about the Prussian Prince who had defeated them eighteen years before. In the Berlin *State Gazette*, Schmidt also accused the Crown Princess and Mackenzie of allowing the throat cancer to spread, when it could have been checked by an operation in the early stages. An anti-Semite, Schmidt even claimed that Morell Mackenzie's real name was Moritz Markovitz, which explained why he was such a bad and cunning doctor.

Dreadfully hurt by these insinuations against the Crown Prince and those devoted to his case, the Crown Princess continued her fight to keep him alive. "As to a certain plot," she informed her mother on November 29, "it has *not* succeeded. They have *not* been able to tear Fritz out of the hands of Sir Morell, Dr. Krause and Dr. Hovell—*nor* to drag Fritz to Berlin, put him under incompetent Doctors, and *force* the operation on him, which would either kill him or reduce him to the *most* AWFUL existence you can imagine. They *cannot* therefore force Fritz to resign as they would, nor get rid of me!"[21]

More than the Crown Prince's life was at stake. The peace of Europe depended on his throat. Lord Salisbury was extremely worried, especially because Prince William's attacks on Mackenzie and his mother's treatment of his father seemed to show great prejudices against England. Such prejudices would be fatal to the policy which both governments wanted the two countries to follow. Salisbury wrote to the British Ambassador in Berlin, "Between us and Prince William's perhaps unchecked rule there only stand now three lives." The Emperor was ninety and failing, Bismarck was seventy-three, and the Crown Prince was menaced by a disease that did not spare.[22] If William succeeded, he would probably support Russia against England on the Eastern Question and plunge Europe into war. Only Bismarck could stop him.

Yet all that winter, the Crown Prince hung on in San Remo—and the aged Emperor hung on in Berlin. Both seemed determined to see each other out. The Emperor was plagued by the intrigues of the reactionaries hoping to make him accept Prince William as his immediate successor, but he would not put aside the rights of his son, however much the courtiers claimed a spurious ancient law that no Hohenzollern could succeed who was not of sound body. The Crown Prince and Princess were also beset by spying and intrigue in their villa, packed with doctors and informants. When Queen Victoria sent out the trusted Lady Ponsonby to report back to her, she was told that no letters could be transmitted without stringent checks to see that no one had tampered with them.[23]

Queen Victoria herself communicated with the Crown Prince and her daughter by cipher telegram. Only her son-in-law and his wife knew the code numbers, and they personally decoded the messages and replied by the same cipher, reporting daily on the state of the Crown Prince's throat. One important paper had to be copied out by the Crown Princess herself before it was returned to Queen Victoria by a royal messenger. Nobody could be completely trusted in the whole household. "I *can not now* get rid of people, who cabal and intrigue against me," the Crown Princess wrote to her mother, "but when I have the power and liberty to do so, it *must* be done. . . . At Potsdam and Berlin it will be FIFTY times worse!!"[24]

However, the illness of the Crown Prince was a matter of desperate concern. The future of Germany and of Bismarck depended on whether the heir to the throne lived a little longer. Not everybody was a spy in the household, only those who considered it patriotic to resist the English influence and the forced optimism of the Crown Princess and Mackenzie. They looked incredulous if any hopeful sentence was uttered; they were in touch with those in Berlin who seemed determined to put everything the Crown Princess did or said in a bad light. They made no secret of the fact that, in their eyes, patriotism consisted of devotion first to Germany, next to the Emperor and thirdly to Bismarck, to whom they sent every detail and gossip often consisting of pure invention.[25]

The Crown Princess may have hoped to get rid of the disloyal members of her household but she could not get rid of the reporters swarming outside the Villa Zirio. The indiscretions of the newspapermen drove her mad. "We cannot *move* or sneeze without telegrams being sent *right* and left," she complained. "It is really TOO *odious,* complicates our existence and makes so much mischief, creates such confusion. They have printed two harmless letters of a perfectly *private* nature Fritz and I wrote a little while ago, and now they begin to comment on them!"[26]

The Crown Princess continued to sort through her husband's essential papers. She wanted them stored in a safe place and preserved from prying eyes. She meant to keep everything that demonstrated his past importance. The three volumes of the Crown Prince's *War Diary* which showed how much Bismarck had to depend on his support to make his father Emperor in 1871, were smuggled out by Dr. Hovell. In spite of orders from Berlin for police and customs officials to intercept him, he reached the British Embassy in Berlin, and the volumes were sent to Queen Victoria by royal messenger. The escapade confirmed Bismarck's opinion that the English doctors around the Crown Prince were also British agents.

This was an excess of caution on the part of the Crown Princess; nothing in the *War Diary* was incriminating, only unflattering to Bismarck's claim that he had been the sole creator of the German Empire. Yet she was right to be afraid that, if her husband were to die, she would be under attack. She was being blamed for everything because of her supposed prejudices against all things German—particularly German medicine. Her elder children were her harshest and most outspoken critics; they believed that they had been deliberately alienated from good old Prussian values. Every discussion ended with their conclusion: "You are wrong—you must be wrong because you are English."[27]

꼬

"So they already look upon me as dead," the Crown Prince wrote bitterly in his diary.[28] His second son, Henry, brought a letter from his elder brother William, curtly stating that the Emperor had given him authority to sign state papers on his father's behalf if too ill to do so. The Crown Prince himself had not been consulted or informed, and Bismarck's letter to him arrived after his son's presumptuous message. In his reply to the Chancellor, the Crown Prince stood firm: he was in sound mind and in full possession of his physical strength, he wrote to Bismarck. "In view of the confidence I have in you, I beg you both urgently and frankly to have consideration for me in future, in spite of my absence, and to get in touch with me before taking any decisive steps."[29]

The weakening Crown Prince now relied on the Chancellor who had, after all, opposed the larynx operation. "It is better to fall into the hands of God than of men," Bismarck answered the Crown Prince. He personally would rather expose himself to the dangers of a disease than of surgery, and the six months since Ascension Day tended to prove him right. With God's help, the Crown Prince's strong constitution would withstand the march of the disease for a long time.[30]

So Bismarck seemed to take the side of the few who believed that the Crown Princess was preserving her husband's life by refusing the throat operation. He did not even support the old Emperor in wanting the Crown Prince recalled to Berlin. He had a much freer hand without the heir to the throne being there. His expressed wish to prolong the Crown Prince's life was genuine, for he could manage better under an Emperor Frederick than under his impetuous son.

On January 17, 1888, the Crown Prince had a violent fit of coughing and spat out a large fragment of his larynx. Virchow again found no evidence of cancer in the expelled tissue, and Mackenzie went so far as to tell the Crown Prince that the throat malady might only be perichondritis. But on February 8, the patient could hardly breathe. His windpipe was blocked. "Oh God!" he complained at last, "I can't bear it any longer." A tracheotomy was performed by Bergmann's assistant, Dr. Bramann, who inserted a metal tube in the Crown Prince's throat below the blockage. This canula in the windpipe allowed the sick man to breathe more easily and his wife continued to hope for his life.

Soon after the successful operation, Bergmann arrived, and immediately picked a quarrel about the type of canula being used. He wanted large ones made of lead, while Mackenzie preferred smaller ones made by the local silversmith to his design. Bergmann's canulas irritated the Crown Prince's throat until he began bringing up bloody matter, which another analyst diagnosed as definitely cancerous. Mackenzie himself accepted this diagnosis, while Bergmann remarked that he was doing his best "to keep this abominable colleague within the bounds of medical decency."[31]

The Crown Prince could not speak for himself, and the Crown Princess had to struggle to keep her mouth shut. "Of course, I am tongue tied," she wrote to her mother. "I dare say nothing against the infallible wisdom of the German medical authorities, or I should be torn to pieces." For three weeks the Berlin doctors took charge of the treatment of the Crown Prince, and his condition deteriorated rapidly. He looked dreadfully ill and altered—thin, sunken, fallen away and pale.[32] The Crown Princess was sure that he would recover only if Mackenzie and Hovell were allowed to treat him again. Evidently, Bergmann had lost her and her husband's confidence and was soon forced to withdraw from the case, leaving it to the English doctors to do their best and worst.

Prince William came to San Remo again, with the Emperor's request that his son should come back to Berlin if humanly possible, because he felt his own death was near. Bergmann told Prince William that his father had only six months to live. The journey back to Berlin would be his last. The Crown Princess refused to move her husband form San Remo; at this moment it would be utter madness. So Prince William returned to Germany alone, to find that his old grandfather was passing away. On March 7, he sent a telegram that the Emperor was very weak after a bad night, and the Crown Prince should return.

The Prince of Wales was visiting San Remo. His mother wanted a direct report on the Crown Prince's condition from her eldest son, who could also bring back all the important information and messages from her daughter. He gave his sister the strength and comfort she needed to accept the return to Berlin. The Crown Prince must be present at his father's deathbed even if it proved to be his own. She sent a cipher telegram back to Queen Victoria that the decision had been taken.

ABSOLUTELY IMPOSSIBLE TO REFUSE TO GO TO BERLIN UNDER THE CIRCUMSTANCES, AT ANY RATE FOR A SHORT STAY. SIR MORELL THINKS THAT THERE IS A RISK BUT HE TRUSTS HE WILL BE ABLE TO AVERT REAL DANGER.

The old Emperor lay on his camp bed with his usual red neckband, shabby from his many campaigns, wound around his neck. His wife Augusta sat beside him, herself crippled with rheumatism and a blood disease, hardly able to move. She sent for a miniature of her husband's first love, Elise Radziwill, so that he could look on it as he died. It might have been an act of charity or of revenge. He could see the face of young beauty in his weak hand, and the face of aged majesty sitting in judgment over his deathbed.

Toward evening on March 8, before the return of his son, the Emperor passed away. As the bells rang his knell, a telegram was sent to San Remo, which arrived at eleven o'clock the next morning. The old Emperor was dead. The new Emperor was condemned to die. In spite of his weakness and the tube in his windpipe, he put on his general's uniform with the orange sash and star of the Black Eagle, and presented himself to his wife, now the German Empress, and his awed household. He took off the star of the order and pinned it to his wife's dress. She burst into sobs at last and clung to him; it was her medal for her devotion in keeping him alive, for her endurance and her concern. He scribbled a message on a pad for Mackenzie: "I thank you for having made me live long enough to be able to reward the valiant courage of my wife."

That was the truth of the matter. Medical knowledge was so limited in the nineteenth century that many, like Lord Byron, died of the doctors' attentions. Half the battle of keeping a patient alive was the bolstering of his confidence and morale, and throughout the new Emperor's long illness, his wife and Mackenzie had encouraged him day after day to get through another month. Her hope and care gave him the will to live on. Brave soldier that he was, he could not have stood it without the sustaining faith of his wife and the soothing treatment of the English doctor. If the German specialists were right in saying that Mackenzie should have diagnosed cancer earlier, they were wrong to insist on a brutal operation that might have killed the patient immediately and certainly would have mutilated him and lessened his will to live. Bismarck himself agreed that the best strategy was a delaying action for as long as possible. God should be trusted more than the knife. This was the strategy of the new Empress and the English doctors, and although their optimism was false, it did support the sick man through his long sufferings. If, as *The Times* said, his father's longevity was due to the stimulus of implacable routine, his own survival was sustained by certain love and unlikely hope.

Whatever the risk of the train journey to Berlin, the new Emperor had to go, or appoint Prince William as Regent in his place. And that, after his eldest son's presumption, he would not permit. In the time left to him, he intended to do all he could to secure the future of his family and of Germany. His son would have to stand by, waiting to take over as he had waited for so long. Prince William would also stand against all that his father tried to do; he told Count Eulenburg that his father's reign, or rather his mother's through her husband, would mean the ruin of Germany.[33]

The Empress thought it would be the salvation of Germany, so often delayed, so precarious now. She had to make her husband live. She and Mackenzie set off with the new Emperor by special train to Berlin, even though Bismarck warned the British Ambassador that public feeling was so incensed against the London doctor that he would hardly be safe.[34] The new Empress ignored these warnings as she ignored her own unpopularity at court. Mackenzie was the only specialist she trusted. And she was determined that he would stay with her to prolong her husband's life.

They traveled through the cold and snow toward the north. At Leipzig, Bismarck met the imperial train. As he tried to kneel to kiss his new master's hand, the Emperor drew him up into a silent embrace. The journey ended at Charlottenburg, where there was both a palace and the royal mausoleum. In that resting place, the light shone down through azure windows onto the white Carrara marble sarcophagi of the dead kings and queens of Prussia, while niches waited for the German emperors and empresses soon to follow them.

12

The Short Reign

THE EMBALMED body of the old Emperor in its sable-covered coffin was borne to the ancient Dom Church on the shoulders of sixteen gigantic sergeants of the Foot Guards. The hoofbeats of the escorting Life Guards were muffled in the snow. Flaring torches were held by the soldiers lining the route. Within the church, thousands of wreaths were strewn on the flagstones. The princes and dignitaries crushed the laurel and the bay leaves underfoot as they moved in line toward the coffin beneath the candelabra. The dead Emperor lay with his head resting on two white satin pillows, dressed in his Foot Guards uniform and wrapped in his gray campaign cloak. The line of mourners bowed before the monarch lying in state and paid their last respects.

The Prince of Wales had come from San Remo to Berlin for the funeral. His mother wanted him to wear the only British uniform there, but he had left it behind and had to appear in the uniform of a German Hussar colonel carrying his honorary marshal's baton. When he visited his sister and her husband for lunch at the Charlottenburg palace, he was surprised to find the new Emperor looking quite like his former self with a flushed face and an animated expression—but speechless—mute. To communicate, he wrote rapidly on a block of paper and waited for a reply. He ate well and swallowed easily and did not look like a dying man.

Everyone thought him doomed, except for his wife and Count Seckendorff. The general mood was matched by the weather, gloom without and within. Morell Mackenzie told the Prince of Wales that the new Emperor's condition was very grave; the sick man had a rending cough and was being weakened by all the business of state. "The patient is *worse,*" an aide of the Prince of Wales wrote to Queen Victoria "steadily going down hill—walking now along a precipice—overhanging the valley of the shadow of Death!"[1]

The new Emperor could not risk himself at his father's funeral procession and watched from a palace room. He forbade the aged Bismarck and Moltke to appear, because the bitter cold would also be a threat to them. Huge arches, crowned with the Prussian Eagle and draped in black crepe, were erected along the Unter den Linden. Between them, ropes of twined evergreens joined together square black pillars holding up great cauldrons of flaming pitch. All the people of Berlin seemed to have taken to the streets. There was fighting with the police, and mobs invaded the large houses on the avenues to watch the passing cortége from the upper windows.

At eleven o'clock in the morning, the bells of the Dom Church rang and the tolling was picked up by the bells of every church in Berlin. The funeral service had begun in front of the new Empress and of her son Crown Prince William, who stood in the middle of the nave behind the imperial standard. An observer wrote:

> The Dom presented at this moment an extraordinary display of martial splendour, surpassing, perhaps, any previous spectacle of a similar kind that has been seen in Europe in modern times. The high officers, civil and military, arrayed in brilliant uniforms, surrounded the coffin; the

Imperial and Royal Princes in the nave, notwithstanding the mourning emblems which they wore, presented an equally dazzling appearance; and the general effect was enhanced by the attendant guard of honour, with their drawn swords. The Royal ladies in the left gallery and the clergy before the altar offered the only contrast to the blaze of bright and varied colour which glowed within the walls of the national Cathedral.[2]

After the service, the body of the Emperor was placed on a plain black hearse drawn by eight black horses, the coffin shrouded in a purple velvet pall on which his plumed helmet gleamed. Picked squadrons of cavalry led the way, their red and white plumes dancing above their dark cloaks, the black and white guidons flickering on their lances, while the First Foot Guards looked like armed Capuchins under the white miters of their helmets. Behind the hearse marched most of the kings and princes and grand dukes of Europe in honor of the Emperor who had ruled over the making of the greatest military power in the world.

To the new monarchs, the funeral procession was a reminder of their own mortality. At his palace window, the Emperor Frederick broke down on seeing the hearse.

The new Empress wrote to Queen Victoria:

People in general consider us a *mere passing shadow,* soon to be replaced by *reality* in the shape of *William!!* I may be wrong, but it seems to me as if the party that opposed and ill-treated us so long, hardly think it worth while to change their attitude, except very slightly—as they count on a different future! It is an inestimable blessing to be relieved from a thraldom and tyranny which was exercised over us in the poor Emperor's name, as now the right thing can be done for Fritz's health! But oh—if it is not too late! too late! This agonizing thought haunts me! Yes, we are our own masters now, but shall we not have to leave all the work undone which we have so long and so carefully been preparing?[3]

She would have to leave all her prepared work undone, for her husband's case was terminal. Already she was being accused of wanting to rule through a sick man as a woman Emperor. Even Queen Victoria's Prime Minister, Lord Salisbury, was perturbed that she might try to make her English views a matter of German policy, and wrote to the British Ambassador in Berlin, telling him to keep his distance from the Empress. It was hoped she would not ask for his advice: if she did, it would be reported to Bismarck and be taken for foreign interference; if she did not, it would show that she understood the pitfalls surrounding her and knew where the line of safety lay. She must not be detected trying to shape Germany to an English pattern, or she would incur a most serious risk. Her role must be mildly Bismarckian and intensely German.[4]

Treading delicately she did not fail in her role. The first proclamation of her husband and his open letter to Bismarck showed a wish to rule in a more liberal and constitutional way, but not at the price of offending the Chancellor. He wanted to appoint Liberals as ministers, but he did not yet dare proceed for fear of forcing Bismarck to resign. The Chancellor himself treated the new Emperor and Empress with caution and courtesy, as long as he was left to do what he was doing already.

Yet the Empress soon felt his claws. Bismarck wanted to prolong the period between elections for the Reichstag, but the Emperor delayed signing the bill. Bismarck demanded to see the Empress, who stood between him and her husband's sickroom. He told her angrily that the Emperor was exceeding his prerogative and would make his Chancellor resign if the bill were not signed. The Empress soothed Bismarck and said that her husband would sign the bill, once he understood he was bound by the constitution, so Bismarck quieted down "and drew in his claws like a tiger that had changed its mind and decided not to hurl itself at its victim."

The Emperor did insist on an amnesty, however, particularly for the political offenders arrested and imprisoned through Stieber and other agents of Bismarck. This had been the fate of some of his own liberal supporters. The Chancellor protested that such an amnesty would loose subversives all across Germany, but the Emperor did get his general pardon. When the reactionary Minister of the Interior, Robert von Puttkamer, used his agents to interfere in the Reichstag elections, the Emperor summarily dismissed him, an act of political courage which Bismarck had to accept.

Bismarck still continued his system of surveillance and spying and innuendo and quarantine against the new rulers. Count Radolinski's place as his chief agent was taken over by the Adjutant General Winterfeld. The Emperor had trusted Winterfeld as a staff officer, but the man was ambitious and determined to be on the right side of the regime to come soon. They always had an eye on William—the Empress wrote bitterly about the double-dealers in the imperial entourage— as if he already had one foot on the throne whilst his father had one foot in the grave.[5]

She had her own puny intelligence system inside and outside Germany. She used her confidante, Ernest von Stockmar's widow, as a confidential agent to liaise with the Liberal deputy Dr. Ludwig Bamberger, an honest and principled man, a longtime admirer of the new Emperor, politically astute and well informed. He was consulted about political problems through Baroness Stockmar, who brought back his answers verbally— only occasionally by letter. In her husband's sickness, the Empress confided more and more in her most trusted German adviser, revealing the depths of her isolation and bitterness. "Give me three words spoken by the Empress, the official world says," she wrote to Bamberger, "and we shall turn her into a foreigner, into a traitor, into an enemy of the Reich."[6]

Officially in power with her husband, she could get nothing done, no reforms made, and her resentment and frustration were expressed in long letters to Bamberger. She declared to him that the ministers were not the Emperor's servants, but his enemies. They violently opposed everything he wanted, and he was too ill to force a change of administration. He did not have one devoted political friend near him; all had been deterred or sent away. She was the only one who could tell the Emperor the plain truth. How few at court were willing to support her! Without her and her few friends like Baroness Stockmar and Bamberger, the Emperor would be a total prisoner.[7]

After thirty years of waiting and planning, the Empress found her reign brief and illusory. Time was too short to change anything, the Emperor too ill to do much. Clutching at straws, she even believed that Bismarck was on her side because he treated her decently, saying that he could not do what the Emperor wanted because he was stopped by the other ministers. It was another illusion. Secretly, the Chancellor was thwarting any change because he knew the Emperor would not reign long.

The Crown Princess still had to fight Bismarck on one thing. She had not given up the idea of marrying her Moretta to Sandro Battenberg. Her husband still disapproved of the match, but he was too weak to resist her determination, although privately he let Bismarck know that he opposed it. The Battenberg Prince had been replaced by Ferdinand of Coburg as the ruler of Bulgaria, but Bismarck still asserted that the marriage would lead to a rift with Russia and with England and told the British Ambassador that he would leave office if the wedding took place. He charged that the Empress was aware of his intention to resign and had said there were other chancellors in Germany.[8] He managed to stop the Empress from asking Sandro to visit Charlottenburg and also provoked Crown Prince William into sending Sandro a message: "If you marry my sister, I shall consider you the enemy of my family and my country."

Bismarck assumed that Queen Victoria was still supporting her daughter and granddaughter in the Battenberg match, which was English interference in German diplomacy. So he loosed a virulent attack in the bought press against the Queen and the Empress, accusing them of plotting against Germany for foreign interests. The smear campaign was so poisonous that Queen Victoria, who intended to pay a first and last visit to her son-in-law and daughter in Berlin, was advised by her Prime Minister that it was unsafe to go there. There might be hostile demonstrations and a certain confrontation with the angry Crown Prince William, soon to inherit the throne.

Queen Victoria had a scepter of steel. She was determined to go to Berlin to see her son-in-law the Emperor before he died. Actually, she was already cooling on the Battenberg marriage. She had heard of Sandro's long love affair with Johanna Loisinger; he was no longer in love with Moretta, who had not seen him for four years. The Queen was also a realist and had no intention of causing a crisis in Germany which would lead to Bismarck resigning while his royal master was slowly sinking. Although she resented losing to Bismarck on her own ground, she was not as stubborn as her daughter about it. The royal marriage game was not worth the candle if it could light so many fires abroad. All the same, she was not amused, and complained: "*How* Bismarck and still more William *can* play such a double game it is impossible for us honest, straightforward English to understand. Thank God! we *are* English."[9]

Before the arrival of Queen Victoria in Berlin, the Emperor was brought close to death by his doctors. After a severe coughing fit one night, he found breathing through his canula difficult. Mackenzie had a new lead canula made and, aware of his precarious position in Germany, he asked Dr. Bergmann to insert it. Bergmann brought along a canula of his own without a rounded end to prevent harm to the tissues of the throat. He pulled out the old breathing-tube and thrust in his new one, missing the incision in the windpipe and forcing the canula inside the flesh of the neck. The Emperor began to splutter and bleed copiously. Again Bergmann tried to thrust his canula into the wrong place and had to pull it out. The Emperor coughed and coughed, streams of blood flowing from his throat. The agitated Bergmann pushed his forefinger into the wound to enlarge it, then failed again to insert his canula. He gave up and called for his assistant, Dr. Bramann, to insert a smaller tube, which Bramann did with ease. Finally Bergmann left, and the bleeding from the Emperor's throat subsided after two hours.

Mackenzie was summoned, and according to his account, the Emperor whispered, "Why did Bergmann put his finger into my throat?"

"I do not know, sir," Mackenzie replied.

"I hope you will not allow Professor von Bergmann to do any further operations on me."

"After what I have seen today, sir," Mackenzie answered, "I beg most respectfully to say that I can no longer have the honour of continuing in attendance on Your Majesty if Professor von Bergmann is to be permitted to touch your throat again."[10]

Bergmann's random stabbing with an unguarded tube resulted in an abscess in the patient's neck. Pus flowed out and made the Emperor's condition even more serious. It was the fatal blow, according to Mackenzie. Bergmann's account was completely different, although he was forced to withdraw from the case. He claimed that he had saved the Emperor's life: he had found the Emperor suffocating from maltreatment by the British doctors and had brought him around by putting a finger in his throat and using his assistant's canula. Mackenzie's assistant thought that Bergmann had been drinking and that his roughness was the result of alcohol rather than nerves. Certainly, the Emperor himself never allowed Bergmann to attend him again and wrote on his pad in his own hand: "Bergmann ill-treated me."[11]

It was the Emperor's life, and he had to be the best judge of who was helping or harming him. Undoubtedly, he supported Mackenzie, who now designed an aluminum canula that allowed his patient to breathe easily for the rest of his short days. Unfortunately, politics interfered with medical judgments. Mackenzie came from England and was therefore presumed guilty no matter what he did. Bergmann came from Germany, and was presumed credible no matter what he said. The Emperor did, however, decorate Dr. Krause and Dr. Virchow for their part in his treatment. A dying man does not mind where his medical advisers come from, only what they do to him.

≫≪

When Queen Victoria arrived at Charlottenburg station, the Empress with her children was waiting to greet her. The Queen kissed her daughter and found her looking careworn and thinner, but not ill. She was led by Crown Prince William to a four-horse barouche, which took her to the royal palace. She passed between a guard of honor and beneath the drawn swords of two gigantic sentries to the old rooms of Frederick the Great that had not been used since the last King of Prussia's death, but had now been redecorated by the Empress to receive her mother. The Queen of England then went to see her son-in-law, who was lying in bed, his face unaltered. He raised both hands in pleasure to see his mother-in-law and gave her a nosegay.

Later, at breakfast, the Empress told her mother that she and her husband had never had a quarrel with Bismarck over the Battenberg marriage. "The whole dreadful bother," she said, "had been purposely got up." It was to prove to the new monarchs how powerful the Chancellor was and how insubstantial was their rule. Lord Salisbury was less charitable, writing to the British Ambassador in Berlin that alcohol by day and narcotics at night must have affected Bismarck's brain.[12] Queen Victoria, however, decided to put an end to all misunderstanding between Germany and England over the

Battenbergs by receiving the Chancellor in a private audience, and he was brought to her by the Empress at noon the next day.

The Queen was agreeably surprised to find Bismarck so amiable and gentle. He referred to their meeting at Versailles thirty-three years before. He did not say that their failure to meet for so many decades had allowed him to underestimate her powers in diplomacy. He spoke a great deal of the German army, which could put millions of men in the field in defense of the fatherland against Russia or France. He hoped that the British fleet would help, if Germany were attacked. He only wanted to defend the borders of the present Empire, which was large enough for its role in Europe.

After hearing what Bismarck wanted, Queen Victoria spoke of what she wanted. She said that she was glad there was not to be a regency under Crown Prince William. She did not say that she knew of a plot by William's supporters to make him act for his sick father in order to stop the Empress acting for him, on the principle that the Hohenzollerns, Prussia and the German Empire would not permit a woman to rule them.[13] Bismarck promised the Queen that there would not be a regency. "Even if he thought it necessary, which he did not," the Queen's journal recorded, "he would not have the heart to propose it. I appealed to Prince Bismarck to stand by poor Vicky, and he assured me he would, that hers was a hard fate. I spoke of William's inexperience and his not having travelled at all."

Bismarck replied that Crown Prince William knew nothing about civil affairs at all, but he was certainly clever. "Should he be thrown into the water," the Chancellor declared, "he would be able to swim." The half-hour interview ended with Queen Victoria discussing other personal affairs.[14] She was very probably telling Bismarck that she had persuaded her daughter not to proceed with the Battenberg marriage because of the political complications. In any event, Bismarck came out of the interview smiling and wiping the sweat from his forehead. "What a woman!" he was reported to have said. "One could do business with her!"

This was the long-delayed meeting between the leaders of the two rival systems of diplomacy which kept the peace and the balance of power in Europe. Queen Victoria had shown that she would throw away her trump card, royal marriage, if necessary for the good of her country. "Grandmamma behaved quite sensibly at Charlottenburg," Bismarck told Busch. The Queen needed German friendship for Britain against Russia, and she was prepared to make a sacrifice for it. She even brought about a reconciliation between Crown Prince William and the Empress, who was now considered by the Bismarckians as more of a supporter than her own mother of English interests in Germany.[15]

That night, at the British Embassy, Bismarck showed how much goodwill had resulted from the meeting. He had already told Crown Prince William that the Queen of England's visit was like an officer going round the outposts and seeing that the pickets were all doing their duty. Sitting opposite her at dinner, his mood was ebullient. He noticed a bonbon which was topped by a likeness of the Empress, grabbed it, unbuttoned the top of his coat and placed it against his heart.[16]

The Chancellor had heard that the people of Berlin had turned out in their tens of thousands to cheer and throw flowers at the coach bearing the Empress and her mother to the Embassy dinner. His warnings of hostile demonstrations were proved untrue; the vicious press attacks were unnecessary. They stopped—except for one which slipped through the net—as soon as they had started. The Empress's influence would expire with her husband, and, Mackenzie told Queen Victoria, he would not live above a few weeks, possibly two months, but hardly three.[17]

The next day, in a bitter wind, Queen Victoria took the salute at a march-past commanded by her grandson William. She then said farewell to her son-in-law the Emperor, who kissed her photograph but coughed so much that she had to leave. At the station, her daughter broke down. "It was terrible to see her standing there in tears, while the train moved slowly off, and to think of all she was suffering and might have to go through. My poor poor child, what would I not do to help her in her hard lot!"[18]

She could not help her daughter now, but she could have helped before. Bismarck's deep suspicion of her manipulation of her daughter in England's interests did not survive his meeting with her. As the Crown Prince whispered to the British Ambassador, he wished she had come over to Berlin years sooner. How useful it might have been, judged by the goodwill the visit had achieved.[19] It had briefly stopped the intrigues against the dying Emperor and the slanders against his wife. It had been of the highest value in freely brushing away industriously woven cobwebs, Lord Salisbury was informed. The many spiders had to return to their holes.[20]

⅍

After Queen Victoria's visit, the spring came. The Emperor's health remained stable, even though he could not swallow much more than milk, and he could be taken out for a drive and show himself to the crowds. When the Crown Prince pressed him, he agreed to review a parade led by his son, a ghost emperor watching his successor usurp his command and his glory. The pressure of necessary business was so great that he had to allow William to sign minor state documents for him. But his wife did all she could, often fanning him most of the night before spending the day without rest at letters, telegrams, audiences and keeping au courant with everything.[21]

Although little could be changed in politics, precautions could be taken for the future. The Emperor used his inheritance to provide for his wife and daughters. The Empress sent her mother a copy of a letter which her husband had written to be given after his death to his eldest son. She feared that the original might be destroyed. "Please consider it most secret!" she begged Queen Victoria. On May 2, she also dispatched by royal messenger a box containing her husband's journals and some more papers, which she did not think safe in Germany. They were to be kept in her mother's strong room with the other boxes of confidential documents brought to London at the time of the Jubilee or sent from San Remo. Her reason for storing the papers abroad was, according to her, because of invasion of privacy. All the dead Emperor William I's most secret and intimate papers were being plundered by utter strangers and government agents, sent by Bismarck to see whether there were documents that might compromise his official version of German history.[22]

The precautions taken by the Empress may have seemed excessive, but she knew how vulnerable she was, how exposed and powerless in all but name. She was pretending to rule on borrowed time at a court which only pretended to obey her condemned husband. "*Whatever* Fritz wishes done meets with the most systematic and persistent though silent opposition, plainly showing that these people only submit to the present reign as a *form*, but *resist* it as a reality!" She could only hope in vain. "A *few* months of health or comparative health would enable Fritz to put an end to this."[23]

The Emperor made a valiant effort and came to the wedding of his second son, Prince Henry, to Princess Irene of Hesse, herself a grandchild of Queen Victoria. Stick in hand, he appeared before the assembled guests in the blue damask room of the palace, dressed in full uniform with all his orders. His wife felt her heart turn over; he looked so handsome and dignified but so thin and pale. He welcomed everyone and embraced Irene and Henry. His wife kept back her tears with difficulty and felt with bitter sorrow that they all should never again see him attending such a gathering as Emperor. The wedding was very beautiful, but very sad. The Emperor stood it well and did not have a fit of coughing during the service. The chapel looked charming, full of roses and other flowers. Irene was very moved, her delicate little figure seemed almost bowed down with the weight of the bridal jewels, particularly by the crown. They had all put off mourning for that day, but naturally only wore gray or white.[24]

Through that last May in Berlin, the Empress carried on, her nerves occasionally giving way under severe bouts of neuralgia. She was growing more popular, especially after she insisted on visiting the victims of bad floods in East Prussia. The people might admire her devotion in trying to keep her husband alive, but she had few friends in the government or at court. As Colonel Swaine reported to the Prince of Wales, these were sad times in Berlin. The approaching death of the Emperor made all trim their sails. It seemed as if a curse had come over the country, leaving only one bright spot, a solitary woman doing her duty faithfully and tenderly by her sick husband against all odds. It was one of the most, if not *the* most tragic episode in a country and a life ever recorded in history.[25]

On June 1, the Crown Princess decided to move her husband to die at his favorite home, the Neue Palais, that he had rechristened Friedrichskron, officially after Frederick the Great whose name he himself bore as Emperor and defender of his country. The River Spree bordered the park of Charlottenburg and could carry the Emperor to Potsdam by boat. The royal steam yacht *Alexandra* picked up the imperial family and transported them past cheering crowds on the banks and past the fortress of Spandau through the Havel lakes to the Glienicke Bridge, where they disembarked for Friedrichskron. Before leaving, the Emperor had paid a visit to the mausoleum at Charlottenburg, to see where his father lay, to see where he did not choose to lie.

"How glad I am to be here at last," the Emperor told his wife softly and continuously at Friedrichskron. The weather soon turned warm and fine, and the sick man lay out on the palace balcony or drove in a pony chaise to view the trees and flowers which he had planted with his wife. Their own creations never looked more beautiful to them, the Empress noted. The sun was always said to shine more beautifully just before setting. The nights were not good, his appetite was poor and meals were a torment. Nevertheless, though he was growing physically weaker and more tired, he still retained the liveliest interest in everything. He signed documents, wrote letters and also made entries in his diary, gave instructions and occupied himself with trifles, read all his newspapers through from beginning to end.[26]

He could not hold out for long. It was the triumph of will over body. His last official act was to insist on receiving the King of Sweden. With great difficulty he put on his uniform, but his wasted face and shining eyes announced his coming end. The British Ambassador noticed the smell of death on him and feared the last stage of the tragedy. To his wife, the Emperor looked like Admiral Keppel on his sinking British man-of-war, saluting the French admiral with a broadside although the water was rising higher and higher.

A fistula had appeared in his throat, so that even his milk now passed out through his canula. Mackenzie had to feed the Emperor with milk through a rubber tube, but unfortunately some of it seemed to reach the lungs, causing an inflammation. He could take no more nourishment and became a fevered skeleton. He struggled for breath throughout the night of June 14, and the following morning it was clear that he was dying. His wife gave him some white wine on a sponge to suck. When she asked him if he was tired, his last words to her were a croak, "Oh, very, very . . ."

The imperial family gathered around the deathbed, where he lay unconscious. They could hear only the slight rattle of breath in the canula. In the hour before noon, he woke and began to write on his pad: "Victoria, I and the Chil—" His hand dropped. He gave one final gasp and lay back. He was dead. Mackenzie closed the eyelids with a practiced hand.

"Oh, the look of his dear eyes," his widow wrote to her mother, "the mournful expression when he closed them for ever, the coldness and the silence that follow when the soul has fled. Oh! my husband, my darling, my Fritz!! So good, so kind, so tender, brave, patient and noble, so cruelly tried, taken from the nation, the wife and daughters that did so need him. His mild just rule was not to be."[27]

❧❦

The Empress had enough strength for a last farewell; no more, or she would have gone mad. She returned to her room to find herself a prisoner. "What undignified and abominable things took place on this disastrous day!" she wrote in her diary. "William's first act as Ruler was to have our house, our sanctuary, our quiet house of mourning where death had set up his throne, cordoned off by a regiment of Hussars who appeared unmounted with rifles in their hands from behind every tree and every statue!" He wanted to have Mackenzie arrested immediately, but was stopped by the Minister of Justice. Soldiers were stationed between the kitchen and the telegraph office, so that the servants could not even telegraph to Berlin for crepe and mourning. Winterfeld immediately flung himself on the Emperor's private writing table and desk, tore everything open, and rummaged as if he expected to find traces of state documents, possibly liberal plots. The Empress Frederick turned away from the miserable spectacle with disgust.[28]

The indecency and paranoiac actions of the new Emperor had been provoked. On the eve of her husband's death, the Empress had sent Dr. Hovell to the British Embassy, carrying a portmanteau and a hatbox filled with confidential papers. The Ambassador knew nothing of the contents, but packed them himself in diplomatic bags and sent them off that night with Colonel Swaine directly to Queen Victoria at Balmoral. The spy in the British Embassy had reported Dr. Hovell's mission to Bismarck and to Crown Prince William, whose impetuosity matched his mother's fear. The Crown Prince had reacted by having Friedrichskron surrounded by a cordon of dismounted Hussars while his father was still alive. As soon as he had become German Emperor, a regiment of infantry was ordered at the double to the palace to seal off the place totally.

The Empress could find no defenders except for the British Ambassador and the Minister of Justice Friedberg, who had been honored by her dead husband. When her son demanded that she surrender all state papers to him immediately, she faced him down. All state papers had been returned by the late Emperor after reading or signing them, she said. The rest were private papers. "Those the Emperor has given to me," she claimed. "And I do not suppose that you wish to take them from me." He did not quite dare to seize them or to continue the search for them nor did he have the baggage of the suspect British doctors ripped apart. "You have the power," the Minister of Justice told him "but you have not the right. If you exercise the power, you will begin your reign badly." Had the full search been ordered, the British Ambassador would have felt bound to intervene, and it would have led to a serious diplomatic incident. As it was, the intrusion ended without a scandal as a form of black farce.[29] "There is something medieval in the incident of Dr. Hovell's portmanteau," Lord Salisbury observed drily. "No doubt there was plenty of matter in it to have sent all the Empress Victoria's friends to Spandau."[30]

That was her reason for sending her private papers to safety abroad. She was protecting her liberal friends and Coburg advisers from inevitable persecution by Bismarck. Their advice to her and her dead husband would be seen as a conspiracy against the Chancellor's authority. Her correspondence with her English relatives would also be misinterpreted. The Prince of Wales was immediately ordered to Berlin for three reasons: His official duty was to represent the British crown at the Emperor Frederick's funeral; his other duties were to support his sister through her time of trial and persecution, and also to bring back in his baggage the last of her confidential documents.

Against the wishes of the dead Emperor and his wife, the new Emperor William II allowed a post mortem. He was under pressure from Bergmann, who had to establish that the death had not been caused by his drunken clumsiness in May. It was found that the whole larynx was a gangrenous ulcer, and there were traces of septic bronchopneumonia in the lungs. No mention was made of the abscess caused by Bergmann, that had spread so much that it was diffused all over the throat. The German doctor's reputation was saved, while the Empress grieved that the specialists had dared touch her husband's dear face, his sacred mortal remains.

For a day and a night, the late Emperor was left lying on his deathbed in Friedrichskron. He was swathed in white to the chin, his head bound, his hands crossed on his saber. He looked like the figure of a Teutonic Knight on his tomb. After the post mortem, his remains were shrouded in his military cloak and decorated with his orders and medals before being laid to rest in a coffin in the Jasper Hall of the palace. His wife put in the coffin his favorite miniature of her with a lock of her hair and his wedding ring. "I, his wife," she said, "lie there too!"

The imperial family held a service in the Jasper Hall. The next day, thousands of people came out from Berlin to stand in line and bow to the dead figure. There was no formal lying in state or state funeral, just a simple ceremony in the Friedens-kirche in the park of Sans Souci where he was buried by the side of his dead son Waldemar. The Emperor Frederick had not wanted any pomp and was given none by his son. Life Guards in black uniforms escorted his coffin, muffled drum taps signaled his end, his old chestnut war-charger Wörth followed the coffin, neighing continually. It was said later that no one mourned so much at the funeral as his horse.

The Empress did not attend the final ceremony, but fled with her daughters to the little country house at Bornstadt. She could not stand the memories, the false condolences, the soldiers and the intruders. Bismarck did not even come to call on her, and would not say that he regretted her husband's death. His faithful Busch expressed satisfaction that they were relieved of that incubus, and that his place was now to be taken by a disciple and admirer of the chief.[31]

In her grief, the Empress depended on the support of her brother, the Prince of Wales. She had always been devoted to him. He would be her defender in place of her husband, just as her husband had served after the death of Prince Albert as Queen Victoria's support and ceremonial representative. On June 23, the Prince of Wales cabled Queen Victoria that he had arranged to return to England the next day. It was not advisable to linger longer with his sister. He also did not wish to hear his nephew the Emperor's speech to the Reichstag, which praised the policies of his grandfather and hardly mentioned his father at all.

During the Prince of Wales's stay in Germany, Bismarck and his son Herbert had done all they could to alienate the heir to the English throne. The brief era of good feeling inaugurated by Queen Victoria's visit was abruptly terminated. The Chancellor spoke of the late reign in a manner which was most offensive to the Prince of Wales, the British Ambassador reported. He said that in fact the Emperor had never been competent to reign because of his illness. The country had been governed by the Empress despite the German law.[32] The Ambassador was glad that the Prince of Wales was leaving because he looked at things from a very personal point of view. He had spent most of his time with his sister the Empress, who was embittered against the Bismarcks and her son. This could only have increased his antagonism toward the rulers of Germany.

Queen Victoria did all she could from a distance, writing to her grandson the new Emperor that he should help his mother at this terrible time of dreadful trial and grief. Yet even if he would, he could not. He had a nature as impetuous and willfull as hers, and a pride more easily pricked. He was also surrounded by advisers who insisted that she had always kept far too close to England and could not be trusted. She must now be totally isolated, her contacts scattered and broken. Only then would the Reich be protected from her alien influence.

The Kaiser's mother knew her fate for as long as her life lasted. She lamented in her diary: "Why does such pain not kill immediately?"[33]

13

Old Scores, New Places

"I MUST HAVE A nook of my own, something to arrange and care for—and look after, as all other occupation is *gone*. For thirty years what an interest I have taken in public affairs and politics . . . now that is *all over!!!*"[1] The widowed Empress Frederick knew her fate. Her influence, however small, would be ended; her circle of friends and advisers would be broken and scattered. Even the memory of her husband's short reign of ninety-nine days would be denied and wiped clean. She could only retire and try to record what she thought was the truth.

Her first concern was the safety of the evidence she needed to collect material for a life of her husband. She had little else except her correspondence with her mother and with him. Her letters to the Stockmars and to her confidante Countess Blücher had all been burned, as had most of the other documents which might have proved compromising because of dealings with the German liberal opposition. In a letter written on June 20, 1888, she implored her mother never to surrender the boxes of papers in the strong room at Windsor Castle.

"FRITZ wished you to take care of them and keep them," his widow declared. No matter how much pressure was applied by the new Kaiser and the Bismarcks for their return, Queen Victoria must resist. "They cannot and do not KNOW what is there or where it is *now!* Fritz tore up and burned heaps, both at Charlottenburg, *here,* Baveno, San Remo—and before we left for England last year, so I can give quite satisfactory explanations."[2]

The Empress Frederick's explanations were quite satisfactory. She wanted to preserve those documents necessary to ensure her husband's place in history. She also wanted to protect her liberal advisers. Bismarck wanted only one version of recent German history to survive, the one he would present in his memoirs. In them, he would appear as the sole architect of the German Empire, and the Crown Prince would play an insignificant part in it. As for the liberals who had opposed him, Bismarck had long waited to scatter the remnants of the Coburg group and had taught the new Kaiser to see them as conspirators around the Empress Frederick. The documents which the Empress thought to be private papers were seen by the Chancellor and the Kaiser as the property of the state.

There is still a legal debate in the United States and in England about the ownership of copies of official papers, once a president or a prime minister leaves office. The security of the state is in conflict with the needs of memorialists and historians. Bismarck was certainly not prepared to wait for a legal ruling in his attempts to have all the papers of the dead Emperor seized. When the Kaiser sent Winterfeld, who had ransacked the imperial desk and writing table at Friedrichskron, to announce his accession to his grandmother, the General was cold-shouldered by the English court. The Queen heard that he had complained of it and was unrepentant. He had been a traitor to his old master, never mentioning his name or a word of regret; he had only spoken of his pleasure in being chosen to announce that his new master had succeeded to the throne.[3]

Queen Victoria did not tell Winterfeld of the papers in her possession, and she was most surprised to hear on July 14 that her daughter wanted the three large boxes of papers brought over at the time of the Jubilee returned to Germany. A compromise had been reached with Bismarck's agents that the contents of these boxes should be examined only by her and the Minister of Justice, Friedberg, whom she trusted. Papers judged official should be given up, the rest kept by her. Lord Salisbury did not like the idea, suspecting the unknown contents of the boxes as much as Bismarck did. When the boxes were on German soil, Bismarck might have them all seized. Surely it would be safer, Salisbury advised Queen Victoria, to have them examined and send only those that were to be given up.[4]

The three boxes were, however, returned without being examined in England. The other packets of documents were not. The Empress sorted through the contents with Friedberg, and she also allowed three of Bismarck's men to look through her husband's safe and desk. All the papers of an official or political nature were given up, but she kept the ones that she thought were private. She would store these in a safe place where nobody could get at them. Their being in England at the time of her husband's death had been a godsend, as all the foolish and false people who had been prowling about the palace, ready like Harpies to seize everything, had now dispersed.[5]

By this time, her defense of her husband's reputation had escalated into a major war. The first cannonade was fired by the German doctors led by Bergmann, who published a report on the late Emperor's illness that was a biased attack on Morell Mackenzie. It accused the English doctor of false optimism and actual malpractice, asserting that an early operation for throat cancer would have saved the dead Emperor's life.[6] The report stung Mackenzie into replying with equal bias and self-justification in a book entitled *The Fatal Illness of Frederick the Noble*. Charge was met with countercharge, innuendo with smear. Mackenzie's riposte was confiscated in Germany by the police, an action the Empress Frederick called a perfectly despotic proceeding worthy of St. Petersburg.[7]

The doctors' war was inflated out of proportion by the political campaign to eradicate the memory of the short reign of the Emperor Frederick. The same people, his widow said, who had wanted to kill him by an early throat operation were those who were hounding Mackenzie for having helped her to keep him alive. Her son the Kaiser was a tool in their hands, and prejudiced against all doctors from her homeland. "An English doctor killed my father," he told his entourage, "and an *English* doctor *crippled* my arm—and this we owe to my mother who would not have Germans about her!"[8]

Believing as he did, the Kaiser supported Bismarck's vindictiveness in smashing the last of the Coburg friends of the Empress Frederick. The thought of the pro-English conspirators close to the German throne had preyed on the Chancellor's mind for more than thirty years. His opportunity to strike was given by the indiscretion of one of them, Professor Geffcken, who had taken a copy of the Emperor Frederick's *War Diary* of 1870 and 1871. He had extracts published in the German press which made it clear how much the Crown Prince then had influenced the creation of the German Empire in spite of the hesitations of his father and the objections of Bismarck. As Bismarck had always claimed infallibility and omnipotence, he was furious. Officially, he declared the extracts from the diaries to be forgeries. Unofficially, he accused the Empress Frederick of leaking state secrets to the Coburg conspirators. Geffcken was arrested in Hamburg and put on trial, while she was forced to leave the palace of Friedrichskron, her husband's last resting place. "I feel I must cling to every table, every footstool in his room!" she wrote in her journal.[9] But still she had to go. Everyone thought that the publication of the *War Diary* was her revenge taken on Bismarck's reputation.

Her son the Kaiser was exasperated by her. He bitterly

attacked his father in front of her, asking how he could write down such imprudent things. He also resented his father's not taking him into his confidence because of a belief that he would run off to Bismarck with the story. The Empress Frederick had given up the original of the *War Diary* by mistake with the rest of the official papers in the boxes returned from England. There was no better proof for her enemies that she had nothing to do with the publication,[10] and no better proof that Bismarck knew perfectly well that the extracts from the *War Diary* were no forgery.

The Empress Frederick thought that Geffcken was bound to be convicted of high treason just as Count Harry von Arnim had been. "Justice is a mere farce here!" she wrote to her mother. "Tribunals, Police, Post and Telegraph Office, are the tools of Prince Bismarck, and the greater part of the press too, as he has 16 millions of marks 'secret funds'. The desire to incriminate me must be very strong in Berlin." Baron Roggenbach's house had been searched and private papers taken, while her go-between Baroness Stockmar had been interrogated. All this police activity was an indirect attack on her. "I was Fritz's wife. I am English—and love Germany and its people *too well*. I know *too much*. I can see—and read and hear—therefore I must be . . . calumniated and attacked—it is so easy—as I am defenceless and a lady."[11]

When the case came to trial, Bismarck's prosecutor had to concede that the *War Diary* was genuine and let Geffcken go. The professor had committed an indiscretion, but not treason. In revenge, Bismarck had Geffcken's indictment widely publicized. It named all the Coburg survivors as conspirators against the welfare and safety of Germany, including most of Bismarck's known political enemies: Stosch, Roggenbach, Windthorst, Freytag and the dead Normann. Sir Robert Morier, the prime contact between England and the Empress Frederick and the German liberal opposition, was also mentioned in the Geffcken indictment. He was a special target for Bismarck's hatred, a man thought to be the head of British intelligence in northern Europe—although, unknown to Bismarck, the Kaiser's friend Colonel Swaine was now playing this role. Morier was a friend of the Empress Frederick and a direct contact with Queen Victoria. If there were an English conspiracy in Germany, it was most vulnerable in the person of the fat diplomat at St. Petersburg.

Through articles planted in the German press, Morier was accused of having betrayed German troop movements to Marshal Bazaine in 1870. This was said to have led to a French victory at Vionville, where Prince Frederick Karl lost 16,000 men. The disclosure came from the German military attaché at Madrid, who was responsible for paying a pension to the exiled Bazaine. Bismarck's son Herbert garbled the information, asserting that Bazaine had defeated the Crown Prince. The implication was that the Crown Prince had endangered his own men by passing military information to his wife, who had passed it on to her sister Princess Alice in Hesse-Darmstadt, and so to Morier. The truth was that Morier had sent only two telegrams containing military information from Darmstadt before the battle, detailing the probable positions of the headquarters of the three German armies then advancing on France. The information had been passed on to the British Ambassador in Paris and may have been intercepted and decoded and interpreted. Bazaine himself, in a letter to Morier, categorically denied that he had received any military information from Darmstadt. The telegraph authorities confirmed that Morier had only sent the two coded telegrams to London. The accusation was a deliberate smear by the Bismarcks' propaganda machine. Its aim, as a letter to *The Times* of London pointed out, was to show that the Emperor Frederick was in the habit of blabbing to the English who turned his confidences to a treacherous and malevolent use.[12]

The aim was also to hit at the pro-French Prince of Wales, who was close to Morier and who had quarreled with the Bismarcks and with his nephew the Kaiser. Angry at his uncle's championship of his English mother, the Kaiser had deliberately snubbed him by refusing to meet him during a state visit to Vienna. Now the Prince of Wales insisted to Queen Victoria that the Kaiser should apologize for the snub and the Bismarcks retract their allegations against Morier. He got no satisfaction, only a deadlock. Anglo-German relationships reached a low ebb, and Lord Salisbury wanted a reconciliation. Morier demanded vindication and used *The Times* to clear his name, starting a press war in Germany between the remaining liberal papers and those of the right wing. He had the best of the controversy in print, but no apology came from the Bismarcks.

To the British Ambassador in Berlin, Bismarck confessed how seriously he took Morier's role as a spymaster and intriguer. He said that Morier had been in constant communication with a group which included Geffcken and Roggenbach and Stosch, who were trying to overthrow the government. "It is a habit with me to stand by my friends," Bismarck said, "and to be hostile to my enemies without counting the cost." Morier was nothing to him except in Germany, where he wished to destroy the man's influence forever. He ended the discussion by classing the Empress Frederick with the group working against him.[13]

Bismarck extended his accusations of spying to a former foe, the Dowager Empress Augusta. Although she was old and dying, he could never forget a sense of injury. Her dead *Kabinetsrath* Doctor Brandis was accused of passing on to Morier secret messages about the war for transmission to England.[14] In one spreading stain of indictment and insinuation, he blackened the names of both the previous Empresses, their groups of advisers and friends, the leading members of the German liberal opposition, the British Ambassador at St. Petersburg, and the British crown. It was the death-blow to the survivors of the Coburg group. Their last hopes had died with the Emperor Frederick, and they were now being scattered to the far corners of Germany and of Europe.

Not satisfied with this, Bismarck hounded Prince Alexan-

der of Battenberg out of the country. During the short reign
of the Emperor Frederick, the Chancellor had deterred him
from giving the Battenberg Prince the command of a German
regiment and a position at court. Now he incited the new
Kaiser against Sandro, who was accused of being a British
agent. The Kaiser made it clear to the Prince that he would
never receive a post at court or in the German army or be
allowed to marry the Kaiser's younger sister. This ill treatment
provoked Prince Alexander into marrying his mistress Johanna
Loisinger. He renounced his royal title for that of Count Harte-
nau and went to Austria, where he was given the rank of
Lieutenant Colonel. He died two years later, a broken man.

In November, the Empress Frederick left for England to
stay with her mother throughout the winter. She took her
three younger daughters with her, also the private papers she
had preserved from the three large boxes returned to Germany.
"No one need know it," she wrote to her mother, "and I
have a *perfect* right to do with my own property what I like!
They are *not* safe here!" She would have to work on a full
life of her husband in secret. They would not be wiped out
of the history of Germany by the Bismarcks; their thirty years
of struggle deserved a record. The attack on their friends and
the seizing of their letters and the lies in the press would
not obliterate the truth. She thought that Richelieu's famous
saying suited Bismarck, "Give me but *one* WRITTEN LINE
in a man's handwriting, and I will make it suffice to bring
him to the gallows." But Bismarck did not quite have the
whole Spanish Inquisition at his disposal. In spite of his reign
of terror, the facts would out.[15]

☙

The situation was so charged that the new Kaiser had almost refused to allow his mother to go to England for the
long winter stay with Queen Victoria, but he had not dared
finally to provoke his powerful grandmother even more than
he already had. Soon after his accession, she had sent him a

long letter of advice which he had snubbed and ignored, feeling he was being treated as a grandson and not as German Emperor.[16] Bolstered by Bismarck's fury at more proof of interference from England, he had delayed answering the letter, and when he did reply, he ran down his father's reign, saying that he had had to spend months clearing up the paperwork after the complete stagnation he had inherited. He also insisted on setting aside a decent period of mourning in order to meet the Emperors of Russia and Austria and the King of Italy before coming to England. "The fate which sometimes hangs over nations," he grandly informed his grandmother, "does not wait till the etiquette of court mournings has been fulfilled."[17]

Queen Victoria was so piqued by his impertinence to her and his bad behavior to her widowed daughter that she refused to invite him to England at all. She certainly would not postpone the Empress Frederick's visit, as Lord Salisbury suggested, just to mollify her grandson and the Bismarcks. "You all seem frightened of them," she scolded Lord Salisbury, "which is not the way to make them better."[18] Her bereaved daughter must come over, and the Queen of England would take the unprecedented step of meeting her at Port Victoria to do her honor.

In fact, the three months that the Empress Frederick spent in England did much to ease the tensions in Germany. Queen Victoria advised her daughter to try and bear her son's thoughtlessness and the slanders of his advisers. Even he hoped that the absence might heal the breaches between them. "My mother and I have the same characters," he admitted to the British Ambassador in Berlin. "I have inherited hers. That good stubborn English blood which will not give way is in both our veins. The consequence is that if we do not happen to agree, the situation becomes difficult."[19]

He urged Queen Victoria to allow him to visit her with a German naval squadron. She was still offended, but much wiser than her eldest daughter in recognizing political necessity. Lord Salisbury had pointed out that English public opinion would not tolerate a diplomatic rupture with Germany because of personal quarrels within royal families.[20] Queen Victoria replied that, while she could not forget the events of the past twelve months, she hoped that her manner to her grandson would not show her true feelings. If the peace of Europe depended upon an open show of friendship between Germany and England, then the Kaiser could come to the Solent with his warships.[21] Even her daughter would finally approve. The relations of England and Germany should not suffer, the Empress Frederick told her mother, in spite of Prince Bismarck's wickedness and William's folly.[22]

The German Emperor still had to make his peace with his English uncle and his mother, whose ill treatment had made Queen Victoria's blood boil. "When a young man is in the wrong and he happens besides to be an Emperor," the Prince of Wales wrote to his elder sister, "it is not palatable to admit it! But I have built him so many golden bridges that if he will not cross them—it is not *my* fault!"[23] Like his mother, the Prince of Wales was ultimately prepared to put his country before his pride, something which the Kaiser still had to learn.

Lord Salisbury also insisted that diplomacy came first, and urged the Prince of Wales to pocket his dignity in order to keep on good terms with the Bismarcks and the Kaiser. There were no apologies from Germany, only further insensitive actions. The worst of them was the removal of the name of Friedrichskron from the old Neue Palais when the Kaiser took it for his own palace. This new effort to erase the memory of the Emperor Frederick hurt his wife and her defender the Prince of Wales. "It is really *too* monstrous!" he wrote to his sister. "Could you not have protested? There are certain things that almost surpass all comment! And it is almost best to be silent in words—though our thoughts are all the more intense!"[24]

Silence was golden, indeed, and a fresh uniform was very

heaven to the new Kaiser. As a warlike peace offering, he wanted to make Queen Victoria the colonel of a German regiment of dragoon guards—an honor never before offered to a foreign sovereign. In return, the English Queen took advice from the Prince of Wales and gave the Kaiser his secret desire, the title and uniform of a British admiral. "Fancy wearing the same uniform as St. Vincent and Nelson," he wrote to the British Ambassador in Berlin. "It is enough to make one quite giddy. I feel something like Macbeth must have felt, when he was suddenly received by the witches."[25]

He and his sailor brother Prince Henry were greeted by the British fleet at Spithead with a full naval review, followed by special army maneuvers at Aldershot. The Prince of Wales was present and discreet, while Queen Victoria was gracious and welcoming at Osborne. She seemed to be taking Colonel Swaine's advice: "Treat the grandson as the Emperor and he will remain grandson. Treat the Emperor as grandson and he is lost as such for ever."[26] Immense care was taken to show him the respect that he felt was his due. In fact, he irritated the Prince of Wales immensely by making him stand aside in his own domain, the Royal Yacht Club at Cowes, to allow the imperial visitor to go through the door first.

The effect of the visit to England was immediate. The Kaiser swung as emotionally and as violently as his mother often did. He no longer feared English influence, but desired it. Lord Salisbury complimented Queen Victoria for making the Kaiser such a changed man. On his return to Germany, the Kaiser invited the British Channel Fleet to visit the German navy at Kiel, where he went to inspect the British ironclads and invited their officers to attend a reception at the Empress Frederick's. His English mother was an advantage at last, if he could inspect her country's fleet.

She felt a stab of jealousy at her son's success in England and with her mother. She did not want to hear about the visit, which seemed to her a change of opinion by her own family. Queen Victoria had to receive graciously all the Kaiser's advisers who had behaved so disgracefully and abominably and treacherously to her and her husband. It was more difficult for her that her son was making the court and the Bismarcks do what she had always tried to do—to achieve a good understanding between Germany and England. These new friends of her homeland were the same people who had denounced her as too friendly to England, and who had abused her husband unjustly and ungratefully for remaining true to his principles. It was ironic and sad.

She was grateful to her mother for advising the Kaiser not to listen to lies against his mother. But it was too late, his mind had been thoroughly poisoned against his parents. She could not say a word against him as most of her entourage were his creatures; her old friends and advisers had been cut off from her. Everyone was always trying to make her think the Kaiser was right.[27]

She did actually have a few loyal people near her in her household. Count Seckendorff and the Countess Perponcher had been with her for decades, while the Countess Brühl and the able Baron Reischach had gained her confidence and remained with her. She exaggerated her isolation because of the obvious fact that she was being excluded, even by her own mother, from the center of diplomacy. Anglo-German relations were no longer affected by her hope of her husband's inheriting the throne, and her personal sufferings could not be allowed to disrupt them. Queen Victoria and the Prince of Wales were now dealing with the Kaiser face to face, and the Empress Frederick was unnecessary to that direct royal diplomacy. The Prince of Wales might come to Homburg to spend three weeks with her privately in September 1889, to mollify her about the Kaiser's visit to England, but he could not restore her lost position of importance. Her eldest son had not only inherited the German throne, but also replaced her special connection between the German court and the English one.

The Kaiser's new interest in the English relationship and

in the British navy was in the national interest. As a young man, he had sent back to his German grandfather detailed sketches and reports on the forts, docks, armaments and ironclads at Portsmouth.[28] As an admiral of the British fleet, he would study it—so he told his English grandmother—as if it were his own.[29] Although he asserted that he wanted the British navy to remain the strongest in the world, he secretly wished to build up the German fleet to be superior, and to do that, he needed to know about British marine technology. Without being accused of spying, he and his aides could be privileged observers who might report back to the German admiralty.

It was understood that royal visitors need not be shown things which were militarily sensitive. When Prince Henry of Germany visited Gibraltar in 1889, he was banned from seeing the ridge of the Rock, where new fortifications were being constructed. He took it in good part, quite captivated rather than repelled by the firm but well-mannered regrets that even His Royal Highness could not be allowed to pass.[30]

The Kaiser's naval interests led him to pay a visit to Greece and to Turkey later in 1889. He wished to attend the wedding of his sister Sophie to Prince Constantine, Duke of Sparta and heir to the throne. While he was at Athens, he went to inspect the British Mediterranean squadron lying offshore, and showed the greatest interest in and knowledge of the complex characteristics of ironclads.[31] In a speech on board, he admitted that the German navy was dependent on the British one for instruction and example. He took it upon himself to advise his grandmother to increase the size of the Mediterranean Squadron from five to twelve first-class battleships in order to counter the French fleet at Toulon. Through his friend Lord Charles Beresford, he even sent a strategical scheme to Lord Salisbury based on the tactics of the German navy.

His British admiral's uniform did, as he admitted, get hold of him.[32] In point of fact, he had replaced his mother and father as Queen Victoria's royal intelligence source on foreign armaments. While being discreet about what Germany was manufacturing, he gave her information on American cruiser specifications along with Russian and French experiments in new small arms. According to his sources, Britain should immediately begin building two dozen ironclads for its own security, while the French and the Russians would be unable to go to war for some four years because of their botched rearming.[33]

The Empress Frederick was also at her daughter Sophie's wedding in Greece, as was the Prince of Wales. She was reminded of her own wedding as her daughter and the Duke of Sparta stood at the altar wearing their golden crowns, before walking three times around it with their lighted tapers. Briefly, she felt important again, but was soon reminded of the passing of the old order when she was summoned back to Germany from Italy for the funeral of the Dowager Empress Augusta. For once, she wrote to her mother, the sight of the dead woman was not unpleasant.

> You would have thought she was *just* going to a fête or a soirée! Her face was *so calm* and peaceful and had grown *younger*. There seemed not a wrinkle, and the eyes that used to *stare* so, and look one through and through were closed, which gave her a gentler expression than I ever saw in life. The false hair in ringlets on her brow, the line of the eyebrows and eyelashes carefully painted as in life—a golden myrtle wreath on her head, and an ample tulle veil, were well arranged, flowing and curling about her head and neck and shoulders—hiding her chin and her hands folded, her bracelets on and her wedding ring. The cloth of gold train lined and trimmed with ermine which she wore for her Golden Wedding was very well folded and composed about her person and over her feet, and flowed far down on the steps in front! She looked *wonderfully well*, and really almost like a young person. I felt if she could have seen herself she would have been *pleased*. She was the "Empress," even in death, and sur-

rounded with all the stiff pomp and ceremony she loved so much.[34]

The most formidable of the Coburg group at court except for herself was gone. The Dowager Empress had usually opposed Bismarck and had usually lost to him; the Empress Frederick was now left more alone in her beliefs. As if to prove how utterly her old supporters had joined Bismarck, Gustav Freytag wrote a pamphlet called *The Crown Prince and the German Imperial Crown,* which was even more malicious than the turncoat Coburg Duke Ernest's second attack on his former allies, *The 99 Days.* Freytag not only damned the Emperor and Empress Frederick, but also said that Prince Alice of Hesse-Darmstadt had helped her sister to pass German military information to the French during the war of 1870. To show repentance for his past loyalty, Freytag even sent the scurrilous pamphlet to Bismarck for approval before its publication.

This was Bismarck's swansong in revenge. What he had done to others would soon be done to him. When the Kaiser wanted new labor legislation, Bismarck unwisely opposed it, and spoke of the dangers of socialism growing by appeasement. He wanted the Reichstag to pass anti-socialist measures and offered his resignation if he did not get them. The Kaiser would have accepted the resignation, but he had no replacement ready. He remained courteous, but he was inwardly seething. He was not his aged grandfather or sick father, necessarily dependent on the powers and infallibility of Bismarck. He wanted social reforms, larger armies and navies and more colonies, and he was not prepared to be balked by an aging Chancellor, however indispensable he was meant to be.

Matters reached a crisis when the Kaiser called for an international labor conference in Berlin, and the Chancellor tried to stop it through his usual underhand methods. He told the British Ambassador that he could not agree to what the Kaiser was doing and had decided to resign some of his posts. His imperial master had no doubts. "He thinks he can do all things and he wishes to have the entire credit all to himself."[35] From the Kaiser's point of view, socialism had to be controlled and led, not ignored or resisted. Bismarck's policy was to allow socialism to progress until it was necessary to call out the troops and to sweep the streets with grapeshot. This might have been possible in the time of the Kaiser's grandfather, but not now. For a young monarch, such a policy would be a disaster. "It would have been said," the Kaiser told the British Ambassador, "that my only idea of governing was by bayonets."[36]

Unable to tolerate Bismarck's opposition which seemed to be threatening the dynasty, the Kaiser made him resign on the pretext of bad health. He conjured up a diagnosis as dangerous as that which had threatened his father's life. He was assured, he wrote to Queen Victoria, that if the Chancellor had kept on a few weeks longer, he would unfailingly have died of apoplexy. With deep regret, therefore, the Kaiser had decided to part from Bismarck in order to keep him alive.[37] Such splendid hypocrisy was worthy of Bismarck himself. It was, Lord Salisbury thought, a curious nemesis for the Chancellor: he had been overthrown by the despotism he had created. No German constitution could save him from dismissal by a young Emperor who wanted to be his own Chancellor, Chief of Staff and his own minister in every department—a task beyond any human powers.[38]

So the Chancellor was retired as thoroughly as the Empress Frederick. He had visited her before his fall, possibly hoping for her mediation, possibly trying to prove she was still in a plot against him. He had told her then that the trouble was the Kaiser's habit of accepting advice from all sides instead of from him alone. The Empress Frederick kept her own counsel, but thought him necessary for Germany and the peace of Europe. Actually, his removal caused no flutters. There seemed still an utter absence of movement all over Europe, Lord Salisbury wrote to Queen Victoria at the time.[39] The Chancellor was no more irreplaceable than anyone else.

As if sorry for himself or for what he had done, Bismarck paid another courtesy call on the Empress Frederick—the call that his ambition had stopped him from making after her husband's death. "He did not exactly complain," she wrote to Queen Victoria, "but I think he feels very deeply that he has not been treated with the *consideration* due to his age and position. We parted amicably and in peace, which I am glad of—as I should have been sorry—having suffered *so* much all these long years under the system—that it should appear as if I had any spirit of revenge."[40]

His system, which had broken her, had broken him. The stage was now cleared for the Anglo-German diplomacy of the next two decades, which would be a traditional mixture of the royal and the ministerial. On the one side were Queen Victoria and the Prince of Wales, who would become king in time, and their foreign secretaries. On the other side were the Kaiser and a succession of imperial servants. To emphasize his policy of direct diplomacy, he hastened down to meet Queen Victoria on her visit to Darmstadt in April 1890. He wanted to reassure her that he would manage better without Bismarck. "He said it would have been impossible to go on with him," the Queen wrote in her journal, "and that his violence in language and gesture had become such, that he had to put a stop to it. He was sorry to say that Bismarck was intriguing with Russia behind his back."[41] This last reason was a sop to his grandmother, whose suspicion of Russia was a constant in her long diplomacy.

Although the Empress approved of Bismarck's replacement, General Leo von Caprivi—a prospective Minister of War under her husband—she did not approve of her son's autocracy. He seemed to be acting like a German Tsar and governing by ukase. The system had not changed; Bismarck was gone, but William had learned from him to play the despot.[42] Fortunately, two of the outstanding quarrels between mother and son were resolved. The ill-starred Moretta was betrothed to Prince Adolf zu Schaumburg-Lippe and could begin to put aside all memories of her Sandro. And with her provision from her dead husband and the proceeds of a legacy, the Empress Frederick could afford to refuse the minor grace-and-favor residences offered by her son and build herself a house at Kronberg near the Rhine in the forested Taunus hills. There, on an estate of 250 acres, she had a German architect design for her Friedrichshof, which would house the art treasures and papers she had been collecting for so long.

She wanted a home that would be no schloss, but more of a large English country house with a small tower or two like Osborne. She gave her architect instructions that nothing about it should catch the eye, but that it should hold the look. She told her mother that Friedrichshof was nothing extraordinary, but solid and in good taste. In style, it was a mixture of Tudor, Italian Renaissance and eighteenth-century classical, yet comfortable without appearing too grand. Her pride lay in her park, cut out of the forests and so already filled with old chestnuts and cedars and larches and firs. And she had planted a rose garden among the flower beds, where she loved to walk.

Her retirement to a country estate so far from Berlin signaled her retreat from politics. Except for an occasional trip abroad, she would become the country lady that a part of her had always wanted to be—the role of the widow of Balmoral and Osborne that her mother had played for many years after the death of the Prince Consort. She made a hurried journey to Greece for the birth of her daughter Sophie's first child, which was born prematurely after a difficult labor among the usual accusations about the incompetence of the doctors. Later, Sophie was received into the Greek Orthodox Church, which provoked an outburst from her brother the Kaiser, who would not give up any sister's allegiance to him as head of the German Church. "Whether I go to hell or not is my own affair," she told the Kaiser from the safe distance of Greece.[43]

Relations were so good between the Kaiser and England after he had acquired Heligoland in exchange for a few claims in East Africa that he agreed to allow his English mother to go on a semi-official visit to Paris in 1891. She was meant to arrange for the exchange of contemporary works of art between Paris and Berlin, but her nostalgia got the better of her discretion. Instead of confining herself to visiting studios and choosing pictures for the exhibition, she went on visits to the places her husband had occupied during the siege of the French capital. She had only intended pilgrimages in his memory to Versailles, where the German Empire had been proclaimed, and to St. Cloud, destroyed by artillery. She provoked a storm of chauvinism in the national press and almost had to flee to England. Her brother, the Prince of Wales, commiserated with her. The French, he wrote, were not to be depended upon and lacked the chivalrous feelings for which they were once famous.[44]

She was never again used in affairs of state. She was condemned to retirement until she would die. The last decade of the century was a magnificat for Queen Victoria's long reign and a demonstration of her expertise in helping to keep the peace of Europe. Her eldest daughter could have no part in it, because she was no longer privy to any intelligence which might help her mother. The Empress Frederick wrote to Queen Victoria about her elder children.

> We *could* have made the young Generation ours by bringing them in contact with the influences of another better, deeper, and higher intellectual and political atmosphere. . . . The Chain was snapped in two—their beloved Father with his influence and authority is gone to join our beloved Papa—and I am only a powerless and useless relic of the past—a shadow—of what once *might* have been—and never came—and who is to gather up the broken threads of the slender web we had been YEARS weaving—only to see it torn up—and trampled under foot in the most ruthless manner—I know not![45]

14

Retirement and Requiem

HE WEB of Anglo-German understanding had always been tenuous. Queen Victoria and her eldest daughter might have thought that the English and the Germans were natural allies because of linked dynasties and shared faiths and cultural affinities, but the differences between the two countries were fundamental. Economics, political structures, communications and the differing natures of their elites pushed the two nations into competition and misunderstanding.[1] The individual efforts of the English Queen and her daughter began to appear futile as Germany, which had always refused to be England's pupil, now became its rival.

When the Empress Frederick retired to her Friedrichshof, the German economy was already outstripping the British one. Bismarck's game with overseas colonies became a matter of national prestige. Imperialism might seem irrelevant to the ousted Chancellor, but it was important to the Kaiser and his countrymen, and the young Emperor was determined to spearhead national feeling, instead of denying it. Half-English

as he was, he could not seem to placate England. Fearing pa-
tronage by his mother's homeland, he wanted to be superior;
he intended to unite his nation by outdoing hers.

By choosing to rule personally, the Kaiser found his personal choices ruled largely by social and economic forces beyond his control. Queen Victoria could covertly influence
politics and diplomacy, she could not decide them. The Kaiser
could decide, but at the risk of public exposure. By taking
power from Bismarck, he lost freedom of choice, for he could
not dissociate himself from his government's demands as
Queen Victoria could. It was particularly true in his relationship with his grandmother's country; he may not have wanted
personally to provoke Queen Victoria, but he felt that national
interests dictated his assertions. Because Britain had its empire
and strong navy and overseas trade, he could not deny his
country the same things just because they might seem a threat
to his mother's homeland.

The Empress Frederick was against Germans having colonies in Africa. In her opinion they did not understand how
to manage or govern them—only the British did—and the
campaign to acquire them excited false patriotism. And with
its huge army, why did Germany also need a huge fleet? Her
eldest son's one idea was to have a navy larger and stronger
than the British navy, although this was really pure madness
and folly. She hoped she could make him see how impossible
and needless it was.[2]

The Kaiser did not see how impossible and needless it
was. He was always irritated by his mother's references in
front of him to "our fleet," when she was referring to the
British fleet. His royal yacht *Hohenzollern* was really a gunboat.
On his yearly trips to the Cowes Regatta, he would inspect
the ironclads drawn up to greet him with broadsides and bunt-
ing, and he insisted on visiting the dockyards at Portsmouth
and on sending over German admirals to check on the launch-
ing of new battleships. Although he protested that he wanted
the British fleet strong enough to defeat all other navies com-

bined, his expanding warship program worried his grand-mother and her admirals with the prospect of an arms race. She was no fool about his use of his British admiral's uniform to pry into naval secrets. She once had to warn Lord Salisbury against the commander of one of her own battleships. "Lord Charles Beresford should be watched and not be told or shown anything," the Queen instructed, "as I know it for a fact (the Duke of York told me) that he writes every week to the German Emperor who is better informed about our navy than I am."[3]

If the Kaiser could not assert himself too strongly against his grandmother, he could against his uncle the Prince of Wales. Not only did he insist on taking precedence on every occasion they met, but he enjoyed racing his yacht *Meteor* against his uncle's *Britannia* for the Admiral's Cup. He won twice and crowed about his victories in telegrams to Queen Victoria. On one occasion, he was accompanied to the Regatta by two cruisers named *Weissenburg* and *Wörth* after his father's victories against France, which made his pro-French uncle indignant and led to attacks on German tactlessness in the British press. The Prince of Wales and the Kaiser were so different in temperament and character that they continued to underestimate and dislike each other. The Prince of Wales thought the Kaiser a liar and a bully, while the Kaiser thought his uncle a banal courtier.[4]

Behind the scenes, the conciliatory Prince of Wales wanted to keep his imperious nephew sweet on England and to give him the marks of respect he craved, but which Queen Victoria liked to withhold from him to show her power. In 1894, the Kaiser made it known through Colonel Swaine that he wanted a British army officer's uniform to add to his admiral's one. "This would never do," Queen Victoria declared. "He is far too much spoiled already."[5] Her ministers agreed with her, her son did not. The Prince of Wales understood the importance of rank and title in the Kaiser's mind. He was touchy over those matters himself. In the end, after mounting pressure from her son and grandson, Queen Victoria gave way with bad grace.

She granted the Kaiser his desire at an occasion which put herself at the head of the united family at her dead husband's German homeland. She went to Coburg in April 1894, to attend the wedding of her only Hessian grandson, Grand Duke Ernest Louis, to her granddaughter Princess Victoria Melita of Saxe-Coburg-Gotha. She was surrounded by four generations of her royal relatives, including one great-grandchild. There were so many of them that there had to be two sittings for dinner at the schloss. In the family group portraits taken during her stay, she looked like an aged queen bee with the Kaiser on her right and the Empress Frederick on her left and her three sons standing behind her among the serried ranks of the family. She condescended to make the Kaiser an Honorary Colonel of the Royals, especially as he had sent a squadron of her Prussian regiment of dragoons all the way to Coburg to honor her. The Kaiser was quite overwhelmed, he declared, at the idea that he could now wear besides the blue admiral's uniform the traditional British redcoat.[6]

This display of family unity overemphasized the kinship and harmony between the thrones of Europe, particularly as the Tsarevitch Nicholas announced his engagement to the bridegroom's youngest sister Princess Alexandra of Hesse. In fact, diplomacy and peace-keeping through royal marriages were declining factors in international affairs. The industrial powers of England and Germany were finding each other to be competitors for the markets of the world, and the growing industrialism of Russia was causing strains within the structure of that retrograde society which threatened the throne of the Tsars. The products of the machines and the rise of the working classes manning them were demanding new methods of dealing with internal and international affairs. Materialism menaced royalism, economics was the enemy of crowns.

There was a family and a political falling out after the

Coburg gathering. Before then, the Kaiser had gone out of his way to conciliate his grandmother and his mother, and settled most of the outstanding family quarrels. The Guelph Fund, which Bismarck had used to finance his press manipulation, was restored in part to the Duke of Cumberland, the King of Hanover's heir. The Kaiser gave his mother for restoration the old castle of Kronberg in the Taunus hills, which adjoined the grounds of her newly built Friedrichshof. As another mark of reconciliation, he went to the wedding of his last unmarried sister Mossy to Prince Frederick Charles of Hesse. And he continued flattering his grandmother in England by calling her the Nestor or Sybil of Europe's sovereigns, revered by all, feared only by the bad.[7]

Yet from 1895 to 1898, the Kaiser's family pride and colonial ambitions prejudiced his relations with Queen Victoria and with her country. He agreed with national sentiment in supporting the independence of the Boers in the Transvaal, which led to his imprudent telegram of congratulations to President Kruger for forcing the surrender of the Jameson Raiders without having to ask for the help of friendly powers. He was so furious at the raid that he even thought of returning his British uniforms, saying that they were only fit to be worn by South African *banditti*.[8] Queen Victoria was even more incensed and sent her grandson an angry telegram, accusing him of being very unfriendly toward England. "It would have been far better to have said nothing."

Indignation against the German Emperor was so great in England that he could not make his annual visit to Cowes. In fact, he did not visit England again for three years. Quite deliberately, Queen Victoria provoked his fears, inviting the new Tsar and Tsarina to Balmoral, where the Kaiser was not able to visit her. She began a private correspondence with the Tsar and made her distrust of the Kaiser clear to the Russian ruler. "I am afraid that William may go and tell things against us to you," she warned the Tsar, "just as he does about you to us. If so, pray tell me openly and confidentially."[9]

She wanted to prove her intelligence system superior to the young Kaiser's, whom she did not even invite to her Diamond Jubilee.

In response, he did not try to alleviate colonial and international conflicts between the interests and the industries of the two powers. Although he kept on corresponding privately with Queen Victoria as her most dutiful and devoted grandson, he offended her by his violent hostility toward his sister in Greece over a Cretan crisis. She was also annoyed by his insistence that England should join him in sharing out the Portuguese Empire and the Pacific islands. Colonial and commercial rivalries were playing their part in the bad feelings between Germany and England in the middle of the decade. Yet personal pride also counted. As Colonel Swaine commented, the principal culprit was the Emperor himself. He could not recover from his annoyance that the Kruger telegram had exactly the opposite result from what he anticipated. He had been convinced that a country with no army corps would not stand up to him who had twenty corps on a peace footing. All the same, Swaine thought that war between the two countries was improbable. The elephant could not fight the whale.[10]

That the rifts betweeen the two nations could be widened by the personal feelings between their two sovereigns was offensive to the English Prime Minister, Lord Salisbury. Like Bismarck, he deplored the fact that the Kaiser would deal directly with Queen Victoria and allow personal feelings to influence his country's diplomacy. When he heard that the Kaiser had called him an enemy, he wrote to the British Ambassador in Berlin:

> It is a great nuisance that one of the main factors in the European calculation should be so ultra human. He is as jealous as a woman because he does not think the Queen pays him enough attention. I believe that in a true constitutional spirit he holds me responsible for all the personal decisions of my Sovereign. This is very unfair. . . . Yet Her Majesty, in dealing with her own personal move-

ments and proceedings, is quite as despotic as the Emperor William is in dealing with foreign affairs.[11]

The Kaiser was further infuriated by Queen Victoria's appearance of acting as head of the family even in German affairs. The question at issue was the succession to the Duchy of Coburg, presently held by her son Alfred, whose heir had died. Her third son, Prince Arthur, was next in line of succession, and the Queen approved of him becoming the legitimate heir. The Kaiser, however, felt it necessary for the English Prince to learn German, reside in Germany, and serve as an officer in the German army. If not, the Reichstag might pass a law declaring that foreign princes were incapable of succeeding to a German throne.[12]

"He has got it into His Imperial Head," the British Ambassador reported back from Berlin, "that He is neglected by the Royal Family, or rather to use his own expression, that they treat him as a *quantité négligeable*."[13] All would be well if Queen Victoria invited him to come to England for her eightieth birthday, or if that was impossible, to Cowes. He received the Cowes invitation to smooth his ruffled feathers.[14] At the Wartburg castle in Thuringia, he told the Duke of Coburg and Prince Arthur that any heir to the Duchy would have to be educated as a German prince if he wished to succeed. Faced with this ultimatum, Prince Arthur resigned his claim in favor of a nephew, the young Duke of Albany, who immediately left Eton to be educated in the ways of his adopted country.

This placation of the Kaiser was not enough. He now asserted that British warships had bombarded German property in Samoa. The action was a taint on the national honor and an attack on his self-respect. In the most astounding letter in this whole period of direct royal diplomacy, he denounced Lord Salisbury by name to Queen Victoria. If he did not get satisfaction from the British government over Samoa, he threatened serious consequences. Neither he nor the German people would accept being treated as if they were from Portugal, Chile or Patagonia. He wanted redress or he could not visit England; public opinion would not allow it.[15] Instead, he received a reprimand from Queen Victoria. She had passed on his letter to Lord Salisbury, who agreed with her that it was quite new for a sovereign to attack in a private letter the minister of another sovereign. Queen Victoria declared herself greatly astonished. "I never should do such a thing," she asserted, "and I never personally attacked, or complained of Prince Bismarck, though I knew well what a bitter enemy he was to England and all the harm he did."[16] She had conveniently forgotten that she had attacked Bismarck to the Kaiser's grandfather as the *"one person"* who wanted to break the peace of Europe—though it was true, she had not named him. She knew the correct form of international accusation.

An accident to the Kaiser's wife gave him a good reason for not appearing at Cowes, but in November, he did cross the Channel on a courtesy visit to Queen Victoria. The Queen found him sensible and kind, and a good understanding was reestablished. It was just in time, for the Boer War was about to begin and England needed every friend on the continent of Europe that it could muster. "The German Emperor wants to be our friend," the British Ambassador in Berlin was told, "but he would like to be our *only* friend."[17]

It was a curious reversal of the War of 1870. Then Germany had been condemned for its military superiority and atrocities against civilians. Now Britain was accused of worse behavior, of raising vast armies to crush a few Boer commandos, and of herding Boer women and children to die in concentration camps. The Kaiser, however, remained Britain's only friend in Europe and refused offers from the Russians and the French to intervene and force England to make peace. The war, he declared, had set many stones rolling and no one could say where they would stop, but he would not forget that he was the devoted grandson of Queen Victoria. He would not join in any combination against her. He would be glad to think that he had in any way contributed to the last years of her reign being passed in peace.[18]

He did, however, listen to an appeal from the Boers, when they were losing the war. He was asked to act as a mediator in negotiating terms of peace. He accepted as long as both sides wanted it, but when Queen Victoria replied that her whole nation was with her in fixed determination to carry the war through without any intervention, he understood and repeated his determination "to see that you shall have fair play."[19] There would be no intervention by Germany or anyone else. "The Teutonic People," he told Colonel Swaine, "must stand shoulder to shoulder, or the Slavs will destroy us."[20]

Undoubtedly, the special relationship which Queen Victoria had developed with her first grandson since his childhood played an important part in preventing the great powers of Europe from coalescing to exploit England's weakness during the Boer War. Bismarck had died in 1898, and with his death, the great promoter of the balance of power in Europe was gone. The new Chancellor von Bülow did little to check the Kaiser's temporary support of England until he should have a navy powerful enough to challenge it on the seas. The Empress Frederick was ill and in retirement at Kronberg. A direct relationship between the Kaiser and his grandmother was possible even though commercial and international rivalries led to bad blood between the two nations. The Prince of Wales aided and abetted in this burial of bad feelings, so necessary for England's security, so personal in Germany's strategy.

The sudden failing of Queen Victoria's health in the middle of January 1901, showed that the Kaiser's devotion to his grandmother was no sham. Canceling celebrations for the bicentenary of the Prussian kingdom, he hurried on a special train to Osborne to be present at her deathbed. "NO *notice* whatever is to be taken of me in my capacity as Emperor," he said to the Prince of Wales. "I came as grandson."[21] For the last two-and-a-half hours of Queen Victoria's life, he stood beside her left shoulder at the head of her bed. When she died and the new King had to go to London to attend the accession Council, the Kaiser made the arrangements for the lying in state and ordered the Union Jack draped around the walls of the room where his grandmother's coffin lay, all covered with floral wreaths. He stayed away from public affairs in Berlin to remain in England for the state funeral. His uncle was so moved by his behavior that the Kaiser found himself raised to the rank of British field marshal. Even Lord Salisbury, for so long the enemy, met him in amity.

Queen Victoria's death seemed to have brought about the understanding between England and Germany which had been the desire of her long life of diplomacy, yet it could only be a temporary understanding between the two industrial and commercial rivals, governed in their different ways. On his way back to Berlin, the Kaiser stopped at Homburg to visit his mother, who was now also stricken with an incurable cancer. They had become reconciled over the past few years, but he could not stay with her long. He had to return to Berlin, where he found himself unpopular because of his show of devotion to the Queen of England. Public opinion in Germany allowed less and less to the personal feelings of sovereigns.

The Empress Frederick's cancer appeared after a bad riding accident she had suffered three years previously. Her horse had reared, the Empress had fallen off the wrong side onto her head. Her riding habit had caught on to the saddle so that she was trapped between the horse's hoofs, and the frightened animal had trampled on her right hand. The injuries did not seem to heal and cancer was diagnosed.

She had been active and happy in her retirement until then, making her country house into a museum of her taste and a shrine for her husband's memory. "One loves one's own things too much," she used to say. "One strokes them with one's eyes." Portraits of the House of Hanover and her

closer German relatives lined the walls, busts of her husband
and of her dead child Waldemar stood over the great Italianate
fireplaces. Collections of books and coins, medals and photo-
graphs, silver and old oak absorbed her time and showed her
interests. She became the benefactress of Kronberg, building
a hospital and an old peoples' home and a modern school,
and restoring the ancient castle and church in the town. She
made a memorial park for her husband and unveiled his statue
there in 1899. If she could not help to run the affairs of a
nation, she could organize her own estate and neighborhood.

Her unwilling isolation from her country's affairs was revealed at the Villa Imperiale at Homburg, where she was visiting her brother, the Prince of Wales. An American journalist
was granted an interview. She launched into a monologue
on America and Anglo-German relations and internal problems in Germany. Hour after hour passed, while the Empress
Frederick held forth. Never for a moment did the stream of
talk stop. The journalist remembered Carlyle's words on Ma-
caulay: "Flow on, thou shining river." He listened and did
not perceive the loneliness of a brilliant and powerful woman,
who needed any outlet for her opinions, so carefully guarded
at home, so needlessly neglected by her son, the Kaiser.[22]

She was not entirely alone. Count Seckendorff had remained with her to the end as head of her household, and
he traveled with her on painting expeditions to Italy, where
she created landscapes and portraits for the walls of Friedrichshof. Her remaining attendants were loyal to her, especially her chamberlain Baron Reischach, who was the first
to know that she had cancer. She told her mother and daughters that it was only chronic lumbago.

As her symptoms became clear and she wasted away, she
could not hide the truth any longer. Her three younger daughters left their husbands to come and nurse her between them.
Her son the Kaiser now found the time to pay her frequent
visits, and her brother and defender the King of England came

to visit her at the end of February 1901. His nephew received him with state honors at Frankfurt and then withdrew with unusual tact to leave his uncle alone with the dying Empress. She and the King had much to say to each other and little time.

"You are so brave and good for the heavy trial and pain which it pleases God to inflict you with," the King wrote to her. "After dear Mama you are the one person in the world who ought not to suffer, for if anyone from her life and virtues is more prepared to go straight to heaven, it is yourself! It often seems to me that it is the bad people that prosper in this world—and not the good ones!"[23]

On August 5, the Kaiser was standing beside his mother's bed when she breathed her last. A butterfly flew in through the open window and circled the face of the dead Empress and flew out over the rose garden she loved. She had lived long enough to see an Anglo-German understanding between her son and her brother; although it was temporary and unsatisfactory and full of stress and misunderstanding, it was a truce that would allow the new century at least a decade of respite.

Her life may have seemed rather a waste, a long preparation for a role which she would never play. She had been trained for a throne. Her marriage had been arranged to influence the creation of a liberal and constitutional and united Germany, but she had been thwarted by the interminable reign of Emperor William I and the intolerable rule of Bismarck. She could have echoed her brother's lament to her when he was unable to move because of a torn ligament: "I hardly like to ask them when I am likely to change my position—anyhow the French saying is applicable—*Qui sait attendre?*"[24]

She knew how to wait even less well than her brother did. She was always impetuous and forthright. Her many great qualities withered away in her long attendance at a foreign court, which gave her no more understanding than she gave it. She was always a stranger in a strange land except in time of war. Her heart remained in her homeland. Though she tried to be a good Prussian and a good German, she could not forget her essential Englishness from which she derived so many wounding comparisons. She was a double patriot in an age that increasingly demanded commitment to a single nation.

Personal royal contacts across artificial frontiers were her birthright, because the kings and queens of the new nations were sometimes foreign born. These personal contacts were still maintained by her brother in England and son in Germany. The Emperor was told that, if there were any disagreements between the two governments, he should write to his uncle the King, who would do his best to smooth matters down.[25] While these last exponents of the art of royal diplomacy were alive and were corresponding with the Tsar and the Austrian Emperor and the King of Italy, there was an alternative system of intelligence and conciliation which helped to prevent the outbreak of the First World War in Europe. That war did not come until King Edward VII was dead. By its end, the international contacts of royalty and aristocracy would be destroyed along with their power.

The Empress Frederick was fortunate to live in an age when her life was still important for her two countries. As it was, she was a woman who was destined to act between her mother and her husband, to work for them both and to be suspected for that. She was loyal to a fault, but loyal to two people in two different nations. She was the heir to a tradition that was the victim of the rise of the modern state. Bismarck was the architect of the unity of Germany, and his commitment to his country made him resist anything he thought alien and persecute anyone he thought a threat to his authority. Both the pride and the misfortune of the Empress Frederick was to be the eldest daughter of Queen Victoria. She could never forget it, nor could Bismarck.

For a Princess Royal trained in England and wedded to Prussia, it was a tale of two countries. It was the best of times, it was the worst of times, it was the spring of hope, it was the winter of despair, she had everything before her, she had nothing before her, until her time was over.

Reference Notes

List of Abbreviations

RA
: The Royal Archives, Windsor Castle.

PRO
: Public Records Office.

FO
: Foreign Office.

LETTERS
: *The Letters of Queen Victoria, A Selection from Her Majesty's Correspondence,* First Series, 1837–1861, edited by A. C. Benson and Viscount Esher (3 volumes, London, 1907). Second Series, 1862–1885, edited by G. E. Buckle (3 volumes, London, 1926). Third Series, 1886–1901, edited by G. E. Buckle (3 volumes, London, 1930).

FURTHER LETTERS
: *Further Letters of Queen Victoria,* from the Archives of the House of Brandenburg-Prussia, edited by Hector Bolitho (London, 1938).

QUEEN VICTORIA'S JOURNAL   Preserved in the Royal Archives.

ENGLISH EMPRESS   *The English Empress, A Study in the Relations between Queen Victoria and Her Eldest Daughter,* by Egon Caesar Conte Corti, with an Introduction by Wolfgang, Prince of Hesse (London, 1957).

KRONBERG ARCHIVES   These consist of the Archives of the Princess Royal, later Empress Frederick of Germany. The letters and papers are kept at Friedrichshof, Kronberg.

NOTE:

The confidential letters and papers sent by the Emperor and Empress Frederick to Windsor Castle were all returned to Germany. They are no longer in the Royal Archives.

CHAPTER 1

1. *The Greville Memoirs, 1814–1860,* ed. L. Strachey and R. Fulford, 8 vols. (London, 1938), 4, p. 338.
2. *Letters,* I, 1, p. 237. Queen Victoria to Leopold, King of the Belgians, October 12, 1839.
3. Idem, January 5, 1841.
4. See Princess Catherine Radziwill, *The Empress Frederick* (London, 1934), p. 45.
5. *Letters,* I, 2, p. 126. Queen Victoria to Leopold, King of the Belgians, September 29, 1846.
6. Radziwill, *Empress Frederick,* p. 29.
7. *Denkwürdigkeiten aus den Papieren des Freiherrn Christian Friederich von Stockmar* (Braunschweig, 1872), p. 358.
8. RA, M 12/5.
9. RA, M 12/39.
10. *Denkwürdigkeiten,* p. 391. Also see RA, M 12/14.
11. See RA, M 12/50, 55, 62.
12. RA, M 13/68. Lady Lyttelton's Journal, August 24, 1845.
13. RA, M 14/50. Queen Victoria for Miss Hildyard, December 17, 1846.

14. RA, M 13/55. The Princess Royal to Queen Victoria, October, 1844.
15. RA, M 12/35.
16. RA, M 13/75, 70. Lady Lyttelton's Journal, September 6, August 27, 1845.
17. Baron Ernest von Stockmar, *Memoirs of Baron Stockmar*, 2 vols. (London, 1872), 2, p. 207 note.
18. *Letters*, I, 2, pp. 183–184. Queen Victoria to Leopold, King of the Belgians, March 1, 1848.
19. Idem, pp. 177–179. The King of Prussia to Queen Victoria, February 27, 1848.
20. RA, M 15/98, 105.
21. *Queen Victoria's Journal*, May 1, 1851.
22. Sir Theodore Martin, *Life of the Prince Consort*, 5 vols. (London, 1875–1880), 2, p. 385.
23. *Further Letters*, p. 25. Queen Victoria to the Princess Augusta of Prussia, June 19, 1851.
24. Idem, p. 44. April 2, 1854.
25. For a fuller understanding of the role of the military attaché, see Alfred Vagts, *The Military Attaché* (Princeton, N. J., 1967).
26. Erich Marcks, *Bismarck, eine Biographie 1815–1851* (Stuttgart, 1951), p. 472.
27. See *George, Duke of Cambridge*, ed. E. Sheppard, 2 vols. (London, 1907), I, p. 197.
28. RA, M 13/78. Lady Lyttelton to Queen Victoria, December 9, 1845.
29. *Queen Victoria's Journal*, September 30, 1855.
30. *Letters*, I, 3, p. 187. Queen Victoria to Leopold, King of the Belgians, September 22, 1855.
31. RA, Z 61/9. Lord Clarendon to Queen Victoria, September 27, 1855.
32. RA, Z 61/12. Queen Victoria to Lord Clarendon, September 24, 1855.
33. *The Times* (London), October 3, 1855.
34. RA, Z 61/22. Lord Clarendon to Queen Victoria, October 3, 1855.
35. RA, Z 61/29, 36. Lord Augustus Loftus to Lord Clarendon, October 9 and 10, 1855.
36. RA, Z 61/46, 47. See the King of Prussia to the Princess of Prussia, January 3, 1856, and her reply to him.
37. RA, Z 61/69. Queen Victoria to Lord Palmerston, March 26, 1856.
38. Quoted in Egon Corti, *The English Empress* (London, 1957), p. 29.
39. *Queen Victoria's Journal*, July 16, 1857.
40. Anon., *The Empress Frederick: a Memoir* (London, 1913), p. 44.
41. RA, Z 67/92. Prince Albert to Lord Clarendon, November 26, 1857.
42. Prince Albert to Prince Frederick William, February 24, 1857, Kronberg Archive.
43. *Letters*, I, 3, p. 321. Queen Victoria to Lord Clarendon, October 25, 1857.
44. See *Correspondence between General Leopold von Gerlach and the Delegate to the Federal Diet, Otto von Bismarck* (Berlin, 1893), p. 313, April 8, 1856.

45. RA, T 1/136, 161. The Princess Royal to the Prince of Wales, September 18, 1856, and July 10, 1857.
46. See RA, M 17/31 and 33. The Prince of Wales to Prince Albert, March 25, 1856.
47. Queen Victoria to the Princess Royal, July 28, 1858, Kronberg Archive.
48. RA, T 2/107. The Princess Royal to the Prince of Wales, December 21, 1859.
49. RA, Z 261. Queen Victoria, "Remarks, Conversations and Reflections," Prince Albert's birthday, 1857.
50. RA, Z 291/20. Idem, December 20, 1857.
51. RA, Z 261. Idem, January 8, 1858.

CHAPTER 2

1. RA, T 1/195. The Princess Royal to the Prince of Wales, December 31, 1857.
2. Walburga, Lady Paget, *Scenes and Memories* (London, 1912), pp. 62–64.
3. *Queen Victoria's Journal,* January 25, 1858. See also RA, Z 261/31 and 32.
4. RA, Z 261/36.
5. RA, Z 5/6. The Princess Royal to Queen Victoria, February 2, 1858.
6. RA, Z 261.
7. Martin, *Prince Consort,* 4, p. 169.
8. *Dearest Child: Letters between Queen Victoria and the Princess Royal, 1858–1861,* ed. R. Fulford (London, 1964), pp. 31–32.
9. RA, Z 70/4. Lady Howard de Walden to Lady Caroline Barrington, February 4, 1858.
10. RA, Z 62/103. Lord Bloomfield to Lord Clarendon, February 6, 1858.
11. RA, Z 70/9. Baron E. von Stockmar to Queen Victoria, February 7, 1858.
12. For accounts of the ceremonial entry, see RA, Z 70/11 and 19, in which Lady Churchill and the Grand Duchess of Mecklenburg-Strelitz write back to Queen Victoria about her daughter's reception in Potsdam and Berlin.
13. RA, Z 70/17. Lady Bloomfield to Queen Victoria, February 10, 1858.
14. RA, Z 70/26. The Grand Duchess of Mecklenburg-Strelitz to Queen Victoria, February 14, 1858.
15. RA, Z 70/39. Lady Churchill to Queen Victoria, February 24, 1858.
16. *Dearest Child,* pp. 50–52, February 20, 1858.
17. *Queen Victoria's Journal,* March 4, 1858.
18. *Dearest Child,* pp. 64–65, February 27, 1858.
19. RA, Z 1/8. The Princess Royal to the Prince Consort, February 20, 1858.
20. RA, Z 261/74–76.
21. *The Greville Memoirs,* 5, p. 201.
22. *Dearest Child,* p. 138, *note.*
23. RA, Z 261/69.

24. The Prince Consort to the Princess Royal, December 1, 1858, Kronberg Archive.
25. Idem, December 22, 1858, Kronberg Archive.
26. *Dearest Child*, p. 141. October 27, 1858.
27. RA, Z 63/117. Sir James Clark to Queen Victoria, January 31, 1859.
28. RA, Z 261/94.
29. RA, Z 261/91–92.
30. RA, Z 7/91. Lady Bloomfield to Queen Victoria, March 5, 1859.
31. RA, Z 7/113. The Princess Royal to Queen Victoria, April 16, 1859.

CHAPTER 3

1. Queen Victoria to the Princess Royal, February 5, 1859, Kronberg Archive.
2. Idem, April 9, 1859, Kronberg Archive.
3. RA, Z 7/113. The Princess Royal to Queen Victoria, April 16, 1859.
4. RA, Z 7/120. The Princess Royal to Queen Victoria, April 30, 1859.
5. RA, Z 8/6. The Princess Royal to Queen Victoria, June 16, 1859.
6. Queen Victoria to the Princess Royal, June 18, 1859, Kronberg Archive.
7. RA, Z 2/23. The Princess Royal to the Prince Consort, June 18, 1859.
8. RA, Z 2/25. Idem, June 25 and July 2, 1859.
9. RA, Z 2/26. Idem, July 9, 1859.
10. RA, Z 8/17. Idem, July 16, 1859.
11. RA, Z 2/29. The Princess Royal to the Prince Consort, February 18, 1860.
12. RA, I 31/85. The Prince Consort to Lord John Russell, March 18, 1860.
13. RA, I 30/2. Sir A. Malet to Lord Clarendon, June 24, 1857.
14. RA, I 30/77. Sir A. Malet to Lord Malmesbury, June 30, 1858.
15. Queen Victoria to the Princess Royal, April 2, 1860, Kronberg Archive.
16. Quoted by Sir Theodore Martin, *The Life of the Prince Consort*, 5, p. 196. The meeting took place on September 25, 1860
17. See William II, Emperor of Germany, *My Early Life* (London, 1926), pp. 9–13.
18. RA, I 33/78.
19. RA, I 37/63. Lord Clarendon to Lord John Russell, November 2, 1861.
20. RA, Z 4/2. The Princess Royal to the Prince Consort, January 19, 1861.
21. RA, I 34/20. The Princess Royal to Queen Victoria, January 2, 1861.
22. RA, I 34/21. Idem, January 4, 1861.
23. RA, I 34/29. Colonel Ponsonby to Sir Charles Phipps, January 7, 1861.
24. RA, Z 4/1. The Crown Princess of Prussia (The Princess Royal) to the Prince Consort, January 11, 1861.
25. RA, Z 10/63. The Crown Princess to Queen Victoria, March 4, 1861.
26. RA, I 35/24. The Crown Princess to the Prince Consort, March 15, 1861.
27. RA, Z 4/10. Idem, March 8, 1861.

28. Queen Victoria to the Crown Princess, March 16, 1861, Kronberg Archive.
29. *Further Letters,* p. 117.
30. RA, Z 12/15. The Crown Princess to Queen Victoria and the Prince Consort, September 25, 1861.
31. RA, Z 12/23. The Crown Princess to Queen Victoria, October 19, 1861.
32. RA, Z 4/36. The Crown Princess to the Prince Consort, November 16, 1861.
33. Queen Victoria to Benjamin Disraeli, memorandum, 1862, Hughenden Papers, Hughenden Manor.
34. Queen Victoria to the Crown Princess, December 18, 1861, Kronberg Archive.
35. RA, Z 12/4 and 50. The Crown Princess to Queen Victoria, August 20 and December 15, 1861.

CHAPTER 4

1. Theodore Juste, *Le Baron Stockmar* (Brussels, 1873), p. 59.
2. *Letters,* 2, 1, p. 11. Leopold, King of the Belgians, to Queen Victoria, January 16, 1862.
3. RA, I 38/96. Lord Palmerston to Lord John Russell, March 9, 1862.
4. RA, I 38/114. Lord Augustus Loftus to Lord John Russell, March 13, 1862.
5. RA, Z 13/16. Idem, May 17, 1862.
6. Major General F. W. Hamilton to Lord John Russell, February 22, 1862. Queen Victoria had obviously asked for the information on the Prussian army as the Major General referred to his figures and wrote, "I trust they are drawn up in conformity with the wishes of Her Majesty."
7. *Further Letters,* pp. 123–126. Queen Victoria to the King of Prussia, March 26 and April 23, 1862.
8. Queen Victoria to the Crown Princess, May 27 and July 2, 1862, Kronberg Archive.
9. Quoted in Egon Corti, *English Empress,* p. 94. The letter was sent on September 19, 1862. The original is in the Kronberg Archive.
10. Prince Otto von Bismarck, *Reflections and Reminiscences,* 2 vols. (London, 1898), 1, pp. 291–293.
11. RA, Z 14/8. The Crown Princess to Queen Victoria, November 1, 1862.
12. RA, Z 14/11 and 15. Idem, November 8 and 23, 1862.
13. *The Correspondence of John Lothrop Motley,* ed. G. Curtis, 2 vols. (London, 1889), 2, p. 105.
14. RA, Z 14/22. The Crown Princess to Queen Victoria, December 17, 1862.

15. *Die Gesammelten Werke Bismarcks,* ed. H. von Petersdorff et al., 18 vols. (Berlin, 1924–35), 15, pp. 194–195.
16. RA, Z 14/27. The Crown Princess to Queen Victoria, January 3, 1863.
17. *Aus dem Leben Theodor von Bernhardis,* 6 vols. (Leipzig, 1895), 5, p. 128.
18. *Letters,* 2, 1, pp. 68–69. Queen Victoria to Leopold, King of the Belgians, February 24, 1863.
19. Queen Victoria to the Crown Princess, February 14, 1863, Kronberg Archive.
20. *Journals and Letters of Reginald Viscount Esher,* ed. M. Brett, 2 vols. (London, 1934), 1, pp. 160–161.
21. *Letters,* 2, 1, pp. 66–69. Queen Victoria to Lord Granville, February 23, 1863.
22. RA, Z 15/15. The Crown Princess to Queen Victoria, April 28, 1863.
23. William II, *My Early Life,* p. 5.
24. *Europäischer Geschichtskalendar, 1863,* ed. H. Schulthess (Nördlingen, 1864), pp. 130–131.
25. RA, Z 15/18 and 20. The Crown Princess to Queen Victoria, May 11 and 16, 1863.
26. RA, I 40/56. Lord Palmerston to Queen Victoria, May 29, 1863.
27. RA, Z 15/19. The Crown Princess to Queen Victoria, April 7, 1863.
28. RA, I 40/57. Idem, June 1, 1863.
29. There is a full account of the exchange of letters between the Crown Prince and the King of Prussia in Corti, op. cit., pp. 103–106.
30. RA, I 40/62. The Crown Princess to Queen Victoria, June 8, 1863.
31. Queen Victoria to the Crown Princess, June 8 and May 24, 1863, Kronberg Archive.
32. RA, I 40/80. The Crown Princess to Queen Victoria, June 11, 1863 (misdated June 21, 1863).
33. Ibid.
34. Queen Victoria to the Crown Princess, June 13, 1863, Kronberg Archive.
35. Corti, *English Empress,* p. 105.
36. RA, I 40/68. Sir A. Buchanan to Lord John Russell, June 13, 1863.
37. RA, Z 15/35. The Crown Princess to Queen Victoria, June 29, 1863.
38. M. Busch, *Bismarck: Some Secret Pages of His History* (London, 1899), p. 460.
39. RA, Z 15/36. The Crown Princess to Queen Victoria, July 3, 1863.
40. See Fritz Stern's important *Gold and Iron: Bismarck, Bleichröder, and the Building of the German Empire* (New York, 1977), pp. 30–31.
41. *Letters of the Empress Frederick,* ed. Sir F. Ponsonby (London, 1928), pp. 46–47.
42. RA, I 41/1. The Crown Princess to Queen Victoria, August 1, 1863.
43. RA, I 42/2. Queen Victoria to the Crown Princess, August 5, 1863.
44. *Memoirs and Letters of the Rt. Hon. Sir Robert Morier,* ed. Mrs. R. Wemyss, 2 vols. (London, 1911), 1, p. 343.
45. *Letters,* 2, 1, p. 310. Leopold, King of the Belgians, to Queen Victoria, September 21, 1863.

46. RA, I 41/32. Lord Clarendon on the Congress of Sovereigns at Frankfurt, August 27, 1863.
47. RA, I 41/43. Minute by Lord Granville of a conversation with Bismarck at the Rosenau, August 21, 1863.
48. RA, I 41/45. Queen Victoria's memorandum on her meeting with the King of Prussia, August 31, 1863.
49. Queen Victoria to the Crown Princess, September 5, 1863, Kronberg Archive.
50. RA, Z 15/50. The Crown Princess to Queen Victoria, September 8, 1863.
51. Quoted in A. J. P. Taylor's brilliant biography *Bismarck: The Man and the Statesman* (London, 1955), p. 59.
52. Corti, *English Empress*, p. 112.
53. Ibid, p. 113.
54. *Letters*, 2, 1, p. 117. Queen Victoria to Leopold, King of the Belgians, November 19, 1863.

CHAPTER 5

1. RA, Z 16/16. The Crown Princess to Queen Victoria, February 8, 1864.
2. *Letters*, 2, 1, p. 145. Lord Palmerston to Queen Victoria, January 8, 1864.
3. Queen Victoria to the Crown Princess, February 3, 1864, Kronberg Archive.
4. Idem, February 13, 1864, Kronberg Archive.
5. RA, Z 16/37. The Crown Princess to Queen Victoria, April 13, 1864.
6. RA, Z 16/41. Idem, May 11, 1864.
7. *Letters*, 2, 1, pp. 282–283. Queen Victoria to Leopold, King of the Belgians, June 30, 1864.
8. RA, Z 16/50. The Crown Princess to Queen Victoria, May 26, 1864.
9. See Corti, *English Empress*, p. 125.
10. Queen Victoria to the Crown Princess, March 2, 1864, Kronberg Archive.
11. RA, Z, 16/61. The Crown Princess to Queen Victoria, July 16, 1864.
12. *Further Letters*, pp. 152–153. Queen Victoria to the Queen of Prussia, July 13, 1864.
13. RA, Z 16/65 and 74. The Crown Princess to Queen Victoria, August 16, 1864.
14. Queen Victoria to the Crown Princess, January 27, 1865, Kronberg Archive.
15. Elisabeth zu Putlitz, *Gustav zu Putlitz*, 2 vols. (Berlin, 1894), 2, pp. 40–50.
16. RA, I 42/8. R. B. Morier to Lord John Russell, November 12, 1864.
17. RA, Z 17/29. The Crown Princess to Queen Victoria, January 21, 1865.

18. *Alice, Grand Duchess of Hesse: Biographical Sketch and Letters,* ed. Princess Helena of Schleswig-Holstein (London, 1884), p. 112. Princess Alice to Queen Victoria, December 11, 1865.
19. *Letters,* 2, 1, p. 271. Queen Victoria to Leopold, King of the Belgians, August 3, 1865.
20. RA, Z 17/82. The Crown Princess to Queen Victoria, August 1, 1865.
21. See Corti, op. cit., p. 145. Bismarck's remark against him was recorded by the Crown Prince in his diaries, selections from which were published in Leipzig in 1929.
22. *Die Gesammelten Werke,* 14, p. 707. Bismarck to Thile, October 23, 1865.
23. RA, I 42/10. Lord Napier to Lord John Russell, November 18, 1865.
24. Queen Victoria to the Crown Princess, April 5, 1865, Kronberg Archive.
25. *Letters,* 2, 1, pp. 449–450. Queen Victoria to Lord Charles Fitzroy, July 20, 1867.

CHAPTER 6

1. Bismarck, *Reflections and Reminiscences,* 1, pp. 164–65.
2. RA, I 43/75. Lord Cowley to Lord Clarendon, March 10, 1866.
3. RA, I 43/30. Consul General Crowe to Lord Clarendon, February 21, 1866.
4. *Diaries of Frederick III,* February 19 and 23, 1866, Kronberg Archive.
5. RA, Z 18/26. The Crown Princess to Queen Victoria, February 20, 1866.
6. RA, I 43/47. Lord Augustus Loftus to Lord Clarendon, March 3, 1866.
7. RA, I 43/98 and 100. Lord Augustus Loftus to Lord Clarendon, March 17, 1866.
8. RA, Z 18/34. The Crown Princess to Queen Victoria, March 16, 1866.
9. RA, I 43/101. Lord Clarendon to Queen Victoria, March 18, 1866.
10. RA, I 43/105. The Crown Princess to Queen Victoria, March 20, 1866.
11. RA, Z 18/39. Idem, April 4, 1866.
12. RA, I 43/105. The Crown Princess to Queen Victoria, March 20, 1866.
13. Queen Victoria to the Crown Princess, March 24, 1866, Kronberg Archive.
14. RA, I 43/118. Lord Augustus Loftus to Lord Clarendon, March 24, 1866.
15. RA, I 43/124. General Grey to Earl Russell, March 26, 1866. General Grey was the Queen's personal adviser on domestic and foreign and household affairs.
16. RA, I 43/130. Earl Russell to Queen Victoria, March 27, 1866.
17. RA, I 43/142. Queen Victoria to the Crown Prince of Prussia, March 28, 1866.
18. RA, Z 18/38. The Crown Princess to Queen Victoria, March 31, 1866.
19. RA, I 43/143. The Duchess of Coburg to Queen Victoria, March 28, 1866.

20. RA, I 43/187. Lord Augustus Loftus to Lord Clarendon, April 7, 1866.

21. See Alan Palmer's excellent summary of Bismarck's maneuverings before the war against Austria in his *Bismarck* (London, 1976), p. 114. See also Bismarck, *Reflections and Reminiscences*, 2, p. 64.

22. RA, I 44/5. Queen Victoria to the King of Prussia, April 10, 1866.

23. RA, I 44/24. Lord Augustus Loftus to Lord Clarendon, April 14, 1866.

24. Full details of this temporary success of the Coburg intrigue can be found in RA, I 44/51, Consul General Crowe to Lord Clarendon, April 19, 1866. Another version of the intrigue from the Austrian point of view is in Chester W. Clark, *Franz Joseph and Bismarck: The Diplomacy of Austria Before the War of 1866* (Cambridge, Mass., 1934), pp. 375–379.

25. RA, I 44/72. Lord Clarendon to Queen Victoria, April 25, 1866.

26. RA, I 44/95. Lord Augustus Loftus to Lord Clarendon, April 28, 1866.

27. RA, I 44/171, Lord Augustus Loftus to Lord Clarendon, May 12, 1866.

28. RA, Z 18/46 and 48. The Crown Princess to Queen Victoria, May 9 and 16, 1866.

29. Queen Victoria to the Crown Princess, May 12, 1866, Kronberg Archive.

30. RA, I 44/132 and 156. Lord Augustus Loftus to Lord Clarendon, May 4 and 5, 1866.

31. RA, I 44/144. Memorandum of Queen Victoria on her meeting with Lord Clarendon, May 6, 1866.

32. RA, Z 18/47. The Crown Princess to Queen Victoria, May 12, 1866.

33. Queen Victoria to the Crown Princess, May 9, 1866, Kronberg Archive.

34. RA, I 44/155. Lord Clarendon to Queen Victoria, May 7, 1866.

35. Queen Victoria to the Crown Princess, May 19, 1866, Kronberg Archive.

36. The Crown Princess to the Crown Prince, June 11, Kronberg Archive.

37. RA, Z 18/60. The Crown Princess to Queen Victoria, June 19, 1866.

38. William II, *My Early Life*, p. 5.

39. RA, Z 18/66. The Crown Princess to Queen Victoria, July 9, 1866.

40. RA, Z 18/63. Idem, June 30, 1866.

41. Busch, *Bismarck*, p. 196.

42. RA, I 45/141. Colonel Walker to Sir Henry Stanley, July 4, 1866.

43. Cardinal Antonelli actually said, *"Casca il mondo."* The quotation comes from Stern, *Gold and Iron*, p. 88.

44. RA, I 46/21. Lord Augustus Loftus to Sir Henry Stanley, July 14, 1866.

45. The Crown Prince to the Crown Princess, July 20, 1866, Kronberg Archive.

46. Quoted in Corti, *English Empress*, p. 155. His account of these negotiations from the Crown Prince's point of view is important.

47. The Crown Prince to the Crown Princess, July 25, 1866, Kronberg Archive.

48. Bismarck, *Reflections and Reminiscences,* 2, p. 52.
49. RA, I 46/139. Princess Alice of Hesse to Queen Victoria, July 31, 1866.
50. RA, I 46/124. Robert Morier to General Grey, July 29, 1866.
51. RA, I 46/156. Princess Alice of Hesse to Queen Victoria, August 6, 1866.
52. RA, I 45/147. The King of Saxony to Queen Victoria, July 6, 1866.
53. RA, I 46/110. Queen Victoria to the King of Saxony, July 28, 1866.
54. *Letters,* 2, 1, p. 356. George, Duke of Cambridge, to Queen Victoria, July 7, 1866.
55. RA, Z 18/65 and 72. The Crown Princess to Queen Victoria, July 16 and 27, 1866.
56. RA, Z 18/76. Idem, August 10, 1866.
57. Queen Victoria to the Crown Princess, August 12, 1866, Kronberg Archive.
58. RA, I 46/124. Robert Morier to General Grey, July 29, 1866.
59. RA, I 47/16. The Crown Princess to Queen Victoria, August 19, 1866.

CHAPTER 7

1. Quoted in Rudolf Olden, *History of Liberty in Germany* (London, 1946), p. 106.
2. RA, I 48/96. Lord Augustus Loftus to Lord Clarendon, memorandum on a meeting with the King of Prussia, December 12, 1868.
3. RA, I 48/115. Lord Augustus Loftus to Lord Clarendon, memorandum on a meeting with Bismarck, April 17, 1869.
4. RA, Z 19/85. The Crown Princess to Queen Victoria, April 20, 1867.
5. Queen Victoria to the Crown Princess, April 24, 1867, Kronberg Archive.
6. *Further Letters,* pp. 163–64. Queen Victoria to the King of Prussia, April 22, 1867.
7. RA, Z 20/1. The Crown Princess to Queen Victoria, April 29, 1867.
8. RA, Z 20/13. Idem, June 10, 1867.
9. Queen Victoria to the Crown Princess, July 6 and 10, 1867, Kronberg Archive.
10. *Letters,* 2, 1, p. 369. Queen Victoria to the Prince of Wales, October 16, 1866.
11. The Crown Princess to the Crown Prince, November 9, 1866, Kronberg Archive.
12. RA, Z 19/67. The Crown Princess to Queen Victoria, March 2, 1867.
13. RA, Z 23/23. Idem, March 2, 1869.
14. RA, Z 24/42. Idem, May 25, 1870.
15. RA, Z 20/74. Idem, December 10, 1867.
16. RA, Z 23/16. Idem, February 6, 1869.
17. RA, Z 24/5. Idem, October 7, 1869.
18. RA, Z 19/21. Idem, November 17, 1866.

19. RA, I 48/47. Idem, August 27, 1867.
20. RA, I 48/59. Sir Henry Stanley to Lord Derby, October 3, 1867.
21. RA, Z 19/20. The Crown Princess to Queen Victoria, November 16, 1866.
22. Queen Victoria to the Crown Princess, March 2, 1870, Kronberg Archive.
23. RA, Z 24/10. The Crown Princess to Queen Victoria, October 31, 1869.
24. RA, Z 24/25. Idem, January 14, 1870.
25. Queen Victoria to the Crown Princess, February 13, 1867, and March 5, 1870, Kronberg Archive.
26. RA, Z 20/34. The Crown Princess to Queen Victoria, August 17, 1867.
27. William II, *My Early Life*, p. 18.
28. RA, Z 23/8. The Crown Princess to Queen Victoria, January 16, 1869.
29. RA, Z 23/11. Idem, January 26, 1869.
30. RA, Z 21/42. Prince William of Prussia to Queen Victoria, May 20, 1868.
31. William II, *My Early Life*, pp. 36–37.
32. RA, I 48/142. Lord Clarendon to Queen Victoria, January 26, 1870. When the Disraeli ministry lost an election and Gladstone became Prime Minister, Queen Victoria tried to stop Lord Clarendon's appointment as Foreign Secretary by what Gladstone called a "Court maneuver."
33. RA, I 48/148. Lord Augustus Loftus to Lord Clarendon, February 8, 1870.
34. RA, I 48/174. Idem, March 18, 1870.

CHAPTER 8

1. Busch, *Bismarck*, p. 6.
2. Idem, p. 16 (my italics).
3. RA, I 63/1. The Crown Princess to Queen Victoria, March 12, 1870.
4. RA, I 63/94. Lord Augustus Loftus to Lord Granville, July 16, 1870.
5. RA, I 63/73. Lord Lyons to Lord Granville, July 12, 1870.
6. Busch, *Bismarck*, p. 20.
7. French Ministerial Statement as reported by Reuter's and printed in the *Pall Mall Gazette*, July 14, 1870.
8. Bismarck, *Reflections and Reminiscences*, 2, pp. 95–100.
9. RA, I 63/70. Lord Augustus Loftus to Lord Granville, July 14, 1870.
10. RA, Z 24/70 and I 63/89. The Crown Princess to Queen Victoria, July 13 and 16, 1870.
11. *The War Diary of the Emperor Frederick III*, ed. A. Allison (London, 1927), pp. 4–7. July 12–15, 1870.
12. RA, I 63/79. Lord Granville to Queen Victoria, July 15, 1870.

13. RA, I 63/116. The Crown Princess to Queen Victoria, July 18, 1870.
14. RA, I 63/129. Queen Victoria to Lord Granville, July 20, 1870.
15. RA, I 63/128. Queen Victoria to the Crown Princess, July 20, 1870.
16. RA, Z 24/74. The Crown Princess to Queen Victoria, July 26, 1870.
17. RA, I 63/170. Sir Robert Morier to Queen Victoria, July 25, 1870.
18. RA, I 63/176. The King of Prussia to Queen Victoria, July 26, 1870.
19. RA, I 64/20. Sir Robert Morier to Lord Granville, July 31, 1870.
20. RA, I 64/94. The Crown Princess to Queen Victoria, August 9, 1870.
21. Quoted in Stern, *Gold and Iron,* p. 263. Chapter Eleven, "The Fourth Estate," is a brilliant examination of Bismarck's manipulation and corruption of the press.
22. RA, I 64/16. General Walker to Lord Augustus Loftus, July 30, 1870.
23. RA, I 64/34. Sir Robert Morier to Lord Granville, August 1, 1870.
24. *War Diary,* p. 19, August 1, 1870.
25. RA, I 64/84. General Walker to Lord Augustus Loftus, August 8, 1870.
26. *War Diary,* p. 63, August 19, 1870.
27. RA, Z 25/2. The Crown Princess to Queen Victoria, August 4, 1870.
28. Busch, *Bismarck,* p. 40.
29. Idem, p. 43.
30. *War Diary,* p. 88, September 1, 1870.
31. Busch, *Bismarck,* p. 66.
32. *War Diary,* p. 91, September 1, 1870.
33. Busch, *Bismarck,* pp. 60–61.
34. RA, I 65/42. The Crown Princess to Queen Victoria, September 6, 1870.
35. RA, I 65/33. Lord Lyons to Lord Granville, September 6, 1870.
36. RA, I 65/150. Lord Lyons to Lord Granville, September 19, 1870.
37. *War Diary,* p. 75, August 28, 1870.
38. RA, I 67/9. The Crown Princess to Queen Victoria, November 6, 1870.
39. *War Diary,* p. ???, December 14, 1870.
40. Bismarck, *Reflections and Reminiscences,* 2, p. 123.
41. *War Diary,* p. 241, December 31, 1870.
42. Queen Victoria to the Crown Princess, July 20, 1870, Kronberg Archive.
43. Quoted in Palmer, *Bismarck,* p. 157.
44. RA, Z 25/44. The Crown Princess to Queen Victoria, January 17, 1871.
45. RA, I 68/68. Princess Alice of Hesse to Queen Victoria, January 25, 1871.
46. Bismarck, *Die Gesammelten Werke,* 14, 2, p. 810.
47. RA, I 67/104, Mr. Odo Russell to Lord Granville, December 18, 1870.
48. RA, I 68/142. The Crown Princess to Queen Victoria, March 4, 1871.
49. RA, I 67/89. Mr. Odo Russell to Lord Granville, December 14, 1870.

CHAPTER 9

1. Busch, *Bismarck*, p. 213.
2. RA, I 49/39. Mr. Crowe to Lord Granville, November 15, 1871.
3. Felix Philippi, quoted by Gordon A. Craig, *Germany, 1866–1945* (New York, 1978), p. 81.
4. RA, I 50/30. Lord Odo Russell to Lord Derby, October 16, 1874. See also Russell's letter to Lord Granville, October 18, 1872, in *Letters from the Berlin Embassy, 1871–1874*, ed. P. Knaplund (Washington, D.C., 1944), p. 71.
5. RA, Z 25/63. The Crown Princess to Queen Victoria, March 24, 1871.
6. RA, I 50/31. Colonel Ponsonby to Lord Derby, November 19, 1974.
7. RA, I 49/140. The remark was made by Lord Odo Russell to Lord Otto Fitzgerald, who wrote back to Queen Victoria as her representative on the occasion of the Queen Dowager's funeral, December 20, 1873.
8. RA, Z 67/52. Queen Victoria to Prince William of Prussia, August 28, 1874.
9. RA, Z 28/55. The Crown Princess to Queen Victoria, August 29, 1874.
10. RA, Z 26/12. Idem, September 9, 1871.
11. Busch, *Bismarck*, pp. 306–307.
12. RA, I 49/98. Lady Emily Russell to Queen Victoria, March 15, 1873.
13. Quoted in Taylor, *Bismarck*, p. 147.
14. RA, I 50/11. Sir R. Morier to Lord Granville, March 27, 1874.
15. RA, I 49/93. Lord Odo Russell to Lord Granville, March 2, 1873.
16. *Letters*, 2, 2, p. 155.
17. RA, Z 64/78 and 82. The Crown Princess to Queen Victoria, December 19 and 26, 1876.
18. Queen Victoria to the Crown Princess, October 30, 1877, Kronberg Archive.
19. *The Times* (London), February 20, 1878.
20. RA, Z 65/31. Colonel A. Ellis to Queen Victoria, February 19, 1878.
21. See Corti, *English Empress*, p. 127.
22. See Lothar Gall, *Bismarck: Der Weisse Revolutionär* (Frankfurt/Berlin, 1980), pp. 508–514.
23. RA, I 50/108. Queen Victoria to Tsar Alexander II, May 10, 1875.
24. RA, I 50/105. Lord Derby to General Ponsonby, May 10, 1875.
25. RA, I 50/116. Lord Odo Russell to Lord Derby, May 11, 1875.
26. RA, I 50/132. Queen Victoria to the Crown Princess, June 8, 1875.
27. RA, Z 29/35. The Crown Princess to Queen Victoria, June 12, 1875.
28. RA, I 50/128. Emperor William I to Queen Victoria, June 3, 1875.
29. RA, I 50/136. Lord Derby to General Ponsonby, June 14, 1875.
30. RA, Z 64/156. Lady Emily Russell to Queen Victoria, February 10, 1877.

31. RA, Z 64/108. The Crown Princess to Queen Victoria, February 10, 1877.
32. RA, Z 28/10. Idem, February 28, 1874.
33. See Gall, *Bismarck,* pp. 516–520, for an analysis of the Kissinger Dictate and of Bismarck's policy after 1875.
34. *Letters of the Empress Frederick,* p. 156. The Crown Princess to Queen Victoria, December 19, 1877.
35. RA, I 51/122. Louise, Grand Duchess of Baden to Queen Victoria, May 11, 1878.
36. RA, Z 30/4. The Crown Princess to Queen Victoria, June 4, 1878.
37. RA, I 51/159. Idem, June 7, 1878.
38. *The Times* (London), August 16, 1878.
39. Busch, *Bismarck,* p. 343.
40. RA, I 53/13. Louise, Grand Duchess of Baden to Queen Victoria, August 14, 1878.
41. Busch, *Bismarck,* p. 356.

CHAPTER 10

1. RA, Z 32/1. The Crown Princess to Queen Victoria, December 15, 1878.
2. RA, Z 65/85. Idem, March 27, 1879.
3. RA, Z 33/16. Idem, June 18, 1879.
4. RA, Z 32/6. Idem, January 1, 1879.
5. RA, Z 31/94 and 95. Idem, September 18 and 26, 1878.
6. RA, Z 33/34 and 34/26. Idem, September 11, 1879, and May 24, 1880.
7. William II, *My Early Life,* p. 67.
8. Ibid., p. 61.
9. RA, Z 64/86. Lord Beaconsfield to Queen Victoria, January 21, 1877.
10. Salisbury MS. Vol. A 61/153–155 Colonel L. V. Swaine's memoranda to Lord Salisbury, November 20, 1887. Christ Church.
11. RA, U 34/8. Prince William to the Crown Princess, July 17, 1879.
12. RA, Z 34/6. The Crown Princess to Queen Victoria, January 26, 1880.
13. RA, Z 34/9. Idem, February 13, 1880.
14. RA, Z 34/40. Idem, August 5, 1880.
15. RA, I 53/26 and 28 and 31. Lord Torrington to Queen Victoria, February 26, 27 and 28, 1881.
16. RA, Z 35/6. The Crown Princess to Queen Victoria, February 28, 1881.
17. RA, Z 35/53. Idem, November 5, 1887.
18. *The Morning Post* (London), January 9, 1882.
19. RA, Z 36/5. The Crown Princess to Queen Victoria, January 18, 1882.
20. *Letters of the Empress Frederick,* pp. 192–193.
21. RA, Z 35/12. The Crown Princess to Queen Victoria, March 28, 1881.

22. Corti, *English Empress*, p. 212. Karl Marx's interviewer was Sir M. E. Grant Duff, M.P.
23. RA, I 53/20. The Crown Princess to Queen Victoria, January 25, 1881.
24. See Palmer, *Bismarck*, p. 226.
25. *Letters of the Empress Frederick*, p. 195.
26. Corti, *English Empress*, pp. 222–223.
27. RA, Z 30/14. The Crown Princess to Queen Victoria, December 1, 1883.
28. J. Rennell Rodd, *Social and Diplomatic Memories, 1884–1893* (London, 1922), p. 50.
29. Busch, *Bismarck,* p. 481.
30. RA, Z 37/1. The Crown Princess to Queen Victoria, September 15, 1883.
31. Busch, *Bismarck,* p. 479.
32. Ibid., p. 481.
33. Corti, *English Empress,* p. 219.
34. Ibid, p. 227.
35. RA, Z 30/26. The Crown Princess to Queen Victoria, October 30, 1885.
36. RA, Z 38/38. The Crown Princess to Queen Victoria, October 5, 1886.
37. See *Mitregenten und fremde Hände in Deutschland* (Switzerland, 1887), also Busch, *Bismarck,* pp. 483–484.
38. RA, I 55/19. Sir Garnet Wolseley to Queen Victoria, January 3, 1886.

CHAPTER 11

1. Corti, *English Empress*, p. 237.
2. RA, Z 39/9. The Crown Princess to Queen Victoria, March 15, 1887.
3. RA, Z 39/23. Idem, May 17, 1887.
4. See the diary of General von Waldersee, May 22, 1887, also Corti, *English Empress*, p. 241.
5. Corti, pp. 307–308.
6. RA, Z 39/23. The Crown Princess to Queen Victoria, May 17, 1887.
7. RA, Z 39/25. The Crown Princess to Queen Victoria, May 25, 1887.
8. Queen Victoria to the Crown Princess, May 20, 1887, Kronberg Archive.
9. RA, Z 39/29. The Crown Princess to Queen Victoria, May 27, 1887.
10. Queen Victoria to the Crown Princess, May 26, 1887, Kronberg Archive.
11. RA, Z 39/33. The Crown Princess to Queen Victoria, June 2, 1887.
12. RA, Z 39/36. Idem, June 4, 1887.
13. RA, Z 39/34. Idem, June 3, 1887.
14. RA, Z 39/25. Idem, May 20, 1887.
15. RA, Z 66/64. Morell Mackenzie to the Crown Princess, August 8, 1887.

16. PRO. Malet Mss., FO 343/8/85–86. Sir Edward Malet to Lord Salisbury, October 15, 1887.

17. Sir Morell Mackenzie, *The Fatal Illness of Frederick the Noble* (London, 1888), pp. 65–66. This is a self-serving work, and of the many rejoinders to it in Germany and elsewhere, the best remains R. Scott Stevenson's biography *Morell Mackenzie* (London, 1946).

18. RA, Z 66/109. Prince William of Germany to Queen Victoria, November 11, 1887.

19. RA, Z 38/88. The Crown Princess to Queen Victoria, November 16, 1887.

20. Stevenson, *Morell Mackenzie*, p. 94.

21. RA, Z 38/97. The Crown Princess to Queen Victoria, November 29, 1887.

22. Malet Mss. FO, 343/2/250–252. Lord Salisbury to Sir E. Malet, November 16, 1887.

23. RA, Z 66/130. Lady Ponsonby to Queen Victoria, December 3, 1887.

24. RA, Z 40/4. The Crown Princess to Queen Victoria, January 11, 1888.

25. RA, Z 66/142. Lady Ponsonby to Queen Victoria, January 13, 1888.

26. RA, Z 38/105. The Crown Princess to Queen Victoria, December 15, 1887.

27. RA, Z 66/136. Lady Ponsonby to Queen Victoria, December 25, 1887.

28. Corti, *English Empress*, p. 254.

29. Ibid., p. 255.

30. Ibid., p. 256.

31. Ibid., p. 262.

32. RA, Z 41/23 and 24. The Crown Princess to Queen Victoria, 26 and 28 February, 1888.

33. Radziwill, *Empress Frederick*, p. 185.

34. RA, Z, 68/11. Sir E. Malet to Queen Victoria, March 9, 1888.

CHAPTER 12

1. RA, Z 68/34. Arthur Ellis to Sir Henry Ponsonby, March 16, 1888.

2. *The Times* (London), March 16, 1888.

3. RA, Z 41/27. The Empress Frederick to Queen Victoria, March 16, 1888. The Princess Royal chose the title of the Empress Frederick of Germany in preference to the Empress Victoria in order to preserve her husband's name and to distinguish herself from her mother, Queen Victoria, the Empress of India.

4. PRO. Lord Salisbury to Sir E. Malet, March 14, 1888.

5. The Empress Frederick's Diary, quoted in Corti, *English Empress*, pp. 285–286.

6. Ludwig Bamberger, *Bismarcks grosses Spiel*, ed. E. Feder (Frankfurt, 1932), p. 351.

7. Ibid., pp. 357–359.

8. PRO. Sir E. Malet to Lord Salisbury, cipher telegram, April 5, 1888.

9. *Letters of the Empress Frederick,* p. 296. Queen Victoria to Sir Henry Ponsonby, April 9, 1888.
10. Mackenzie, *Frederick the Noble,* pp. 148–149.
11. Stevenson, *Mackenzie,* p. 123.
12. PRO. Lord Salisbury to Sir E. Malet, May 2, 1888.
13. Corti, *English Empress,* p. 276.
14. *Queen Victoria's Journal,* April 24 and 25, 1888.
15. Busch, Bismarck, pp. 490–491.
16. Malet Mss. FO 343/9/64–65. Sir E. Malet to Lord Salisbury, April 28, 1888.
17. *Queen Victoria's Journal,* April 25, 1888.
18. Idem, April 26, 1888.
19. RA, Z 68/63. Sir E. Malet to Queen Victoria, May 17, 1888.
20. RA, I 56/45. Sir E. Malet to Lord Salisbury, April 28, 1888.
21. Corti, *English Empress,* p. 291.
22. RA, Z 41/40 and 42. The Empress Frederick to Queen Victoria, April 28 and May 2, 1888.
23. RA, Z 41/46. Idem, May 9, 1888.
24. The Empress Frederick's Diary, May 24, 1888, quoted by Corti, *English Empress,* p. 292.
25. See Radziwill, *Empress Frederick,* p. 215.
26. The Empress Frederick's Diary, quoted by Corti, *English Empress,* pp. 295–296.
27. RA, Z 42/64. The Empress Frederick to Queen Victoria, June 15, 1888.
28. The Empress Frederick's Diary, quoted by Corti, *English Empress,* pp. 302–303.
29. RA, Z 68/106. Sir E. Malet to Queen Victoria, June 16, 1888.
30. Malet Mss. FO 343/9/75–77. Lord Salisbury to Sir E. Malet, June 22, 1888.
31. Busch, *Bismarck,* p. 491.
32. RA, Z 68/131. Sir E. Malet to Lord Salisbury, June 24, 1888.
33. The Empress Frederick's Diary, quoted by Corti, *English Empress,* p. 304.

CHAPTER 13

1. RA, Z 43/1. The Empress Frederick to Queen Victoria, September 13, 1888.
2. RA, Z 41/66. Idem, June 20, 1888.
3. RA, I 56/77. Queen Victoria to Sir Henry Ponsonby, June 27, 1888.
4. RA, Z 68/154. Lord Salisbury to Queen Victoria, July 15, 1888.
5. RA, Z 42/18. The Empress Frederick to Queen Victoria, July 20, 1888.
6. See Professor Ernest von Bergmann et. al., *Die Krankheit Kaiser Friedrich des Dritten* (Berlin, 1888).

7. RA, Z 43/25. The Empress Frederick to Queen Victoria, October 18, 1888.

8. RA, Z 44/33. Idem, April 27, 1889.

9. The Empress Frederick's Diary, quoted by Corti, *English Empress*, p. 316.

10. RA, Z 280/55, 57 and 58. The Empress Frederick to Queen Victoria, September 24, 26 and 27, 1888.

11. RA, Z 280/60 and 61. Idem, October 6 and 8, 1888.

12. F. Greenwood in *The Times* (London), January 5, 1889. For Morier's part, see Agatha Ramm, *Sir Robert Morier: Envoy and Ambassador in the Age of Imperialism, 1876–1893* (Oxford, 1973), pp. 270–304.

13. Malet Mss. FO 343/10/36–40. Sir E. Malet to Lord Salisbury, January 17 and 19, 1889.

14. See *The Times* (London), January 9, 1889.

15. RA, Z 43/27, 29, 30 and 31. The Empress Frederick to Queen Victoria, October 20, 23, 27 and 30, 1888.

16. Ponsonby Mss. FO 800/3/182–183. Colonel Swaine to Sir H. Ponsonby, July 4, 1888.

17. RA, Z I 56/84. The Emperor William II to Queen Victoria, July 6, 1888.

18. RA, Z I 56/95. Queen Victoria to Lord Salisbury, October 24, 1888.

19. RA, I 57/20. Sir E. Malet to Lord Salisbury, March 30, 1889.

20. RA, Z 280/71. Lord Salisbury to Queen Victoria, November 1, 1888.

21. Malet Mss. FO 343/3/20–25. Lord Salisbury to Sir E. Malet, February 20, 1889.

22. RA, Z 43/32. The Empress Frederick to Queen Victoria, November 2, 1888.

23. RA, Add. A 4/4. The Prince of Wales to the Empress Frederick, April 10, 1889.

24. RA, Add. A 4/16. Idem, July 4, 1889.

25. RA, I 57/33. The Emperor William II of Germany to Sir E. Malet, June 14, 1889.

26. Ponsonby Mss. FO 800/3/192–193. Colonel L. Swaine to Sir H. Ponsonby, March 8, 1889.

27. RA, Z 45/26 and 41. The Empress Frederick to Queen Victoria, July 13 and August 17, 1889.

28. See Prince William to Emperor William I, November 14, 1880, reprinted in *My Early Life*, appendix 6, pp. 308–313.

29. RA, Z 46/2. The Emperor William II to Queen Victoria, August 24, 1889.

30. RA, I 57/53. Idem, August 17, 1889.

31. RA, I 57/70. Mr. E. Monson to Lord Salisbury, October 31, 1889.

32. RA, I 57/75. The Emperor William II of Germany to Queen Victoria, December 22, 1889.

33. RA, I 58/21. Idem, February 24, 1890.

34. RA, Z 69/112. The Empress Frederick to Queen Victoria, January 11, 1890.
35. RA, I 58/16. Sir E. Malet to Lord Salisbury, February 12, 1890.
36. RA, I 58/34. Memorandum of a conversation by the Emperor William II to Sir E. Malet, March 27, 1890.
37. RA, I 58/32. The Emperor William II to Queen Victoria, March 27, 1890.
38. RA, I 59/2. Colonel F. S. Russell to Lord Salisbury, February 13, 1891.
39. RA, I 58/39. Lord Salisbury to Queen Victoria, April 7, 1890.
40. RA, Z 69/123. The Empress Frederick to Queen Victoria, March 25, 1890.
41. *Queen Victoria's Journal,* April 26, 1890.
42. RA, Z 49/49. The Empress Frederick to Queen Victoria, December 21, 1890.
43. Corti, *English Empress,* p. 337.
44. RA, Add. A 4/25. The Prince of Wales to the Empress Frederick, February 27, 1891.
45. RA, Z 50/45. The Empress Frederick to Queen Victoria, June 12, 1891.

CHAPTER 14

1. Paul Kennedy's important work, *The Rise of Anglo-German Antagonism 1860–1914* (London, 1981), makes clear how fundamental the differences were between the two nations, and how personal relationships and royal diplomacy could do less and less to bring the countries together.
2. RA, Z 56/20. The Empress Frederick to Queen Victoria, June 21, 1894.
3. Salisbury Mss. A/83/123. Queen Victoria to Lord Salisbury, cipher telegram, October 24, 1898.
4. Salisbury Mss. A/114/51–52. Lord Dufferin to Lord Salisbury, January 10, 1896.
5. RA, I 60/4. Queen Victoria to Sir H. Ponsonby, January 15, 1894.
6. RA, I 60/64. The Emperor William II to Queen Victoria, April 24, 1894.
7. RA, I 59/80 and 98. Idem, May 22, 1892, and January 28, 1893.
8. Salisbury Mss. A/120/67–70. Sir F. Lascelles to Lord Salisbury, January 4, 1896.
9. Quoted Corti, *English Empress,* p. 358.
10. RA, I 61/27 and 60/149. Colonel L. Swaine to Sir A. Bigge, November 16, 1897, and a memorandum of January 1896.
11. Salisbury Mss. A/122/38–39. Lord Salisbury to Sir F. Lascelles, May 10, 1899.
12. RA, I 62/9. Sir F. Lascelles to Lord Salisbury, March 31, 1899.
13. Salisbury Mss. A/121/68–71. Idem, March 11, 1899.
14. RA, Add. A 4/104. The Prince of Wales to the Empress Frederick, April 25, 1899.

15. RA, I 62/14. The Emperor William II to Queen Victoria, May 27, 1899.

16. RA, I 62/18. Queen Victoria to the Emperor William II, June 12, 1899.

17. Lascelles Mss. FO 800/9/ 297–299. Mr. Sanderson to Sir F. Lascelles, August 2, 1899.

18. RA, I 62/83. Sir F. Lascelles to Lord Salisbury, March 9, 1900.

19. RA, I 62/90. The Emperor William II to Queen Victoria, March 31, 1900.

20. RA, I 62/113. Colonel L. Swaine to Sir A. Bigge, December 28, 1900.

21. Lansdowne Mss. FO 800/128/61. The Emperor William II to Sir F. Lascelles, January 19, 1901.

22. George W. Smalley, *Anglo-American Memories* (New York, 1911), pp. 402–408.

23. RA, Add. A 4/217. King Edward VII to the Empress Frederick, June 5, 1901.

24. RA, Add. A 4/71. Idem, August 10, 1898.

25. Lansdowne Mss. FO 800/128/120–121. Sir F. Lascelles to King Edward VII, April 13, 1901.

Select Bibliography

All the archives, papers and books that I have used in this book are listed in the notes. It would be tedious to repeat their titles or catalogue those which I have read, but not used. I would recommend the following as being of particular importance to the understanding of the background of this work:

Bonnin, Georges: *Bismarck and the Hohenzollern Candidature to the Throne of Spain* (London, 1957).

Briggs, Asa: *Victorian People* (London, 1954).

Craig, Gordon A.: *The Politics of the Prussian Army, 1640–1945* (Oxford, 1955).

————: *Germany, 1866–1945* (Oxford, 1978).

Eyck, Erich: *Bismarck and the German Empire* (London, 1950).

Freund, Michael: *Das Drama der 99 Tage: Krankheit und Tod Friedrichs III* (Cologne/Berlin, 1966).

Gall, Lothar: *Bismarck: Der Weisse Revolutionär* (Frankfurt/Berlin, 1980).

Hardie, Frank: *The Political Influence of Queen Victoria* (London, 1963).

Holborn, Hajo: *A History of Modern Germany, 1840–1945* (New York, 1969).

————: *Germany and Europe: Historical Essays* (New York, 1970).

Howard, Michael: *The Franco-Prussian War: The German Invasion of France, 1870–1871* (New York, 1961).

Kennedy, Paul: *The Rise of Anglo-German Antagonism, 1860–1914* (London, 1981).

Langer, William L.: *European Alliances and Alignments, 1871–1890* (2d ed., New York, 1956).

Mattingly, Garrett: *Renaissance Diplomacy* (London, 1955).

Masur, Gerhard: *Imperial Berlin* (London, 1971).

Pflanze, Otto: *Bismarck and the Development of Germany: the Period of Unification, 1815–1871* (Princeton, 1963).

Stern, Fritz: *Gold and Iron: Bismarck, Bleichröder, and the Building of the German Empire* (New York, 1977).

Taylor, A. J. P.: *The Struggle for Mastery in Europe, 1848–1948* (Oxford, 1954).

Wehler, Hans-Ulrich: *Bismarck und der Imperialismus* (Cologne/Berlin, 1969).

For particular biographical material, the following books are recommended:

Anon. *The Empress Frederick, a Memoir* (London, 1912).

Auchincloss, Louis: *Persons of Consequence: Queen Victoria and Her Circle* (London, 1979).

Barkeley, Richard: *The Empress Frederick, Daughter of Queen Victoria* (London, 1956).

Bennett, Daphne: *King without a Crown* (London, 1977).

————: *Vicky, Princess Royal of England and German Empress* (New York, 1971).

Benson, E. F.: *Queen Victoria's Daughters* (New York, 1938).

Bismarck, Prince Otto von: *Reflections and Reminiscences* (2 vols., London, 1898).

Blake, Robert: *Disraeli* (London, 1966).

Bunsen, Chevalier Charles de: *Memoirs* (2 vols., London, 1868).

Bunsen, Marie von: *The World I Used to Know, 1860–1912* (London, 1930).

Busch, Moritz: *Bismarck, Some Secret Passages of His History* (3 vols., London, 1898).

Duff, David: *Albert and Victoria* (London, 1972).

    0

————: *Hessian Tapestry* (London, 1967).

Empress Frederick: *The Empress Frederick Writes to Sophie* (A. G. Lee, ed., London, 1955).

Eyck, Erich: *Bismarck: Leben und Werk* (3 vols., Erlenbach/Zurich, 1941–44).

Fulford, Roger: *The Prince Consort* (London, 1949).

Lee, Sir Sidney: *King Edward VII* (2 vols., London, 1925).

Longford, Elizabeth: *Queen Victoria: Born to Succeed* (New York, 1964).

Magnus, Sir Philip: *King Edward the Seventh* (London, 1964).

Martin, Sir Theodore: *Life of His Royal Highness the Prince Consort* (5 vols., London, 1875–80).

Paget, Walburga Lady: *Scenes and Memories* (London, 1912).

Palmer, Alan: *Bismarck* (London, 1976).

————: *The Kaiser: Warlord of the Second Reich* (London, 1978).

Philippson, Martin: *Das Leben Kaiser Friedrichs III* (Wiesbaden, 1908).

Ponsonby, Sir Fredrick: *The Letters of the Empress Frederick* (London, 1929).

————: *Recollections of Three Reigns* (New York, 1952).

Radziwill, Princess Catherine: *The Empress Frederick* (London, 1934).

Ramm, Agatha: *Sir Robert Morier: Envoy and Ambassador in the Age of Imperialism, 1876–1893* (Oxford, 1973).

Reischach, Baron Hugo von: *Under Three Emperors* (London, 1927).

Richter, Werner: *Bismarck* (London, 1964).

Rodd, Sir Rennell: *Social and Diplomatic Memories* (3 vols., London, 1922).

St. Aubyn, Giles: *Edward VII, Prince and King* (London, 1979).

Saxe-Coburg-Gotha, Duke Ernest II of: *Memoirs* (4 vols., London, 1888).

Stockmar, Baron Ernest von: *The Memoirs of Baron Stockmar* (2 vols., London, 1872).

Taylor, A. J. P.: *Bismarck: the Man and the Statesman* (London, 1955).

Tisdall, E. F. P.: *She Made World Chaos: the Intimate Story of the Empress Frederick* (London, 1940).

Waldersee, Count Alfred von: *Denkwürdigkeiten des Generalfeldmarschalls Alfred Grafen von Waldersee* (3 vols., Berlin, 1922).

William II, Emperor: *My Early Life* (London, 1926).

————: *My Memoirs, 1878–1918* (London, 1922).

Woodham-Smith, Cecil: *Queen Victoria, Her Life and Times* (Vol. 1, 1819–1861, London, 1972).

❧ Index ❧